ABOUT THE AUTHOR

DONALD A. WELLS is Professor and Chairman of the Department of Philosophy at Washington State University, where he has taught since 1948. He received his Ph.D. in philosophy from Boston University in 1946. In addition to articles in scholarly journals, he is the author of GOD, MAN AND THE THINKER: PHILOSOPHIES OF RELIGION (Random House, 1962) and has contributed a chapter, "Religion and Human Potentialities," to *Exploration in Human Potentialities*, Herbert A. Otto, editor (C. C. Thomas, 1966).

Dr. Wells has been active in peace movements since 1935 and was a conscientious objector in World War II. Currently he serves as chairman of a local Citizens for Peace group and as advisor to the Washington State University student Committee to End the War in Viet Nam. He has been a popular speaker in platform debate and on radio and television programs on the issues of war and peace.

THE WAR MYTH

by Donald A. Wells

PEGASUS   NEW YORK

CONTENTS

PREFACE

IN SOME OF THE MYTHS of ancient Greece there runs a mood of inconsolable despair in the face of a cosmic fate that man cannot transcend. For all his insights and courage Prometheus is still cursed to lie bound on a mount in the Caucasus. While a vulture devoured his flesh by day, he took what comfort he could in the expectation that his wounds would heal in the nightly respite allotted to him. Sisyphus wearily rolled his rock up the hill of futility knowing that the labor was useless. Even the optimistic Plato concluded that man was apparently doomed to stupid and fruitless effort. Even though men knew how to emancipate themselves, some inherent surd of irrationality bound them in chains of their own forging. The *Republic* pictures the philosopher as a traveler who takes refuge under a wall from the dust and hail, "content if he can keep his hands clean from iniquity while this life lasts."[1] He had no easy optimism that states would ever establish themselves upon wisdom, even though the wise solutions to civil chaos were fairly obvious. If philosophers became statesmen the end of humanly caused troubles could arrive.

But if the Greeks who saw virtue as teachable and the good

---

[1] Plato, *The Republic*, 496d. Jowett Translation. New York: Charles Scribner's Sons, 1956.

society as a genuine option had their doubts, imagine how utopian the dream of social harmony must seem to modern men who lack these Greek assurances. When we contrast the knowledge we possess about what is politically and socially needful, with the general unwillingness to do what obviously must be done, it is little wonder that counsels of despair overshadow expectations of hope. After all, weaker hearts than Calvin's concluded that men must confront some monstrous flaw within themselves. How else can we explain the invincible stupidity and the ineluctable depravity with which men confront their interpersonal relations? It really makes little difference whether this defect be called *hubris*, original ignorance, or original sin. It is hard to imagine that men knowingly and willingly consign themselves to such misery. How else can we account for the fact that the human race has known how to solve its problems so much longer than it has been willing to have them solved. We confront international anarchy and, knowing that it leads to war, we fear to part with this last vestige of international license. This book is written from the conviction that a significant part of the problem of war and peace is one of motivation. Indeed, it seems that what we lack is willingness rather than information. It is not so much that we do not know about war, but that we do not want to think about it. War is the last socially acceptable outlet for a barbarian species which is not yet willing to be civilized.

One of the consequences that historically follows from lengthy and inconclusive discussion is that the subject of the discussion becomes obfuscated by essentially irrelevant distinctions. No subject demonstrates this semantic decay better, or worse, than that of war and peace. Beating swords into plowshares and spears into pruning-hooks is not, after all, a very complex or difficult step. Nor is the thesis that human life is superior to every abstract principle a particularly devious commitment. But, after several millennia of talk about this problem, where almost no progress seems to be made, where swords are still manufactured faster than healing instruments, and where wholesale slaughter is performed in the pious name of principle, the talk about peace becomes a mere genuflection. The talk is all that there is. There is no longer any substantive content in either the terms or the expectations. Like much religious conversation about God and immortality, the important words seem to have lost any meaningful referents. One corollary of this in religion is that potentially meaningful and humanly centered terms like guilt and virtue are replaced by transcendental terms like atonement and incarnation. The issue of human responsibility which guilt and virtue entail is neglected in favor of academic questions concerning the meaning of Jesus' death or birth. Denominations are born and defended over such general terms, while humane responsibilities remain unchanged. Men could walk with God and they could love their fellow men, but there really wasn't anything that they needed to do as a result of the atonement thesis or the dogma of the virgin birth.

War and peace discussion has exhibited this pattern. Once upon a time it was as simple as "thou shalt not kill." Now the killing is encapsulated in myths of dominoes, communist tyranny, freedom, and democratic doctrines so firmly that we really do not see what we are doing when we napalm villages. Love of neighbor was once envisioned as possible, while it is now described in the language of the incredible. Direct affirmations are replaced by evasions, and what was once crucial is now buried under a mass of concrete trivia. When great issues fall into the hands of the dogmatizers, they become debated without any sense of concern, and myth and reality become blurred and indistinguishable.

Take a few contemporary instances of this tendency to trivialize the sacred by posing preposterous questions. Ordinarily human life is an inalienable right, and a man about to be slain by an assassin is not required to prove why he ought not to be killed. In fact, it is presumed that any assassin who wishes to be heard on behalf of his killing should be dismissed as a moral charlatan. Modern war has reversed this elementary humanitarianism. The citizens of Hiroshima and Nagasaki were expected to prove their right not to be bombed, and even though they were not consulted before the fact, they were reminded of this datum after the holocaust. Meanwhile their exterminators paraded, like Grand Inquisitors after the dreadful deed, their chimerical "justifications" for the human bonfire. It was the same before and after Dresden in World War II, and it is the same in the pillaging of Vietnamese villages. In the absence of a Vietnamese defense for their own survival, American bombers may, without any justification, napalm the villagers out of existence.

Imagine, if you can, an extermination camp like Belsen, and a court hearing where the condemned Jews are required to prove that they ought not to be gassed or burned. In the absence of such proof, the operators are then "justified" in continuing operations. Picture some "impartial" judge weighing the values of Nazism to see if the ends justified the means, and imagine that he condemned the extermination on the grounds that the political system of Nazism was not worth the lives of so many. Obviously, if the system had been democratic, the trial would have found the Storm Troopers innocent, and perhaps even noble. Such a trial reverses normal values, for it presumes every man deserves death unless he can make a case to the contrary. It is this reversal which modern warfare effects in the actions of soldiers. The issues are so confounded by sophistry that the military enterprise is carried out on the assumption that soldiers have a right to kill anyone whose innocence has not been demonstrated. Imagine what Western society would be like if this Gestapo mentality prevailed in police departments and in courts of law the way it does in the deliberations of the Pentagon and the State Department. The whole military establishment and process is an anachronism in our midst. The war "game" is a monstrous charade or a gigantic chess gambit which we have played so long that, like the Roman attitude toward the arena, we have quite forgotten that the players are persons.

Peace is not politically or economically so complex that it requires technical genius to grasp it. Peace is simply an issue which our long discussions have made incomprehensible. The very possibility of peace is predicated on the assumption that it is unnatural, while war gains credence precisely because it is the putatively "natural" way things are done. Here again, a religious analogy is appropriate. Religious experience is commonly lost in the wilderness of theology. While the encounters which religious persons have are indubitable in their occurrence, theological jargon tends to make these personally obvious experiences semantically inexpressible. The obscurantism of some religious discourse is, thus, a pallid substitute for the richness of what religious persons may experience. Much war language works the same mystification when citizens of some bomb-devastated city are informed that, by definition, this was not a hostile action, and that no war is actually occurring. It is in ways such as this that so-called political realists make the idea of peace inconceivable by their unfathomable remarks. One aspect of the unintelligible way in which such issues are assessed is seen in the notion that peace, like medicine, is a nostrum which needs to be tested before it is sold to the public. Until this has been done, war is presumed to be the better option. What an odd locution! Does the simple act of cessation of killing require more defense than the slaughter does?

While there are suggestions as to how to get the human race out of the suicide race, this book is not intended to be a mere blueprint for peace. The real problem is not that men do not know how to avoid war, but that they irrationally want those things that make for war. The chief drives toward war are not unscrupulous war-planners, but inept, unthinking, and callous statesmen and citizens. While blame may surely be due, the intent here is to minimize condemnation and to maximize the insights as to who must assume the responsibility. Perhaps the need for violence will never be eradicated from the human scene, but the need for war can be erased. It may be that the possibility of revolution will always remain as a live last-resort for peoples whose governments have been swallowed up in tyranny. Such occasions, we would hope, would remain the exception rather than the custom. In the international scene, however, we can surely afford to give up piracy. International law, international diplomacy, and international organization can do for world peace what they have already done in their domestic forms for internal affairs. The problem is not to find a sinless nation entitled to cast the first stone, but to find a sinful nation willing to submit to a change in policy. If this book is hard on religion, it is so because religion has offered so much hope but given so little charity, and in the belief that the tattered robe of the one-time Prince of Peace might yet shelter men from their own inhumanity rather than serve as a pious cloak for barbarism.

I owe a special debt of gratitude to Professor John M. Swomley Jr. for his critical, insightful, germane, and scholarly comments on the entire manuscript. The errors of exuberance or insight that remain are, of course, my own. I wish, also, to express appreciation for the stimulation given to me by the men and women, young and old, in the peace movements, who by their dedication and enthusiasm have promoted the sense of humane concern in a world too much dedicated to callousness.

THE MEANING
AND MATTER OF WAR

1 *The Definition of War*

To THE POPULAR MIND there is rarely any doubt when a war is occurring. When the soldiers of one nation are shooting at the soldiers of another nation, then a state of war would seem to exist. When the citizens of one nation are bombing the citizens of another nation, what else would such actions be called other than war? There may well be disputes over intentions, motives, or pretensions in the relations with our neighbors, but how could there be any question when a war is taking place? Speculation on war, however, has ordinarily scorned such obvious common sense in favor of the most incredible sophistry and double-talk that any issue has ever produced.

The twentieth century has witnessed some of the most amazing instances of self-deception on the part of nations with regard to their public actions. The United States can send her troops halfway around the world, it can bomb the villages, napalm the inhabitants, machine gun the soldiers, and, strange to recount, insist that no war is taking place. We have sent United States soldiers to the Dominican Republic and have fired our weapons within the boundaries of their land, and still our public relations experts are able to describe the events as if the U.S. militia had just been sent to Mississippi. Indeed, the myth-making has achieved such a state of utter confusion that the spokesmen for the United States involvement in Vietnam as a non-warlike act are the same ones who protest the temerity of the Justice Department in sending troops to Mississippi. In a world in which such Brobdingnagian nonsense can be uttered in the name of wisdom, it may seem presumptive to raise the subject of war for public reassessment, but it would be even more erroneous to imagine that we have passed the point of rational reflection, and that, like Nazi Germany in the late thirties, our country has been engulfed by a semantic fog that is now beyond penetration. It is the confidence that the voice of simple reason should be spoken and that there are ears to hear and minds to reflect, that prompts the ensuing discussions over the meaning, method, causes, and cures of war.

Why should there have been such a long and vehement discussion over what would appear to have been the only clear element in the whole issue? Ordinarily when we raise the definitional questions, we intend to distinguish what we are talking about from all extraneous matters. It should be elementally simple to determine war from non-war, once we have a definition of war. But this is precisely what the historic discussions of war have failed to supply. There is also a common sense that would dictate that definitions pay some attention to how words are actually used, unless, of course, we are trying to change common usage. It would, for example, be an egregious definition of religion which associated it with non-belief in gods, angels, immortality, saints, or scriptures. It would follow, then, that irreligious persons are those who believe in gods, angels, and so forth. This would be not only odd, but otiose, for religious discussion would no longer be possible. Yet this is the kind of ju jitsu with language that has characterized the maundering discussion of the meaning of war. Why should this have been the case?

There are several factors in history that have stimulated this Mad Hatter's discussion. In the first place, national leaders have been concerned with the assignment of praise or blame on the participants in a war. It was understood that, if a war was taking place, then culpability was an issue. If there were no war, then there should be no question of praise or blame. If a soldier from one nation stabs a soldier of another nation, and this is an act of war, then it is proper to ask who is on the side of justice. If this is not an act of war, then apparently the act is under no judgment, and moral questions are out of order. If a warlike act has been committed, then it would be proper to ask who was the aggressor and who the victim. If it was not a warlike act, then putatively it is a case of police against brigands, and then the moral question has a begging answer.

In the case of legally unrecognized war, so-called neutral nations are to treat all apparent belligerents the same. This means not only that they are to be equally damned or praised, but they can be equally ignored or supported, that any implements of war may legally be sold to nations on both sides of armed conflict. If, on the other hand, war is legally declared, then a nation ceases to be neutral if it gives assistance, and if the aggressor nation can be identified from the nation transgressed against, then it would be improper to aid the offensive nation.

A wealth of writing on the subject of defensive and offensive war takes its plausibility from a presumed definition of war and the belief that there are rules and proprieties which ought to apply. If war occurred, then there were certain conventional responses which a nation was expected to exhibit. Ordinarily, for example, the organized power of the state mustered behind a war. It did not do so in the case of revolution, strikes, bull fights, or duels. It seemed necessary, therefore, to know that an armed conflict was not the action of private parties, else every gunshot would herald a war. It followed from this that there were matters of strategy dependent upon a careful definition of war. There were overtones of belligerence associated with war which it might be convenient to avoid. For example, a nation might wish to exert an economic, political, or moral boycott on another nation without having to declare a state of war. Such actions could then be classified as business, religion, or politics and the whole affair be given an aura of respectability that it might otherwise not possess. Each nation could then declare war when it suited its convenience, and this, in simple language, meant that war was declared when it appeared that we were the innocent victims and the enemy was the vicious aggressor. As long as a nation could, by definition, date the onset of any war, then it could always show that it was acting defensively, while the enemy was acting offensively. No nation would ever be the aggressor in its own history books, and publications have borne this out. The soldiers of one country could then bomb the villages of another nation prior to the declaration of war without being called the aggressors. As soon as the villagers retaliated, we could declare war and then appear as the victims of a brutal and uncalled-for attack.

As we shall see later, the discussion of the concept of the "just war" depended upon each nation having the right to define war as it pleased and when it pleased. The application of the "just war" thesis has illustrated the casuistry to which this has led, for no nation has ever admitted to waging an unjust war. There has been a striking paradox implicit in all of this. War, it has been presumed, is the anarchic right of each nation against all other nations; and yet the discussion of the definition of war has presupposed that there are "rules of war," "laws of war," or some tribunal before which the warlike acts of nations must be justified. Since none of these antecedents has ever significantly been the case, it may be assumed that the point of the whole farcical discussion is to enable the leaders of the nation to explain to their citizens that war always comes through no fault of their own. This is part of the reason why discussions about war are normally carried out in a semantic vacuum, so that the protests of one nation against the actions of another possess the property of unrelated monologues. This is also why we can talk as if fighting between nations is not war, or as if war can exist between nations without there being any fighting. The only general requirement that must be met is that the duly authorized leaders of any country must declare that a war exists before military actions can be called war, and before we need to worry whether diplomatic relations have actually broken down.

War appears to be more of a political or legal concept than a military one. In common usage a state of war is not determined by military strategists, but by political strategists. Indeed, it is exceedingly difficult for soldiers to tell when a war has either begun or ended. In legal definitions, ordinarily, war entails the conflict of armed forces and an attitude of hate toward some enemy. In these senses it can at least be distinguished from old-style diplomacy, where hate was not a component in the machinations and where compromise was a noble strategem to be distinguished from appeasement. If there is no legal acceptance of a state of war, then no matter what degree of military activity is occurring, there simply is no war, by definition. We can see part of the confusion in identifying war when we turn to a typical discussion of the differences in meaning among terms such as "war," "battles," "campaigns," and "armament races."

Quincy Wright noted that from 1480 to 1941 there were 278 wars.[1] The term "battle," as a "lesser military confrontation," was more easy to locate in space and time. In the 18th century battles were identified by the towns in or near which they were fought. In World War I battles were named after rivers, and in World War II they were titled by some geographical place in the country in which they were fought. No one had to wait for a formal political or legal opinion to know that a battle had taken place. In the same work Quincy Wright identified 2,700 battles in modern times. In addition, the term "campaign," as a less concentrated type of military activity, connected by a plan, has also been assumed to designate a clearer state of affairs. Campaigns may not only occur outside of wars but they may be waged without battles. "Armament races," like battles and campaigns, have also been outside the province of duly constituted legal authorities to announce. The rapid build-up of military materials can be determined by any economist who has the information. Again, Quincy Wright calculated that there have been at least 25 distinct arms races in modern history, including two European ones: 1787–1815, and 1840–1871, and two general ones: 1886–1919, and from 1932 to the present.[2] Indeed, both "peace" and "war" are so ambiguous in their designation and use that contemporaries have advocated waging war to end war, waging war to preserve peace, waging peace to end war, and waging peace to bring peace.[3] International lawyers like John Bassett Moore and Edwin M. Borchard speak of "perpetual war for perpetual peace."

Saint Thomas (1225–1274) applied himself to some of these issues entailed in determining that war actually exists, who is responsible for its existence, and what ought to be done in response. His discussion was initiated in terms of the question of interpersonal strife, although the implications of his answers were noted to be applicable to war as well. "Strife," he observed, "is a kind of private war."[4] What distinguishes it from ordinary verbal contention is that physical attack is involved. The aggressor in such physical violence is sinful, while the recipient of the violence may be without sin depending on his intentions and the manner of his defense. It is not a sin to defend oneself with moderation, but to do so with vengeance and with undue vigor may make even the attacked person sinful. This kind of sin may range from a minor venial affair to a mortal sin. The possibility that a person may defend his life sinfully has a special bearing on war, particularly in view of the fact that every war is justified on the grounds of self-defense. Indeed, there would appear to be no other reason for war, if the literature on the subject can be believed. No nation ever admits to aggression. Each claims to be the innocent victim of a baseless attack. Now Saint Thomas believed that the duly constituted authorities may justly declare and wage war. Those who resist such a war of public authority and who defend themselves inordinately are guilty of sin. It is the physical attack, the excessive emotionalism, and the aggressiveness of the conflict that make a contention into a war. All of this sounds better than it means, and the consequence has merely been that an ad hoc explanation will always be possible. The criteria by which the just wars are distinguished from the unjust wars make international discussion impossible, since the rules simply enable each nation to defend whatever position it may officially choose to take.

We are in a position of considerable confusion after all these Thomistic niceties have been noted. While "strife," as personal fighting, is always a sin, "war," as fighting at the request of the prince, seems always to be a virtue. Indeed, to refuse to follow the princely mandate to fight is itself a sin. Thus what must never be done from our own personal inclinations now becomes blessed when done at the inclination of the prince. War is, thus, fighting declared by the proper authorities. They, obviously, do so only when it is to their advantage, and the declaration rests on no identifiable criteria. Indeed, most of the purported discussions of war function as if the term "war" were undefined. This is evident from the fact that we discuss the questions of the just war, acts short of war, kinds of war, causes of war, or cures for war rather than the question, "How do we know that a war actually exists independently of whether it is just, defensive, or aggressive?"

The definition of war, therefore, is conditioned by the wish to appear on the right side of the war, and thus, the general subject of the just war is handled with casuistry, sophistry, and self-deception. It is not that justice or injustice cannot be distinguished in a war, but rather that the nations involved are not in the proper position to make this distinction. As long as each nation acts as its own judge and jury we ought not to expect more than the pettifogging paralogisms which they produce. Since nations commonly wish to attack each other without having to admit publicly that they are at war, considerable ingenuity has been exercised to explain armed actions as not really warlike actions. Success in this semantic game has given rise to a plethora of nominal terminology relative to war. In the absence of war, by definition of course, it is still possible to use such non-warlike expressions as massive retaliation, hot pursuit, residual punch, a respectable military posture, graduated deterrence, nuclear stalemate, peaceful coexistence, or cold war. Even the expression "limited war" may be used between two nations engaged in armed conflict without there really being any admission of war.

A semantically rich and complex "language" has been invented to enable men to talk about human destruction without having to employ the value-laden term "war." It is now possible to discuss our own demise in terms of strictest "objectivity," and to entertain the annihilation of our fellow men as if we were computers playing with punched cards. Strategists can speak of the capacity to explode bombs larger than are required to annihilate the people we have in mind as "over-kill." It appears as a relatively unbloody word, and the discussions carried out by its use are usually dispassionately diffident to the bloodshed it implicitly entails. Tacticians use the symbolism "E.O.E." to refer to that level of nuclear power required to wipe out the whole world, or to bring about "an end of earth." In a world situation where every nation is presumed to be out to destroy the other, and where many have the power to bring about an E.O.E., the Strangelovian policy of getting your death blow in first, though all will perish in any case, is called by the absurd title "forward strategy."

Giovanni da Legnano (d. 1383) identified seven kinds of corporeal wars, which he claimed were recognized by law.

1. Roman war, which is war waged by Christians against infidels.
2. War made by a lawful judge against the rebellious.
3. Presumptuous war, made by the rebellious against a lawful judge.
4. Any war allowed by the authority of law.
5. Unlawful war against the authority of law.
6. Voluntary war, made by a prince without the emperor's permission.
7. Necessary war: i.e. war to repel invaders.[5]

In addition to this list he noted that there were so-called "particular wars," which arose from the infliction of particular violence. But, here again, we are not dealing with the definition of war, but with legal or moral classifications of kinds of wars. These medieval writers did not believe that war needed definition so much as it needed judgment. Since the question did not seem to be, "Is a war occurring?" but, rather, "Who should be blamed for the situation?" all discussion of war was colored by the wish to assign blame and escape censure.

The sixteenth century ushered in the first semi-secular attempts to give some generally acceptable meaning to war. Pierino Belli (1505–1575) delineated three kinds of war: for offense, for defense, and for the recovery of some lost possessions. "We must assume," he stated, "that wars originated among men either through the infliction or warding off of injury . . . each individual looked out for his own interests under no regular code . . . undertaking war at his own charges which it was his right to do, both by the divine law and by the natural law and the law of nations."[6] Here, also, the meaning of war is implicit, rather than explicit. Fighting between nations is assumed to be war. There is little ambiguity on this score. Belli's concern is to classify wars into moral grades, rather than to distinguish war from non-war. But the very difficulty in assigning moral grades to war shifts very easily to a difficulty in the definition of war itself.

Francisco Suarez (1548–1617) did, however, distinguish war from other kinds of armed conflict.

> *"An external contest at arms which is incompatible with external peace is properly called war, when carried on between two sovereign princes or between two states. When, however, it is a contest between a prince and his own state, or between private individuals, it is called a quarrel or a duel. The difference between these various kinds of contest appears to be material rather than formal."*[7]

This emphasis upon war as a state function was affirmed, also, by Alberico Gentili (1552–1608), who remarked that war was "a just contest carried on by the state's armed forces."[8] Hugo Grotius (1583–1645) expressed the same essential thesis in a definition he adopted from Cicero that there are two kinds of contests: by discussion and by force. The latter is war.[9]

But just as it might appear that war is being defined, the emphases shift once again to the question of moral sanction. Cornelius van Bynkerschoek (1673–1743) rejected all the putative definitions of war in favor of the statement that "war is a contest of independent persons carried on by force or fraud for the sake of asserting their rights."[10] Since he believed that every recourse was lawful in war, he effectively insulated war from either moral or pragmatic criticism. As far back as the seventeenth century he affirmed that we may destroy unarmed citizens with poison or incendiary bombs, and by this affirmation effectively made the subject undebatable.

Part of the problem with such analyses as these two centuries produced is that they attempted too much. These critics were so concerned that the definition of war not be used against them that language about war was, of necessity, either pejorative or hyperbole. The definition of war was simply not the concern. What was of interest were casuistic proofs that one's own nation was morally praiseworthy.

A new point is reached, however, with Jean J. Rousseau (1712–1778). He asserted that war is a relation between things rather than persons, and this only when they are in a state of nature.

"War then is a relation, not between man and man, but between State and State, and individuals are enemies only accidentally, not as men, nor even as citizens, but as soldiers; not as members of their country, but as its defenders. Finally, each State can have as enemies only other States."[11]

Any State which attacks another without first declaring war is not an enemy but a brigand, and even if war is declared, no State may kill any members of the other State unless they are bearing arms. Indeed, he observed that it is possible to kill a State without killing any of its warriors. Here we have a halfway useful definition by which we can identify a war even if the leaders of the respective nations refuse to call it such. With this definition, war can be identified independently of the justice of either side in the war, and this avoids the anomaly of undeclared wars not existing.

In 1758 Emmerich de Vattel (1714–1767) endeavored to summarize the modern thinking on the whole question of the meaning of war. He called it a conflict between nations, and he conceded that there was no general law of nations which obliged them to declare war before they attacked. He believed that the 17th century marked the turning point of the requisite that a war be formally declared before it be admitted to exist. If, however, a State wished to legalize war, then it would have to make a formal declaration of war through the conventional channels endowed with the power to make such a decision.[12] In the absence of a formal declaration, or in the presence of a declaration made by an unauthorized source, there is no legal state of war. This casuistry is at least frank, and the definition of war apart from legality is identifiable. The worst that this distinction may lead to is the contrast between legal and extra-legal war, but at least undeclared wars still exist.

The twentieth-century Italian theoretician, Luigi Sturzo, reasserted this same minimal distinction so that undeclared wars may still be identified.[13] He developed this analysis into a claim that war is a right possessed by every State against every other State. When armed conflict exists other than between States we call it variously a vendetta, feud, street-fight, assault, brigandage, raid, private war, family war, tribal war, civil war, colonial war, guerrilla war, or hunting war. He proposed that the term war be reserved for public conflict between States. Even here, however, the term "public" is ambiguous and the term "conflict" ranges over a complex spectrum.

Hans Kelsen has distinguished two basic modern interpretations of war, and in each of them it is assumed that the existence of war is a matter for objective determination. His concern is with the legal status of war. According to the interpretation, war is neither a delict nor a sanction. It is not a delict because war is not forbidden by any general international law. It followed, thus, that any State could war against any other State without violating any law. Obviously no State would violate its own laws in going to war, and, in the absence of international law forbidding war, there could be no question of a delict. On the other hand, war cannot be a sanction either, since there is no international law authorizing war. While every State authorizes its own wars and condemns its enemies, this hardly constitutes a legal state of affairs. War is, thus, beyond legal praise or blame.

The other position held that there was a general international law forbidding war on principle, except where an illegal act, a delict, had been committed. On this account war is either blameworthy, because it is a delict, or praiseworthy, because it is a sanction.[14] How shall we decide between these two positions? On the one hand, war is neither a delict nor a sanction; on the other hand, it is either a delict or a sanction. The options here delineated may be postponed for the moment, since our present concern is not with the justification of war, but rather with the determination that a war does or does not exist.

In summing up this matter of the legal definition of war, Fritz Grob concluded that "there can be no such notion as war in the legal sense."[15] The obstacles he noted to the meaningful use of expressions such as "legal war" or "illegal war" included the simple fact that there is no corpus of rules of war internationally, nationally, or municipally. To be sure, there are statements on war, and proposed rules for the improvement of the atmosphere in which war is waged, but these are, for the most part, the pronouncements of private associations like the Quakers or the Oxford Conference, or pseudo-official documents like the Hague Proceedings which have no authoritative power. During the period between World War I and World War II many peace conferences met and many documents were produced, but none of these can conceivably be considered as providing a basis for laws of war. The Paris Pact of August 27, 1928, for instance, proposed the renunciation of war, but the international meaning of such a renunciation has never been clearly specified. In the absence, therefore, of any laws of war or rules of war, there cannot be any clear meaning to expressions such as "state of war" or "state of peace" in the legal sense. This being so, no applicable meaning attaches to such terms as "act of war," "de facto war," "belligerent," "limited state of war," "imperfect state of war," "partial state of war," or "quasi state of war." Indeed, terms such as quasi, limited, partial, or imperfect have no practical sense at all. Either there is a war or there is no war. A "measure short of war" makes no distinction except in retrospect, and then it refers merely to the last event prior to the first sign of war. If there were criteria of war they would not apply to any putative intermediate situation, and yet, if there is no war, then isn't there a state of peace, and, likewise, if there is no peace isn't there then a state of war? Notions of some limbo between war and peace are either contradictory or unintelligible.

Obviously the Congress of the United States, for example, must decide whether a war is to be announced as officially occurring. Their problem is not to determine whether violence has occurred, but rather, whether the violence shall be called war. The determination of this is not a simple matter of applying a definition, for admission of a state of war carries with it the assignment of praise and blame. This may mean that a set of otherwise identical bombings may in the one instance be called acts of war, and in the other left unspecified. Once war is granted to exist, every nation confronts certain protocols in terms of their responses. If Congress is not ready or willing to face these protocol responses, they simply do not declare a war. The expression "cold war" is one of the ambiguous alternatives to a war declaration. The difference between a "cold" and a "hot" war is not based on the fact that diplomacy instead of bombs is being used but upon the presence or absence of military action. A "cold war" is simply not a war in the legal sense, and, hence, it does not entail the political and economic sanctions of a genuine war. That these things are so bears out the prior observation that war is really a legal, rather than a military, issue.

If there were some sense to the expression "legal war," the existence of some international body which assigned the criterion for legality would at the same time make the expression otiose or contradictory. It would be like the idea of "legal revolution" within a country and by virtue of the laws of that country. This would be an absurd notion. It would seem to follow, thus, that under the rules such as those in the United Nations Charter there could be no legal sense of war. War would simply be a crime.

Even so, there would be no problem in ascertaining whether such a state of affairs did or did not exist.

In addition to the ambiguity of the definitions of war and the obvious sense in which the proffered definitions are weapons in the international anarchic struggle, there are legal obstacles to the acceptability of any definition of war which also includes the element of normative approval. If there is no legal sense in which the expression "laws of war" can be used, then we cannot say that war exists or does not exist. The whole subject of war would be outside of the scope of legal discussion. Within the nation, however, there could be laws permitting the nation to resort to war, and, indeed, nations commonly have the procedure specified by which wars are to be announced. It has yet to be decided, nonetheless, whether war is actually a national right or whether it signifies that all legitimate means have been abandoned. If war is anarchy, then there can be no rules for determining right or wrong in war. Where war is presumed, implicitly, to be each nation's right, there would still remain no legal context in which two nations could war while a third nation adjudicated.

In the absence of any generally accepted definition of war, or in the presence of such a cacophony of disparate and prejudicial definitions of war, perhaps the only alternative is to let each spokesman on the issue of war define the subject to suit his fancy. The problem, after all, is not to solve a problem of definition, but to determine how to resolve international killing and to forestall the potential nuclear Armageddon, whether we call this war or lawn tennis. Obviously, what one nation is willing to call a war may be what another nation insists to be a state of peace, and aggressive and defensive measures will be judged by the perspective of the participants who are making the allegations. In spite of this lack of univocality on the definitions of war, there are events of such importance that, by whatever name we call them, we may agree that they affect the possibility of human survival. The bombing of cities, the killing of persons with machine guns or flame-throwers, the poisoning of the atmosphere by radiation are deeds we would wish to abolish. When two nations meet at the level of the exchange of gunpowder, or when their mutual dealing entails the death of their respective citizens or soldiery, then, by whatever name we call this, we are intent that it not continue. There is, after all, a problem more than definitional posed by the fact that human lives are blasted to oblivion in exercises called "military" on fields called "battle." Our concern is that these acts of violence, made illegal and unnecessary within nations, might also be abolished internationally.

The trend of too much scholarly discussion over the definition of war leaves the impression that the whole issue is being resolved by some debate society of high school sadists. When men and women are being exterminated by napalm, rifle bullet, or bayonet it makes no moral sense to quibble over whether this is being done by war or revolution. Yet the discussions over cold and hot wars, declared and undeclared wars, genuine versus pseudo wars all give the clear impression that if we could just get our definitions straight, we could then either end extermination or perform it with impunity. Does it make any difference whether we wipe out a village by non-war rather than war, if we can agree that villages ought not to be handled like Sodom and Gomorrah? No doubt a legally conditioned mind might feel more secure in the face of human destruction, if, like some Torquemada, it can appeal to a legal rule. Our problems today, however, are not that our definitions are imprecise, but that our descriptions are false and our feelings are deadened by casuistry. Like Mr. McChoakumchild in Dickens' *Hard Times*, who attempted to show by definition that everyone in England lived in luxury, we try to show that if there is no war, by definition, everything must be in good shape, and we try to show this while the bodies fall and the anguished cries of wounded rise to the heavens. For our purposes in this book, armed conflict, arms races, military budgets, weapons research and construction, or the rise of mushroom-shaped clouds amid the fields strewn with human dead are the issue. If by some definition some are able to call these states of affairs "international incidents" rather than "war" the semantic squabble will be here ignored in favor of the more urgent matters of life and death.

II *The Just War*

MOST human history presupposes that wars are one of the legitimate ways by which states are administered, offenders punished, and national aims achieved. As a consequence, the early criticisms of war were not against its use in principle, but, rather, against some particular way in which war was being waged. The aim of such criticism was to keep wars lawful, orderly, humane, or just. In this vein Aristotle (384–322 B.C.) had observed that "the art of war is a natural art of acquisition, for the art of acquisition includes hunting, an art which we ought to practice against wild beasts, and against men who, though intended by nature to be governed, will not submit; for war of such a kind is naturally just."[1] Thus, war against barbarians was always just. Cicero (106–43 B.C.) had urged that the laws of war be obeyed so that men might be better than mere brutes in their fighting. He reminded his contemporaries that war was a human enterprise, and that it ought, therefore, to be subject to humanizing laws. He had concluded that wars for property and for glory were just wars, although those for conquest or national glory alone should be carried out with a minimum of rancor.[2]

The first serious Western effort to apply humane criteria to war practice was that of Saint Augustine (354–430). While he deplored the restless ambition that promoted wars for sovereignty,[3] he did believe that there were conditions under which it was just to extend an empire. If empires could not be morally extended, then nations already under the control of wicked rulers could not be righteously aided in revolt. Even where the war is just, however, the good man mourns the misery caused, and eschews needless slaughtering, plundering, burning, and torturing. Saint Augustine believed that wars before the birth of Christ were far more numerous and severe than were wars after the advent of the Prince of Peace.[4] Augustine, however, claimed that he was not chiefly concerned to tidy up the political affairs of man. The chief warfare of the Christian was against sin, and the major battles were those of the spirit against the flesh. When, for example, he stated: "Better, I say, is war with the hope of peace everlasting than captivity without any thought of deliverance," he was speaking of the battle for salvation and not of military conquest or defense. In spite of this spiritual interest, Saint Augustine discussed war with considerable worldly thoroughness, and he was responsible for the whole notion of the "just war" which subsequent Catholic Christians extended.

The idea that the preservation of property was a basis for a just war emerged in the middle ages, and prudence in war was advised so that the least damage to property would be caused thereby. This was what Saint Thomas recommended in *De Regno* as a general political policy, even though it was not formally applied to war until Franciscus de Victoria did so in the sixteenth century. Saint Thomas believed that war and Christianity were not antagonistic, and he rejected the notion that Jesus was a pacifist. Within this framework he laid down the formal principles of the just war. In the first place, an authoritative sovereign must declare that the war is a just one. In the case of force applied by the monarch within his own country, the word of the monarch that it is needed is ordinarily sufficient. In the case of war, however, more may be required. Thus, a second criterion of a just war is that a just cause is required. This just cause should be clear enough so that the monarch may specify it. This meant that those who are attacked must deserve such an attack. In the third place, the belligerents must have rightful intentions so that

good will be promoted and evil will be avoided. While these remarks may seem grossly vague to modern men, they gained
meaning in the middle ages through the conviction that there
was a divine strategy which vindicated just wars and attacked
unjust wars. Indeed, Catholics are forbidden to participate in
unjust war. The anomaly is that the Catholic leadership within
a nation have never declared the wars of that nation to be unjust.
In the face of the large number of wars, it would be egregious
to claim that they must all have been just. It would be unfair,
also, to conclude that the notion of the just war is an empty
cliché. The unwillingness of the Church to label any war unjust
has been defended on three bases. The church does not wish to
make hasty condemnations which they will have to recant at
some later time. They do not want the church members to be in
a moral bind between their religion and the state. They do not
want to subject church members to political persecution. All three
of these concerns rest on a further presupposition that the justice
of national wars is always a "given." This means that unless the
citizen has overwhelming evidence that a war is unjust he should
assume that it is just. This has lent to discussions of the just war
the aura of prudentialism.

Franciscus de Victoria (1480–1546) extended the scope of the
just war. In answer to the query, "Who may properly declare a
war?" he replied that citizens, states, and kings may all do so
when their person, property, or goods are threatened. In answer
to the question, "What are good reasons for a war?" he listed
several unacceptable ones. Difference of religion, for example,
was not a good reason for a war, and he asserted that Saint
Thomas and all the major Catholic doctors agreed on this. Indeed, odd as it sounds in the face of the Crusades, he knew of
no one of an opposite view.[5] Extension of empire, the personal
glory or advantage of the prince, and trivial wrongs are all
classed as unworthy causes of a just war. After all, it makes no
sense to respond to slight wrongs with the horror, slaughter, and
devastation of war. There is only one just cause of war, and that
is to avenge a major wrong received. Even here the reciprocity

must fit the offense. Under no conditions can we justly turn our swords against those who have done us no wrong. In order, however, to make sense out of some scriptural wars and to justify some papal wars, Victoria conceded that God might in special cases recommend killing inconsistent with all these rules. This alternative, however, casts discussion of the just war to the winds of convenience, since it, in effect, provides for the sanctity of otherwise unjust wars.

Pierino Belli reaffirmed that wars are to be undertaken only for serious and just reasons. He considered the following five as meeting the criteria: a just person, a just matter, a just cause, a just intent, and just authority. What this meant in fact was that any people or nation living under its own laws, and any ruler who is fully independent may declare war legally. Since both the content and the authority, called just, are ambiguous, Belli, in effect, sanctioned any war declared by any sovereign. Even when he intimates that some holy wars have been unjust, and that some church fathers disagree as to what may justly be done, he piously professes that the end of all war is peace, and you cannot really oppose what a sovereign does. At this point "adulation is more acceptable and expedient than candor."[6] After all, the emperor is the guardian and mainstay of the public good. In wars which he declares, it will not be considered homicide to kill. On behalf of such divine killing Belli cites King David, Saint Augustine, and Saint Boniface.

John Calvin (1509–1564) listed five acceptable bases for a just war. These were: to inflict public vengeance by a king, to preserve the tranquillity of a territory, to suppress disturbers of the peace, to rescue victims of oppressions, and to punish crimes.[7] If we wonder how a magistrate can shed blood with piety, the answer is that he does not act for or from himself, but merely carries out the punishments decreed by God. While it is not proper for the godly to wound or hurt their fellow men, it is not considered either wounding or hurting when commanded by God. How could the godly Moses have slain three thousand of his fellows and still be a lover of righteousness? The answer is that since God commanded him to do this slaying his hands were sanctified. Indeed, had Moses been lenient he would have been guilty of an indiscretion. Any monarch entrusted with the care of a people may therefore wage all war necessary to the preservation of land and possessions. While the monarch ought not to be unduly cruel, he ought not to be unduly humane. The Holy Spirit is called as witness that such wars are all lawful.

Balthazar Ayala (1548–1612) included in his list of the just bases of war: the defense of empire, friends, allies, property, to get back what has been taken from you, to put down a revolt, and to take vengeance for a wrong unjustly inflicted. Only a sovereign prince should declare war, and even he must be free from vengeful savagery and a passion to hurt, and to have as his aim peaceful existence and freedom from outrage. Indeed, it is these aims which justify any war.[8] He appeals to a "Law of Nations," canon law, and the law of God as enjoining just wars. In special cases, unspecified save that they are "pressing necessity or the absence of the prince, coupled with the hazards of delay," [9] there is a law of nature which justifies anyone in warding off an enemy. Ayala cites the case of Octavius Caesar, who began war against Antony before a decree from the Senate legitimized it. The Senate later ratified as just what Caesar had done on his own initiative. Apparently, there are strict rules to be followed in times of peace, while the threat of war justifies all that may be thought to be necessary for national survival. The ambiguity of the whole discussion is summed up in his remark that a war is a just one for whom it is a necessary one.

Francisco Suarez (1548–1617) argued from the thesis that self-defense is natural and necessary, and that, hence, defensive war is always just.[10] Even in the case of aggressive war, however, it may be both necessary and just. In this latter case, the war must be fought with moderation and with appropriate sensitivity to the relation of the attack to the reply to the attack; i.e., the punishment should fit the crime. Suarez summarizes the conditions that must be met for wars to be justly waged.

1. The war must be waged by the legitimate authority.
2. The cause and reason for the war must be just.
3. The war must be waged with a sense of proportion; i.e., there is a proper conduct in war.

Alberico Gentili (1552–1608) supplied a similar list of the just causes of a war, and he agreed, also, that just wars may be either offensive or defensive. One consequence of the position that the distinction between aggressor and victim is trivial, as far as just wars are concerned, is his admission that both sides in a war may have justice in their cause. He observed: "It is the nature of wars for both sides to maintain that they are supporting a just cause. In general, it may be true in nearly every kind of dispute, that neither of the two disputants is unjust." [11] Gentili was aware that some of his predecessors, like Baldus and Maximus of Tyre, had held that only one side in any war could be on the side of justice, but he believed that if such were the case, it would be a contingency not a necessity. There is reasonable doubt, to be sure, that someone is on the side of injustice, but it does not follow logically that if one party has a just cause then the other must have an unjust one. In such a case it is no surprise that rules of war should have developed as if war were a game or contest, where all the participants may do their part with honor. This would, of course, be a most peculiar view to take between police and gangsters within a nation, although, perhaps, the rules of chivalry from the middle ages provide a precedent.

Hugo Grotius (1583–1645) considered that defense of self and property were just causes of war. He added, however, that there were situations where it would be praiseworthy not to take advantage of this right of defense. In general, he proposed that "it is not, then, contrary to the nature of society to look out for oneself and advance one's own interests, provided the rights of others are not infringed; and consequently the use of force which does not violate the rights of others is not unjust." [12] Like many of his predecessors he appeals to a "law of nature" to show that war is divinely sanctioned, and he quotes from scripture to show that God himself laid down laws for the proper execution of a war. Even wars not specifically commanded by God can be just. The absence of any clear scriptural statement on the just causes of war Grotius interprets as signifying that the just causes of war are so natural that God assumed they did not need to be mentioned. In addition to the testimony of scripture in support of the justice of wars, there is general agreement among the nations, "and especially among the wise," that defense of one's life is just.[13] Anyone who wishes to rob us of life is clearly in the wrong. This conviction is so deeply rooted in culture that we judge animals by the same standard. Grotius cites Ulpian with favor on the position that if an ox or bull attack another, and if the death of the victim follows, then we judge the attacking bull as culpable. If the attacking bull should die on the horns of the intended victim, this result would be just. Wars are also justified, he held, by the laws of nations, although he admitted that while the laws of any particular nation might justify that nation in its wars, these same laws did not justify the enemy. Grotius held further that the legality of a war did not hinge on whether it had been formally declared, for if the cause of a war is just, it should not matter that there has been no official announcement that war exists.

By the end of the seventeenth century discussion of the just war, in the medieval sense of moral norms by which universal judgments could be made about war, had been transformed. From this time until the League of Nations, no serious juristic attention was given to the justice of wars. For the next two and a half centuries "justice" was a national concept, and each country had carte blanche to justify its own wars. Not until the twentieth century do we find jurists facing again the task of international law which alone makes meaningful international discussion of the justice or injustice of a war. During this intervening period rules of war were developed, but not criteria for determining whether a war was right in the first place. In reflecting on this turn of events Quincy Wright[14] noted an inverse relation between the rigor of rules of war and the observance of them in major wars. The rules laid down, for example, during the Hague conferences are both clear and strict as to how wars are to be fought. The analyses of how wars have actually been waged, however, reveal that virtually no nation ever made much of a gesture in the direction of living up to these rules. Like most modern "sports," the rules of the game are simply part of the obstacles to be hurdled, and success in war is largely a matter of knowing how to by-pass the rules.

It would be difficult to assess whether modern wars are more unprincipled and lawless than their medieval counterparts. That modern wars are more devastating may simply be due to the increased effectiveness of the weapons, rather than to the increased bloodthirstiness of contemporary soldiers. This issue is not merely a matter of a decline of chivalry, a concept that had meaning in the middle ages partly because of the influence of knighthood and the face-to-face nature of battle. The professional nature of medieval soldiers probably had no effect on the putative humaneness of war. In fact it has been claimed in democratic countries that volunteer soldiers tend to be more humane than professionals. Neither of these claims seems to be defensible. If modern warfare appears more bloody than that in the middle ages, it is probably due, in addition to the more effective weapons, to the concept of "absolute" war. In this thesis the entire nation is at war, and this tends to eliminate the distinction between combatants and non-combatants. If the civilians, men, women, and children, are all combatants, it makes no sense to compare medieval and modern war. The Hague Conventions deplored the wholesale bombing of cities in 1899 as inhumane, since the residents were not combatants—while in World War II both sides practiced wholesale bombing of cities, in part on the thesis that every member of the enemy country is a potential threat.

Charles Montesquieu (1689–1755) stated clearly that the law of nations, which he used to justify war, meant simply the law of a particular nation in relation to every other nation. War is a legal right which every nation gives to itself, and, in effect, denies to all others. Montesquieu saw the problem as a relatively simple one to be solved by an analogy.

"The life of governments is like that of man. The latter has a right to kill in case of natural defense; the former have a right to wage war for their own preservation. In the case of natural defense I have a right to kill, because my life is in respect to me, what the life of my antagonist is to him; in the same manner a state wages war, because its preservation is like that of any other being. With individuals the right of natural defense does not imply a necessity of attacking. . . . But with states the right of natural defense carries along with it sometimes the necessity of attacking. . . . The right therefore of war is derived from necessity and strict justice."[15]

Clearly by the time of Montesquieu the issue of the just war depended upon the legality of a war. The medieval concerns with the motives and attitudes of those who wage war are no longer present. We see this expressed in Adam Smith's (1723–1790) account of the conditions under which a war is lawful. Generally speaking, any matter that may constitute a proper lawsuit before a court may be a just reason for a war.

"When one nation encroaches on the property of another, or puts to death the subjects of another, imprisons them, or refuses them justice when injured, the sovereign is bound to demand satisfaction for the offense, as it is the intention of government to protect its several members from foreign enemies, and if redress be refused, there is a foundation for war."[16]

Likewise, failure to pay a debt, and every offense of the sovereign or subjects of one country against the sovereign or subjects of another, may be the just cause of a war. Smith was not sure about quasi-contracts, the breaking of which might lead to war, but this was simply due to the ambiguity of these before courts of law.

William Paley (1743–1805) separated the issues of war into the causes and the conduct of it. His remarks were tempered by the admonition that princes ought not to base their personal glory on the amount of territory they can amass, nor should they ever pursue national honor apart from national interest. He stated the just and unjust causes as follows:

> *"The justifying causes of war are, deliberate invasions of right, and the necessity of maintaining such a balance of power amongst neighboring nations, as that no single state, or confederacy of states, be strong enough to overwhelm the rest. The objects of just war are, precaution, defense, or reparation. In a larger sense every just war is a defensive war. . . . The . . . unjustifiable motives of war, are the family alliances, the personal friendships, or the personal quarrels of princes; the internal disputes which are carried on in other nations; the justice of other wars; the extension of territory, or of trade; the misfortunes or accidental weakness of a neighboring or rival nation."*[17]

He believed that the pursuit of interest was a sound basis for war, since self-interest prompted caution and a weighing of the gains and losses incident to war. National honor, by itself, and apart from national interest tended to be careless, hasty, and stupid.

William Godwin (1756–1836) went into careful detail enumerating the insufficient or unjust reasons for going to war. It is not justifiable to declare war in the hope that one would make his own people more disciplined and more obedient thereby. War should not be undertaken as therapy, nor as an experiment in psychology. When our own citizens visit other states, they should expect to abide by the rules of the countries they are in, and if they show excess boorishness, they ought not to expect their home country to come to their rescue. War is not justified merely because our neighbors are arming themselves, for an arms race is the first result of such a response. National honor is a very inadequate reason for war, since the reputation of a nation ought not to rest in military victory. There are only two causes of war which Godwin considered adequate or just. They are: the defense of one's own liberty, and of the liberty of others. While going to the defense of others may be abused by scoundrels or by men of ambition, the same reasons justifying self-defense apply to the defense of others.[18]

J. G. Fichte (1762–1814) reflected a strong nationalistic bias in his remarks on war. Both the violation of a treaty and the refusal to recognize a state are proper incentives to wage war and there appear to be few limits which cannot justly be transgressed.

> "The right of war, like all rights of compulsion, is infinite. The opponent has no rights because he refuses to recognize the rights of the war-making power. True, he may afterward sue for peace, and promise to recognize those rights. But how shall the other party be convinced that he is in earnest and is not merely looking out for a better opportunity to subjugate him? Hence, the natural end of war is always the annihilation of the opponent; that is to say, the subjugation of his citizens. True, a peace (or rather merely an armistice) may be concluded, because one party or both parties are too much weakened; but mutual distrust remains, and the object of subjugation remains also."[19]

John Stuart Mill (1806–1873) believed that to go to war for an idea, if the war is aggressive, is as immoral as to do so for territory or for revenue. We are as unjustified in forcing our ideas on others as we are in compelling them to economic obedience. There were, however, some instances where intervention in the affairs of another nation might be justified. Such instances might occur in the case of the relations of an advanced to a barbarian nation, since the latter would stand to gain by the intervention of the former. It was precisely this kind of rationale which justified the British empire at that time.[20]

Much of the current modern discussion of the conditions under which just wars can be waged consists in showing that war and peace are complementaries rather than contradictories. R. G. Collingwood considered this with the query, "It has been said that in certain circumstances war may serve the cause of peace. 'How can this be?' "[21] His analysis consisted in showing that war and peace are like black and white, rather than like white and non-white. It followed, therefore, that there is no impossibility of war serving the cause of peace and of being justified when there is no other way available to stem belligerent tyranny. In addition to the concept of the just war, some religious spokesmen include the concept of the pious war. That is to say, the war must be both sanctioned by law and by the gods. This has been true for Islam in the notion of the Jihad, or holy war.[22] It is roughly this same merging of law and God that underlies Emil Brunner's conclusions that divine love prompts the use of force in international relations.

"A State which is not prepared to defend itself by force of arms might just as well hand itself over to a more virile State, which, as a conqueror, does not hesitate to use these violent methods. To deny, on ethical grounds, this elementary right of the State to defend itself by war simply means to deny the existence of the State itself."[23]

Roman Catholic thinking on the question of the just war has covered the whole gamut from the acceptance of the war method as just whenever authority approves to some modern suspicions that the horror of contemporary war makes medieval distinctions inapplicable. John Courtney Murray[24] cited Pope Pius XII in favor of the position that wars of aggression, just or unjust, were morally banned. While Pius did not define what an aggressive war would be, Murray assumed that, as a minimum, the Pope intended to deny that war was a legitimate instrument of national policy. Since this position leaves the question of defensive war unspecified, and since every nation believes itself to be in the position of the defender, the old notion of the just war would still seem to be in operation. John C. Ford, S.J., in an article, "The Hydrogen Bombing of Cities," in the same source, intimated that these new weapons make even the notion of defense otiose since such bombs make the combatant-non-combatant distinction inoperable. A similar query was raised by John R. Connery, S.J., in an article, "Morality of Nuclear Armament,"[25] but here, also, the decision is granted to military men to make. The moralist appears helpless.

A genuinely forthright position, however, was taken by Franziskus Strattman, a German Dominican priest, and long-time director of the Catholic Peace Union. His position was uncompromising enough for the Nazi government in 1940 to deprive him of the rights of citizenship. The First World War showed that a new moral language on war was required. The magnitude of new weapons, eliminating the notion of the non-combatant, and exacting punishment of a cosmic quantity, deny any possibility of a just war. War is altogether forbidden. His mandate proscribes defensive and offensive war both. In the writing of Saint Augustine and Saint Thomas it was the guilt of the enemy that justified killing them. This became so preposterous a notion in the case of most war deaths that it was abandoned by many Catholic moralists as early as the 16th century. In modern war with its total-obliteration, saturation-bombing tactics, it is absurd to claim that citizen guilt, or even national guilt, can cover the havoc which is wrought.[26]

One of the anomalies within Roman Catholic thinking has been the fact that no official Catholic leaders have ever declared that a war of their own nation was unjust. It would seem reasonable to conclude from this fact that all talk about just wars has been mere rationalization. A criterion that has never been applied against one's own nation can scarcely qualify as significant. This situation is, in part, responsible for the doubt expressed by some contemporary Catholics that the simple Thomistic account of the just war can supply any usable concept today. In the face of the destructiveness of modern weapons, the old medieval notion of means and ends commensurate to each other proves to be inapplicable. Some concluded that there were no ends so good that they could be used to justify thermonuclear war.[27] In addition, the nature of modern weapons makes any precise distinction between aggression and non-aggression impossible. Not only is it impossible to determine who fired the first shot, figuratively speaking, but in nuclear war there may be no second shot. The whole concept of deterrence is now ambiguous, since if one uses his deterrence, then its establishment in the first place would be aggression. Expressions such as retaliatory bombing and nuclear blackmail have been used as applying to defensive war. Apparently, therefore, there is little hope that the offensive-defensive distinction will ever prove useful.

Hans Kelsen[28] asked how it could be possible to prove the thesis of the just war, when the only way in strict legal thinking to prohibit a certain conduct within a certain legal system is to apply a specific sanction. The only sanction in the case of an unjust war is war, a kind of war against war. It follows, thus, that war must be a sanction if war is to be a delict, and, therefore, the whole question has been begged. If we consider the documents of the various states, however, it is apparent that statesmen generally consider war to be illegal. This explains why the leaders of any state going to war make such an effort to justify to their respective peoples such an act. While Kelsen sees this as a moral rather than a legal kind of persuasion, he did believe that if there ever does emerge a legal proscription of war, it will have come from the existence of a prior moral prohibition. But, after all, the concept of the just war originally intended moral rather than legal sanction.

There is apparent a marked change between the medieval and the current debates over what constitutes a just war. In the earlier period the concern was with the causes and the means—ends for which and by which the war was putatively fought. In the current period, these issues are replaced with the distinction between aggressive and defensive war. The relatively simple American doctrine of the just war[29] states that any defensive war is just, and any aggressive war is unjust. The only problem, thus assumed, is to determine who started the war in order to ascertain who is unjust. Since history presents every nation, by its own lights, as the innocent victim, we are now in the position of having no negotiable criteria by which any war can be judged. On the credit side, the discussion of aggressive as opposed to defensive war has prompted the rejection of the legitimacy of preventive wars. Still there is a complacency, by medieval standards, about the ends for which just wars may be fought. In part this is a consequence of the preoccupation with who initiated the first aggression. It is rarely admitted that a nation might be transgressed against and still be in the wrong. The presumption is that war is not the real problem. The problem is, rather, did the nation in question resort to war at the right time. Even though medieval thinkers may have proposed a superfluous criterion, they at least did raise the issue of worthy ends, and they assumed that some ends could not be justified. In many current discussions the goals have vanished from the debate. What remains is a tactical question of when it is proper to wage war, and the criterion of propriety is so insular that no tribunal would be able to apply it. It is small wonder, therefore, that many now feel that the notion of a just war is a contradiction in terms.

The indecisiveness of most churches on the matter of unjust wars indicates the degree to which the notion of the just war has lost both content and criteria. Thus, in 1935, the Roman Catholic Archbishop Groeber of Freiburg-im-Breisgau rejected the claims of pacifism, and supported Hitler, on the grounds that Catholics have always left the decision of the justice of war to the legitimate authorities. This clerical rejection of the right of conscientious religious persons to condemn the killing entailed in war commonly rests on the presumption that the wars of one's own nation are always just, unless proved otherwise. This means that unless the citizen has overwhelming evidence that a war is unjust, he must obey the state. But, if the evidence for a war is equally so unspecified, why do we not begin with the thesis that wars are presumed unjust unless proved otherwise? Part of the unwillingness of churches to label unjust any war in which church members participate, stems from a wish not to put church people in a moral dilemma between allegiance to the state and allegiance to the church, and to relieve them from possible persecution. In addition, the churches fear unfavorable criticism for unpopular causes. Thus we have before us a history of the reflection on the concept of the just war with its attendant aim to assess wars by reference to their means and ends. If the medieval theological preoccupation with the idea of the just war seems presumptuous now, it is still a vast improvement over the current theological assumption that the justice of wars is a matter for lawyers and politicians to determine.

The abyss that exists between the pronouncement of the National Council of Churches on Vietnam in December, 1966, and the reflections of the local churches is of cosmic proportions. In spite of the suggestion that the United States is a somewhat innocent victim in Vietnam, the statement issued did bemoan the war. The February, 1966, position of the World Council of Churches on United States involvement in Vietnam was, however, clear in its condemnation of the U.S. and forthright in its proposals for adopting the cease-fire, negotiations, and general theses of both U Thant and the Geneva Accords. The response, however, was disappointing. Paul Ramsey[30] dismissed the recommendations as "Christian counsels of perfection." A meeting in Geneva, July 26, 1966, of the World Conference on Church and Society reported an almost universal condemnation of U.S. policy in Vietnam.

The masses of Christian clergy, however, do not look to such world or national pronouncements for guidance. Religious leaders are not supposed to make commitments on matters of policy, doubtless because the emptiness of the religious message guarantees that its kingdom is not of any world. Perhaps the whole question of just wars has rested on a mistake, from a religious point of view, since to contemplate the possibility of a just war presupposes that wars are either neutral or approvable. If wars are like lynching or concentration camps, then we err fundamentally in looking for just and unjust ways to use them. Clearly one of the great vacuums in religious discussion is over means to ends. If we can agree that spiritual conversion ought not to be done by the sword, we have certainly not witnessed any comparable agreement among clerics or religious laymen that political, social, or economic conversion ought to be pursued with any comparable sensitivity to the means used.

Early attempts to delineate just from unjust wars assumed that war was a moral means to certain ends. The aim was to determine who had the right to declare war, and answers to this question generally conceded that the duly authorized political leaders had this moral right. Since political leaders of two opposing states may both declare the war, it followed that such a war would be just for both sides. As long as the political chief declared the war, it was assumed that any war was just until proved otherwise. In determining which of the properly declared wars were morally just, the criteria ranged from war against barbarians, for property, glory, empire, vengeance, rescue of victims of oppression, to the repulsion of invaders. Generally, the concern, up to the eighteenth century, was with the moral defense of war. Since then thinkers like Charles Montesquieu, Adam Smith, or J. G. Fichte were more concerned with the legal bases of war. If the earlier strictures on the just war were intended for Princes so that they would not declare war for flippant reasons, the later pronouncements on just war were probably intended for the citizens of the nation, or for the neutral nations, so that the wars of any given nation might appear lawful or legal.

The crassness of the amenability of Western religion to Western wars stems doubtlessly from the naïve acceptance of Western culture, or of American culture, as the cosmic norm. Most of the theological double-talk on the just war stems from this chauvinism. If religion gives to Caesar his thermonuclear bombs, then it will be hard pressed, after this concession, to come up with any fruitful advice, since Caesar knows better than religious saints when to take the first offensive step. Perhaps the whole effort to moralize war and then to legalize it rests upon a mistake. This would appear particularly so in the face of the almost complete absence of any religiously identified unjust war, and the almost universal presence of the claim to legality by every nation in any war.

III *The Inevitability of War*

THERE IS A LONG Christian tradition which stems, in part, from an ambiguous remark attributed to Jesus: "And ye shall hear of wars and rumors of wars; see that ye be not troubled: for these things must needs come to pass."[1] The expression "must needs" has been the amorphous locus of a host of contradictory certitudes, many of which pronounce the inescapability of war, primarily because the passage is taken out of context. When this is done it reads like a prediction of doom, rather than like a sign of hope. The biblical scholarship of the last half century would lead one to suppose, on the contrary, that the remarks of scripture presuppose a millennium or an Armageddon, rather than that they intend to characterize human nature as unavoidably bellicose. Christians, nonetheless, have commonly assumed that the remark proves that war is inevitable. In fact, persons with no particular religious persuasion quote this passage of scripture as if it were a law of nature with which we have to learn to live. One wonders whether the authors of the Bible would ever have gone to the trouble of writing at all if they had known that their remarks would be taken so uncritically.

The early history of the Jews was filled with war tales in which God played a most belligerent part. Of course, there were exceptions to this macabre account. Solomon, for example, was chosen over David to build the Temple since his hands were not stained with blood. Wars were common, if not inevitable, even though it was believed that God could, if he would, have ended all wars by his fiat. In the first century of the Christian era, Tacitus, the Roman historian, noted:

> *"Though I would allow that there were some few who in their secret wish prayed for peace in the stead of disorder, for a worthy and blameless Emperor in the room of men utterly worthless and wicked, yet I cannot suppose that Paullinus, wise as he was, could have hoped in an age thoroughly depraved to find such moderation in the common herd, as that men, who in their passion for war had trampled peace underfoot, should now in their affection for peace renounce the charms of war."*[2]

Eighteen hundred years later Herbert Spencer (1820–1903) insisted that "the state of universal warfare maintained throughout the lower creation, to the great perplexity of many worthy people, is at bottom the most merciful provision which the circumstances admit of."[3] If, indeed, war is an expression of both human nature and a cosmic process, then only an ontological change could remove it. Political maneuvers would be superficial palliatives. Tacitus (55–117) had seen that the passion for power did lead to war, and that this passion was innate in man. Men were born to warlikeness in the same sense that they were born to procreate. Peace, like celibacy, therefore, was not the natural state of things, for war was common to all, and hence natural to all. Yet even celibacy, in spite of its putative unnaturalness, has become a way of life for millions. In spite of this, there seemed little confidence that sex was on the way out. What the proponents seem to have forgotten is that war is, after all, accepted as natural only in international relations. Within nations the militant way is looked on with condemnation, and the normal way is pacific and adjudicatory.

A survey of human history indicates that men have been preoccupied with war, even if it may be doubted that they were so inevitably. From 1496 B.C. to 1861 A.D., a period of 3,357 years, there were 227 years of peace and 3,130 years of war. This means that there were 13 years of war for every year of peace, and this is not a very heartening human record. From 1500 B.C. to 1860 A.D. there were more than 8,000 peace treaties, and they remained in force only two years on the average. It would seem, therefore, that if what men do is any guide to what men are, then their warlikeness would seem to be well established.

Saint Augustine (354–430) pictured wars as "stern and lasting necessities,"[4] whose results were, however, misery and horror for the human race. Many wars he saw as the result of the quest for empire, although even good kings waged war. There were, as a result, so-called just wars. Augustine believed that war was a part of the human condition, and, although it was to be lamented, it was unlikely that it would ever be abolished. After all, the ancient Hebrew could say, "Hear, O Israel, and be not in fear of your enemies; for the Lord your God fights for you."[5] There was, obviously, "a time of war and a time of peace,"[6] and God apparently approved of this state of affairs. Jesus, also, had affirmed the ubiquity and eternality of wars.[7] Since war was scripturally recognized, and endorsed by the Roman empire, it would have been surprising had Augustine not recognized at least the temporary need for war. Then, too, Augustine and his Christian brethren confronted the need to justify to non-Christian Romans that the followers of Jesus were good citizens who did their part in the stern necessities of political life. But the Church remained equivocal on war participation. For centuries the Councils issued prohibitions against killing, and stipulated penance for those who, as soldiers, had slain their fellow-man. In spite of this, however, the degree to which war received the early sanction of the post-Constantine Church was something of a measure of the general social acceptance of the compulsions toward war. The same Church which sent its own armies in battle against the infidels was in a poor position to classify war as really unnecessary.

Nicolo Machiavelli (1469–1527) was more impressed with the political necessity of war than with any metaphysical grounds.

This political necessity was, however, so compelling that he urged
the Prince to "have no other aim or thought nor take up any
other thing for his study, but war and its organization and discipline."[8] When he was listing the virtues of Hannibal, his in-
human cruelty in war was important enough for special mention.[9] Princes and republics of contemporary times which are not
prepared for war should be ashamed.[10] And yet, in spite of these
strong comments on the universality of war, Machiavelli saw
good reasons why social change might come about without war.[11]
In fact, one of the reasons that Rome lost her liberty, he maintained, was that she prolonged military commands.[12]

In the long list of the exponents of the thesis that war is inevitable because it is natural, none is so distinguished or thought-
ful as Thomas Hobbes (1588–1679). In the "state of nature,"
meaning prior to any social or political organization, all men
have a desire to hurt others. This derives, in part, from the fact
that all men desire the same things, and that there are not enough
of these things to go around. In a world, therefore, of limited
goods and inhabited by men of unlimited desire, "it cannot be
denied but that the natural state of men, before they entered
into society, was a mere war, and that not simply, but a war of
all men against all men."[13] It is this state of affairs that provides,
for Hobbes, the strongest argument for the need for social and
political organization. Perpetual war is destructive of any enduring permanence in the state of nature. In view of this, Hobbes
asserted, "to seek peace, where there is any hopes of attaining
it, and where there is none, to enquire out for the auxiliaries of
war, is the dictate of right reason."[14]

Hugo Grotius (1583–1645) insisted that "in the first principles
of nature there is nothing which is opposed to war."[15] All creatures are given strength for self-defense and each learns its mode
of fighting from nature. What makes war so inevitable is the
desire to defend oneself in a world where all men are naturally
trying to do the same. This was the same basis to which Benedict
Spinoza (1632–1677) appealed. War is grounded in the state of
nature. What is natural for men outside of political states is also

natural for political states outside of any international tribunal. Commonwealths are enemies by nature. "If, therefore, one commonwealth wishes to attack another and to use extreme measures in order to make it subject, it has the right to attempt this, since all it needs to wage war by right is the will to wage war."[16] This was the same position held by John Locke (1632–1714). In a series of criticisms made of Robert Barclay's abjurations concerning the rights of citizens to wage war irreverently, Locke insisted that "to resist force with force, being the state of war that levels the parties, cancels all former relation of reverence, respect, and superiority."[17]

The appeal to force is a natural right, and it is not abrogated just because men are no longer in a state of nature. Jean J. Rousseau, however, took issue with both Grotius and Locke. As he saw it, men in the state of nature were so loosely associated that neither peace nor war was a possible state. His subsequent explanation of this position makes clear that he was not holding the absurd position that men couldn't really fight except in society. His point was, rather, one of definition of terms. "It is a concurrence of things, and not of men, that occasions war . . . nor can private war between man and man exist either in the state of nature, where there is no settled property, or in a civil state, where everything is under the authority of the laws."[18] Rousseau did not express the prevailing view, however. Most thinkers, like even Immanuel Kant (1724–1804), considered that the state of peace was not the natural one.[19] However much he deplored the state of war, it was, for Kant, the one indigenous to human nature.

During the nineteenth century there was a clash of opinions on the inevitability of war. At one extreme Ralph Waldo Emerson (1803–1882) insisted that war would one day pass away as a sign that man had finally become mature.[20] At the higher stage of development, which will denote his maturity, man will turn the other cheek. This does not mean that a nation of higher men is inactive so that it would fall prey to the first marauding neighbor. Emerson affirmed, rather:

> *"If you have a nation of men who have risen to that height of moral cultivation that they will not declare war or carry arms . . . you have a nation of lovers, of benefactors, of true, great and able men. . . . I shall not find them defenseless, with idle hands swinging at their sides."*[21]

It should be noted, however, that Emerson believed the nation to be composed of individuals, and that he really assumed that war was born in the hearts of such private citizens, rather than in the structure of the state itself. At the other extreme from Emerson was Herbert Spencer, who avowed that war was the irrevocable discipline of nature for the perfection of mankind.[22] The eugenics of the human race required an endless war. Thomas de Quincey (1785–1859) rooted the necessity of war in "a sad overruling principle which it is vain to fight against."[23] This principle belongs to the degraded side of man. In spite of this rather unfavorable evaluation, he believed war to be necessitated in order that an otherwise callow age receive the blessings that only war can bring. Although he anticipated some kind of congress of nations, he did not expect that it would eliminate war. It would, rather, control[24] and purify[25] them.

It was Hegel (1770–1831), however, who presented the most consistent and thorough defense of the inescapability of war, and of its usefulness in the development of nations. The state was, for Hegel, the most significant organization to which persons may belong. It is in the state that man finds his authentic meaning. It follows, thus, that "sacrifice for the sake of the individuality of the state is the substantive relation of all the citizens, and is, thus, a universal duty."[26] Although he was aware that war may, and commonly does, end in desolation, he still insisted that it ought not to be regarded as an absolute evil,[27] since it is through war that men escape from the moral and intellectual stagnation which perpetual peace engenders. Indeed, the military class is the class of "universality."[28] Since Hegel predicated nationalism as the desirable state of affairs, he precluded the possibility of any international tribunal, and saw that, where rival states disagree, war was the only way to settle the dispute. Much of the fatalism about the necessity of war has rested on the Hegelian reification of the life of the nation as what war really preserves. Thus, while war may kill the citizens, it does save the state. Bluntschli (1808–1881) exemplified Hegelianism in his claim that:

> *"Without force a state can neither come into being nor continue. Force is required within, as well as without; where force has produced firm and enduring results, it seeks and commonly attains a connection with right. . . . United with right, it becomes worthy of the moral nature of man."*[29]

This inevitability of war, combined with its virtue-producing properties, has persisted as dogma in the writings of persons of a wide variety of metaphysical and ethical positions. Both Henri Bergson (1859–1941)[30] and George Santayana (1863–1952)[31] portrayed war as instinctually grounded in basic ownership drives and in more general psychic motives. War was simply inescapable. It was the case, Bernard Bosanquet (1848–1923) concluded, that as long as men are self-contradictory creatures who possess a conscience, and at the same time value some things more than the lives of their fellows, there will be war.[32]

While there is some evidence that war is older than civilization, there is also evidence to the contrary, and it has been debated whether man possesses this kind of aggressive behavior because of innate or conditioned causes. While it really shouldn't make any difference, the debate is carried on nonetheless. Most of the so-called civilizing process consists in eradication of ancient custom no matter what its causes may be. William Graham Sumner (1840–1910) summarized his portrayal of the human situation with the remark, "Men have always quarreled."[33] He might have added the obvious fact that men have always lied, stolen, murdered, and raped also; but for some interesting reason no prophet has announced, "There will always be rape and the rumor of rape, but be of good cheer . . ." Sumner did not postulate, however, that man has a warlike character. He noted, for example, that wampum belts and strings of beads were traditionally associated with peace-pacts and prayers for peace. Peter Kropotkin (1842–1921), the Russian anarchist, maintained that primitive men practiced an amazing amount of mutual aid.[34] Indeed, even the lower animals do so. In fact, he proposed that, with the exception of ants, man is the only creature who practices war. Even this fact, however, does not entail any biological instinct for battle.

Some of the real diehards for an ingrained human warlikeness seem to have come from the camp of the religious believers. Nels Ferré, for example, felt that since God had made the world with the potentiality for war, then there must be some divine purpose for it. It must be an expression of and an extension of the cosmic struggle.[35] We must remember, he said, "that God has made this kind of world and that we have no right, therefore, to deny that wars, however indirectly, have somehow a place in it."[36] To lend a further note of justification for his ad hoc account he alluded to the creativeness that accompanies war and to the decadence that peace nurtures.* He praised the Gothic ideal of fighting as being rooted in reality and as an acting out of the simple way that God has made us. With idyllic imagery Ferré portrays happy young animals fighting creatively, and noble humans gaily on their way to boxing matches, football games, or hangings. War is simply another fighting game, and the risks that it entails are therapy for an otherwise decadent species. As one contemporary writer put it, "There seems no more reason for believing that man will ever lose the fighting instinct than that he will ever lose any other basic instinct. . . . Not only is the fighting instinct permanent; the causes which provoke it are equally permanent and unchangeable."[37] Any expectation, therefore, that war could be eliminated was considered to be wishful thinking.

There seem always to have been self-styled and hard-headed men of the world who believed that the nature of things some-

---

*Despite these comments, on other occasions Ferré has called himself a pacifist, thus joining those Christians who have alternately supported and condemned war.

how necessitated war. Strangely enough these thinkers never held this view of permanence for any human act except war. While disease was natural, they admitted that cures were possible. Indeed, unless one has an esoteric view of "natural," anything that happens is natural, and, hence, to make the natural unchangeable would be tantamount to denying change altogether. Perhaps the fact that the world was composed of warlike nations and without any adequate international authority to resolve disputes made it hard for men to imagine that war would become obsolete. Yet, in a world which has had both a League of Nations and a United Nations organization, the fatuous cry of the military men still remains. Even with a U.N. the bellicose-minded ones still assert that contingency rules and that war is a eugenic tool. The Hegelian "slaughter-bench"[38] theory of history prevails even when the conditions that prompted it to be asserted in the first place no longer exist. Struggle is, for them, a fundamental law of nature, and periods of war are the noblest of human history. This inevitability of war has also been predicated on a putative human nature. If warlikeness is a human trait, then the opponents of war will first have to change the way men are before they can ever hope to succeed in abolishing war. This is part of the reason why Reinhold Niebuhr believed that force was necessary in this world, even though such force was not Christian.[39] Many of the traditional religious arguments that man has a moral right to wage war are related to this view of human nature. In Heraclitean fashion war was shown to be universal, and thus right. Given that war was inevitable, Hegel could then claim[40] that there was an abstract right to meet force with force, and Spinoza could claim the right to vengeance.[41] Out of the same premise James Russell Lowell (1819–1891) and William Ellery Channing (1780–1842) constructed a moral right for war. Treitschke (1834–1896)[42] could then avow that war was both moral and justifiable, and that peace was both impossible and immoral. Henry Sidgwick (1838–1900) affirmed not only that nations had rights to go to war, but that they also had the right not to be subject to any international tribunal.[43]

The thesis of war's inevitability has been bolstered and obfuscated by claims that there were character-building virtues of war. While these claims did not entail that war was necessary, they did make the apparent unavoidability of war more palatable. Francis Bacon (1561–1626) praised war as making for the health of the nation.[44] Both Hegel[45] and Treitschke[46] affirmed this claim. Hegel said that the warriors were the chief deterrent to national debility,[47] a position shared by Gustav Schmoller (1838–1917), professor of political science at Halle, Strasbourg, and Berlin. Even David Hume (1711–1776) believed that war developed character in soldiers.[48] One finds it hard to visualize, nonetheless, character developing in one-legged, one-armed, maimed, burned, and deformed soldiers. Long before imagination becomes as vivid as reality, the temptation is to put up with lazy, characterless men, if the only way to improve man is to maim him physically and psychologically. Adam Smith believed that war was the noblest of arts, as well as the most complicated.[49] DeMaeztu[50] credits war with having produced popular government, national solidarity, and human brotherhood. All of these appeals to the virtue-producing attributes of war have commonly been strengthened by appeals to religion. God has been rallied to the support of war for a variety of reasons, and even the survival of religion has been rested on the chariots of war. If, therefore, God has planned war for the execution of some divine plan, it should be no surprise that churches are bulwarks for militarism, and among the chief endorsers for wars fought by their respective nations. In this spirit Helmuth von Moltke (1800–1891) wrote in a letter to J. K. Bluntschli, December 11, 1880, that "war is an element of the world order established by God. It fosters the noblest virtues of man, courage, self-denial, obedience to duty, and the spirit of sacrifice; the soldier gives his life. Without war the world would stagnate and sink into materialism."[51]

In view of all these claims concerning the inevitability of war it would appear that the necessity is conditional. War is enjoined because we accept anarchy, nationalism, warlikeness, an instinct to pugnacity, human egotism, or a divine law blessing the warmakers. It is not so much the nature of war that offers such cosmic opposition to the peacemakers as it is the nature of the assumptions that make for war. The current concern of men like Norman Cousins that "modern man is obsolete"[52] stems from the imminent probability of nuclear annihilation which our preoccupation with warmaking entails. The tenor of some writing on war suggests that man welcomes his own obsolescence, labors for his own demise, or else is abysmally masochistic. Listen, for example, to the kind of self-deceptive double-talk with which the American public is assailed: "It is unlikely that this war can be stopped in any case. The only chance of stopping it is by carrying through a policy the fulfillment of which would remove the causes of war. This can be done only by a constant readiness for war; and readiness for war, far from making war more probable, is the indispensible means for decreasing its probability to the lowest figure."[53] It is surely more than an odd locution to speak of war preparation as peace preparation, for then napalm and diplomacy become the same methods, and bombing our opponents is the same as international adjudication. Perhaps there is a covert presumption that spreading war is like spreading disease germs; namely, that the patient may develop an immunity. If there were any likelihood of there being anti-bodies to bombs as far as the victims are concerned, then the analogy might make some sense. In fact, there is some meaning to the hypothesis, but it makes it even more necessary that war be abolished. Each escalation in a war, each new village bombed, and each new attack on an enemy fortification does result in an escalation of inhumanity, or in an inoculation against sensitivity. In the same bland voice with which the news announcer reports the imminence of the Christmas season, he reports the wiping out of enemy villages. We can watch a television program relating the efficiency of the ambulance units in picking up wounded soldiers, patching them up, and sending them back to the front lines and the common response is, "How nice that they are so efficient, helpful, and humane." One unit wounds them and the other patches them up until, like Prometheus, we may suspect that the vultures ought not to be confused with the healers. But these nice distinctions tend to be lost in the general callousness which the exigencies of killing produce.

The amphibolous casuistry which praises God and humanitarianism and drops the napalm suggests that it is not human nature or metaphysical reality that entails war, but rather that the inevitability of war derives from human stupidity. If men can talk of abolishing war with more war, banishing force with super-force, saving life with bullets, and securing the future with thermonuclear explosions there may, indeed, be little hope that man can save man from an ultimate Armageddon. Perhaps, as Berdyaev (1874-1948) concluded, a world of sin is a world which must wage war, and thus that there is no escape.[54]

This survey of the inevitability claims for war is, of course, only one side of the picture, and the chapter on the Christian attacks against war help to balance this. For every claim that men are warlike there is the counter evidence of the masses of citizens who are so far removed from this sentiment that they must be drafted before they will fight at all. We discuss these factors in the chapter on the supposed psychological drives to war. If, however, the human race is determined to vanish in a thermonuclear blast, it should at least identify the sources of the pressures that have led them to this brink. There are, after all, no necessities in nature, human or non-human, and this is a simple message of confidence which modern science has given us. War gains its plausibility from antecedent human enterprises and commitments, and not from any purported nature of war. If, in the last analysis, war is the only recourse, then it must be that we want those things that make for war, and the blame lies with us and not with the stars.

IV *Patriotism and the Military Spirit*

PATRIOTISM HAS BEEN CALLED the last refuge of a scoundrel, and, at the other extreme, as the ultimate expression of a socially conscious and responsible citizen. The military spirit, commonly inseparable from patriotism, has frequently been characterized as noble when expressed by our allies, and as villainous when practiced by our enemies. Nowhere is chauvinism more blind than in military evaluations. The aggressive spirit of battle is uncouth when exemplified by a Hun or a Vandal, while the same spirit is civilizing and humane when our own side expresses it. During most of the history of Western man there has been a close relation between military willingness and prowess, on the one hand, and patriotic sentiment and activity on the other. To be patriotic, in common usage, means to be a soldier. It is, thus, that the promotion of valor through military academies is at the same time patriotic education. Our concern here is with this identification of patriotism and the military spirit, as well as with the critics of this equation.

One of the earliest defenses of war was that it was a sign of national piety, and the unwillingness or hesitation about war was a sign of a spiritual weakness marking national decay. In the days of the Peloponnesian War Pericles (d. 429 B.C.) urged battle for this very reason.

*"If you give way, you will instantly have to meet some
greater demand, as having been frightened into obedience
in the first instance; while a firm refusal will make them
clearly understand that they must treat you more as equals.
Make your decision therefore at once, either to submit before
you are harmed, or if we are to go to war, as I for one think
we ought, to do so without caring whether the ostensible
cause be great or small."*[1]

Quite apart from the end defended, Pericles asserted, the means
of war are glorious, worthy, and signs of national commitment.
War is the one national effort for which there are no criteria
which justify critique. When war has been undertaken, then debate becomes unpatriotic. Thucydides (471–400 B.C.), therefore,
urged a strong military as essential for national survival. The lack
of a powerful army was both a cause and a consequence of
political degeneracy and personal weakness. War built the kind
of character that a nation needed: obedient, uncritical, passive
in carrying out orders, and fanatic in its own cause.

Yet as far back as Aristotle it had been recognized that military training was not good preparation for peaceful governing.[2]
Indeed, most of the ancient tyrants were demagogues precisely
because they were military men, and unversed in the art of
rhetoric.[3]

*"There was once a law in Macedonia that he who had not
killed an enemy should wear a halter, and among the Scythians
no one who had not slain his man was allowed to drink out
of the cup which was handed around at a certain feast.
Among the Iberians, a warlike nation, the number of enemies whom a man has slain is indicated by the number of
obelisks which are fixed in the earth round his tomb. . . . Yet
to a reflecting mind it must appear very strange that the
statesman should be always considering how he can dominate
and tyrannize over others."*[4]

This fear of Aristotle has prompted many contemporary theoreticians to urge a sharp separation between the civilian and military functions of government. In spite of this, however, there is very little concern over whether military leaders ought to be elected to posts of civilian authority. From the point of view of some endorsers of the martial spirit, it is a mistake to separate the military and civilian functions of government. After all, the aims of military strategy ordinarily entail victory in the shortest possible time no matter what happens politically. The aims of political strategy, on the other hand, may prolong discussion in a way inimical to military conquest. Civilians may, because of their political reservations, obstruct the military commander who is simply trying to kill his opponents. The military leader has an end which he euphemistically calls "winning the war," while the political leader has an end which he calls "winning the peace." Indeed, the confusion has become so abysmal that military leaders speak of their efforts as "peace offensives," and they designate their armies as "peace-keeping forces."

This bit of play on words makes military officers into ambassadors of peace, and tends to make conventional diplomacy into an ineffective game. In part, this linguistic somersault reflects a doubtful analogy between armies and police forces. But armies function in the absence of law, while police function under law. An army which increased the war tempo would ordinarily be praised for success, while a police force which increased the overt attacks of criminals might well be subjected to investigation. Where police brutality may incite a riot, this is action that is condemned. While when an army incites the enemy to attack, this may be praised as sound strategy. Armies commonly increase the likelihood of war. Police forces, on the contrary, would rarely be accused of increasing the chances for the commission of crime.

Aristotle assessed the proper function of the class of warriors in the political state. He asked whether those who determine matters of law should also be the same persons who compel obedience. Should these two classes be distinguished, or should both functions be given to the same persons? He answered this question conditionally.

> *"There is no difficulty in seeing that both functions will in one way belong to the same, in another, to different persons. To different persons insofar as these employments are suited to different primes of life, for the one requires wisdom and the other strength. But on the other hand, since it is an impossible thing that those who are able to use or to resist force should be willing to remain always in subjection, from this point of view the persons are the same; for those who carry arms can always determine the fate of the constitution. It remains therefore that both functions should be entrusted to the same persons, not, however, at the same time, but in the order prescribed by nature."*[5]

The perennial problem, however, has been to determine that mystical order prescribed by nature so that we know when men function best in their appropriate capacities. Surely there is no doubt that in the passions evoked by battle, and in the battles evoked by passions, it is difficult to keep clearly in mind one's appropriate function. What, for example, is the proper moment for the politician to become a general? Queen Elizabeth (1533–1603) is said to have inspired her lagging soldiers by riding into their midst and vowing, like some Joan of Arc, to be the "general, judge, and rewarder of every one of your virtues in the field."[6] Is this what Aristotle had in mind? If, as he claimed, the men who have the arms can determine the constitution, then either the politician had better be the military commander in fact, or else military men should be carefully quarantined from politics.

The proper role of standing armies can scarcely be determined apart from this problem of political and military leadership. Adam Smith (1723–1790) saw standing armies as entailing both risks and advantages. He was aware that men of republican interests were commonly suspicious of standing armies. Since armies function as lobbies against the legislature, they are threats to republican liberty. This fact had been borne out many times in the past. It was claimed to have been the standing armies of Julius Caesar which destroyed the Roman republic, and those of Oliver Cromwell that dismissed the Long Parliament. In spite of these examples of concern, Smith concluded that:

> "Where the sovereign is himself the general, and the principal nobility and gentry of the country the chief officers of the army; where the military force is placed under the command of those who have the greatest interest in the support of the civil authority, because they have themselves the greatest share of that authority, a standing army can never be dangerous to liberty."[7]

Love of country, however, has usually been found to be a deceitful principle from which to make constructive programs. As William Godwin (1756–1836) suspected,[8] the insight into the meaning and importance of liberty is best grasped in times of peace. War demands such obedience, and military involvement escalates callousness to such a degree that analysis of the worthiness of ends or the appropriateness of means appears like hair-splitting armchair speculation. The eve of battle is hardly the pedagogical environment for serious political decisions.

At least part of the battle over the equivocal interchanging of the terms "militarism" and "patriotism" comes from the fact that each "ism" extols the same virtues but for opposite ends. The double-entendres of Friedrich Nietzsche (1844–1900) in his exhortation to be warriors of knowledge, rather than mere soldiers of knowledge,[9] can hardly be expected to produce other than mystification. In another context he spoke of the will to power as entailed in being a living organism; and yet he considered arguments to defend the right of self-defense as "brought on by moral narcotics."[10] While, on the one hand, he saw the military state as maintaining the traditions of the past in its development of a strong type of man, it is by no means obvious that Nietzsche intended to approve of this state of affairs. When he called nationalism "bovine"[11] and the arguments for empire founded on "threadbare and discredited ideas" he would seem to be doubting this easy identification of patriotism and the military spirit. Unfortunately, too many writers on the subjects of patriotism and militarism feel called upon to be terribly subtle, and thus they add to the confusion rather than clarify it.

What precisely is the function of the military? John Stuart Mill (1806–1873) thought that it was "the last resort against the despotism of the government."[12] While he was aware that soldiers soon lose compunctions about killing foreigners, he apparently considered this enthusiasm for their work as helpful to nationalism, and hence as supportive of patriotism. Even a social Darwinian like Herbert Spencer, however, suspected there was a genuine conflict between the two types of function.

> *"There is, of course, a close connection between the sentiment of justice and the social type. Predominant militancy, by the coercive form of organization it implies, alike in the fighting body and in the society which supports it, affords no scope for the egoistic sentiment of justice, but, contrariwise, perpetually tramples on it; and, at the same time, the sympathies which originate the altruistic sentiment of justice are perpetually seared by militant activities."*[13]

Leo Tolstoy (1869–1945) was even more determined to root out the militant type of patriotism on the grounds that it, more than anything else, made universal peace impossible. He concluded that "to destroy war, destroy patriotism."[14] The difficulty of persuading citizens that chauvinistic patriotism is wrong is that they must first be convinced that war is wrong. The evils of war, however, are so ubiquitous and commonplace that military leaders are commonly the first ones to admit them, while yet girding themselves for the next conflict. "Seas of blood," Tolstoy observed, "have been shed over this passion; and will yet be shed for it, unless people free themselves of this obsolete relic of antiquity."[15]

Under the guise of patriotism, not only is the training of the art of killing sanctified, but any means to do the killing is permitted. Men can patriotically operate gas chambers as easily as hospitals, flame throwers as easily as microscopes, and they can drop napalm on villages as neutrally as they can drop pamphlets. Patriotism permits all these things to be done, and, what is more important, they can be done by good citizens.

Emma Goldman (1869–1940), in this regard, saw patriotism as "conceit, arrogance, and egotism."[16] Men can be trained to accept the job of spying, stealing, lying, and killing for their countries, and few seem to doubt that such enterprises are as "patriotic" as those of educating, healing, adjudicating for their countries. The cost of military patriotism is so great, and the human waste is so profound, that one would expect men of intelligence to have rejected it. The military enterprise survives, however, partly because it has the people's toys, and war is the game they play with these toys. If the military is, indeed, the best security for peace, as the military patriots affirm, then why isn't the most helpful citizen the one with a rifle? Why should we suppose that the powers of evil abroad are any different in kind from those at home? Actually the Minuteman mentality draws precisely this inference, and his paranoia about the world is matched by an equal paranoia at home. It would be too easy to dismiss Emma Goldman's remarks as about what we should expect from an anarchist, for the problem remains no matter who calls attention to it. The military patriot commonly looks at such dissent as, of course, unpatriotic, and demonstrates, therefore, his wish to poison the well of discussion and to protect himself from the inconvenience of having to answer hard questions. Much of the dissent, nonetheless, stems from a concern with human brotherhood and an anguish in the face of endless war, and it advocates that patriotism, if it is to be saved at all, be separated from military activity.

Military patriotism is, however, a hardy plant and has never been in danger of being rooted out by the simple expedient of showing that it is harmful, destructive, or decadent. Thorstein Veblen (1857–1929) pointed out that "once a warlike enterprise has been entered upon so far as to commit the nation to hostilities, it will have the cordial support of popular sentiment even if it is patently an aggressive war."[17] The arguments normally mustered, in the name of patriotism, bear witness to the vacuity of the base on which this patriotism rests. Patriotism all too casually equates the nation's material welfare with its honor, and promotes actions that drive a nation to colonialism in the name of saving its reputation. Military success becomes equated with cultural survival, and devotees from Hitler and Churchill back in time to Pericles and Moses have all made this point. Patriotism is basically chauvinism no matter what its language of expression. It contributes to the divisions that separate nations under the guise of glorifying nationalism, insularity, and territorial pretensions—all set to martial music. Toward the end of World War I Karl Liebknecht described the military spirit as extolling "the obedience of the corpse."[18] Indeed, the claims of this kind of patriotism are so implausible that indoctrination becomes a matter of decoying or deceiving the public. Liebknecht continued his indictment of the military mentality:

> *"The proper 'spirit' needed by militarism for its purpose against the foreign enemy consists of a crazy jingoism, narrow-mindedness, and arrogance; the spirit it needs for its purposes at home is that of a lack of understanding or even hatred of every kind of progress, every enterprise and movement even distantly endangering the rule of the actually dominating class."*[19]

Part of the whole military deception consists of the uniform with its badges and medals, and the status that comes with the wearing of them. The status that comes with clothes is particularly appealing to the lower classes, the psychologically insecure, and the mentally unfit. He saw the soldier as isolated from ordinary society and from normal contacts with the opposite sex. This insulation was furthered by the emergence of a special military history of the world situation. Thus the soldier does not need to be bothered by lay discussions of the facts, by the daily press, or by university professors. The psychology of military persuasion constitutes an attempt to "tame men as they tame animals. Thus the recruits are drugged, confused, flattered, bribed, oppressed, imprisoned, polished, and beaten."[20] In addition to what military training does to the individuals under its tutelage, it fosters an anti-labor attitude through the use of militias as strike-breakers. The fact that this has occurred has prompted many socialists to categorize the military as the private army of the bourgeoisie in its economic battle against the proletariat. Either the military is naïve, or else it is class-conscious.

Josiah Royce (1855–1916) commented on this kind of anti-social training:

> *"Let his elemental passion for conflict hereupon fuse with his brotherly love for his own countrymen into that fascinating and bloodthirsty form of humane but furious ecstasy, which is called the war-spirit. . . . But one reason why men love this spirit is that when it comes, it seems at once to define a plan of life, a plan which solves the conflicts of self-will and conformity."*[21]

Royce assessed the military masses as being politically inert and as lacking in social drive. If this had ever been the case then, it surely is not the case now. At no time since the middle ages has the life of a soldier been more of a profession, and never have military men been in a more strategic position to rule. Although he saw soldiering as irrelevant preparation for political leadership, John Dewey (1859–1952) knew that the position of military power did control the selection of political leaders.[22] This fact accounts, in part, for the failure of most ambassadors to be diplomats. Men who can wage war well are not, by virtue of this talent, equipped to wage peace or to engage in the compromises required at the conference table.

Immediately preceding World War II the proposal to introduce compulsory military training brought forth from the bellicose patriots a new wave of arguments in favor of the conscript life. In a letter to *The New York Times*, August 27, 1940, Colonel Hugh H. Young, then a surgeon at Johns Hopkins Hospital, and a clinical professor at the university, praised military training as a eugenic boon. "Systematic physical training, hygienic and sanitary education, along with military training would be of incalculable benefit to our young men, increase their vigor, materially lengthen the span of life, and develop in them a pride of country and right thinking."[23] He saw the program as a bulwark against subversive thinking, whose meaning he left conveniently unspecified. The lengths to which the military complex has gone in this program of military indoctrination has been documented extensively by John M. Swomley, Jr., in a recent study on *The Military Establishment*.[24] Norman Thomas, in a reply to the supporters of compulsory military training, believed that he knew perfectly well what the armigerents had in mind by subversion. Thomas asked the question about subversion, and received a military reply that the army preserved order at home by keeping the labor movement in its place. The experience of other nations augurs poorly for compulsory military training making a constructive contribution. Such training did little democratic good in Japan, Russia, Germany, or Italy; nor did it eliminate disloyalty or promote freedom in France, Belgium, or Holland. Conscription is more proper to serfs than to free men. A similar query was raised by Robert M. Hutchins, then President of the University of Chicago. He doubted not only that the army and navy were the best agencies to educate the youth in either physical or mental health, but also, as he observed, the military rejects the sick anyway, and therefore does nothing for them. If military men are healthier than the general run of the citizens, it merely means that they have been selected out of the nation as the most healthy to begin with. What is more crucial for Hutchins, however, is that military training unfits a person for democratic living. The military trains for obedience, for unquestioning acting on orders from superiors, and for non-participation in decision-making. None of these attributes is of the least democratic value.[25]

In his history of war, Charles Oman described the havoc wrought in states after the hardy, unscrupulous war veterans, accustomed as they were to loot and plunder, returned to the peaceable life. "The best of soldiers while the war lasted, they were a most dangerous and unruly race in time of truce or peace."[26] John Laird also raised serious questions about the social damage to democratic values which ardent militarism had brought about.

> *"Suppose, for example, a warlike State, organized for the glory of its arms, and allow, as many assert, that this bellicose efficiency may really be a good. If so, and if military aims have precedence in time of peace as well as in time of war, it is plain that the women of the community are to be regarded essentially as the mothers of warriors; that the boys are fighting men in posse; that the civilians are the tools of the body militant, gathering its supplies, manufacturing lint and uniforms and poison gas. The old and useless exist upon sufferance, and in time of stress should be exterminated."*[27]

Modern Western culture is not consistent enough for such extremes. What in fact occurs is usually some program to extend the life of the aged, and promoted along side of another program for the quicker elimination of the youth. Few societies have ever been as single-minded as Naziism. The fact remains, however, that military training does exhibit characteristics markedly different from those of ordinary public education. In a post World War II study of military education it was concluded that it differed from its academic counterpart in being controlled by a special-interest group which acted as a selector of facts, and because its aim was directed toward organized violence.[28] The military graduate had a mission which stemmed in part from his esoteric information, and the execution of this mission involved the person emotionally in a way ordinary education rarely does. G. F. Nicolai referred to this derogatorily as "the last great carouse of which even a degenerate nation can dream."[29]

Even public educators, however, must face the question of military teaching, since they also are expected to inculcate various kinds of quasi-patriotic sentiments. In periods of national involvement in declared or undeclared wars, this patriotic training seldom presupposes any critical assessment of the situation. Good citizenship descends to a matter of genuflection before verbal drum-beating. The impression is given that there is no peace-time patriotism, and that only active soldiers are loyal to their country. In no other time, and under no other condition, is the dictum "my country right or wrong" more aptly and more blindly appropriate. In a pamphlet called *Puppy Patriotism,* put out by the New York League of Women Voters, one aspect of this identity of soldiery and patriotism was elaborated.

> "In the military training classes brought since the war into the schools and colleges we are including an attractive and decorative feature, girl auxiliaries with girl officers playing at learning how to fight. To anyone who has seen war, to anyone who has imagination to perceive what it means, this popping in of young girls in natty uniforms, with light-weight arms, is a travesty, even a sacrilege. . . . It makes a game of what is, whether wrong or right, the ultimate sacrifice. We wonder that girls of intelligence can be found to lend themselves to so undignified a part, and we wonder that the boys have not realization enough of the gravity of what they are undertaking to resent this turning of the whole business into opera bouffe."[30]

It was this playing at the game of mercenary in the context of nationalist hortatory that G. B. Shaw called a "prodigious mass of humbug,"[31] and that Melman saw as contributing to the dehumanization of values and to a "robotized American society."[32] The military life is so self-hypnotic that the theorist of war, Karl von Clausewitz (1780–1831), could aver without embarrassment that "even when the likelihood of success is against us, we must not think of our undertaking as unreasonable or impossible.[33]

Students are not the only ones to face problems of clashes of conscience in war-time education. Many faculty members are asked to aid the war-efforts by virtue of their peculiar talents. When the danger seems imminent enough scientists may be expected to offer their services, as they did in World War II, to the development of nuclear bombs, chemical defoliants, and biological germ war. If the *Bulletin of Atomic Scientists* is any criterion of academic sentiment, then the scholarly community has done soul-searching enough to regret having been corrupted. Some German professors had similar pangs of conscience at being the designers of gas-chambers and the creators of poisons for human destruction. Independently of the ends which professors may espouse, they face decisions in which relative values are at stake. If some biologists are hesitant to lend their aid to building germ bombs, others have felt the same about thermonuclear bombs. This reaction of repugnance toward one kind of weapon, but not to another equally lethal kind, is doubtless of more psychological than moral interest. Since victims cannot be deader than dead, it would be difficult to show that stabbing is less humane than burning, or that gassing is less humane than shooting.

During the nineteen-thirties professors tended to assume that some kind of world organization was desirable. The exigencies of World War II, however, weaned most of them from the more naïve forms of this expectation. After the War "realism" was preached, and today, such realism is practiced by leaders in the State Department, who would travel almost anywhere in the world before they would make the short journey down to the United Nations headquarters in New York City. Part of the new realism supports the role of the Pentagon as the mentor of national security. Before the War there was considerable worry within the government that the military might undermine our democratic freedoms. The new concern, however, supports the military in the name of democratic freedom. Prior to the outbreak of World War I, the elder Moltke predicated that a politician should become silent the moment mobilization for war begins, and he should not renew his political functions until the military authorities have given their permission. While World War II was waged with considerable docility on the part of faculties, the same cannot be said for the war in Vietnam. During World War II, as one historian of the time reported, "the issue between soldiers and governments takes the form of an interdepartmental argument."[34] Current disputes about Vietnam within governmental circles can scarcely be classified as docile, although they are by no means widespread.

This blurring between the military and political roles was well exemplified in Spain in the Carlist War, where military obedience carried with it an obligation to compel political agreement among the politicians. While this may seem to be an exceptional case of a possible result of an internal revolution, modern states face the real and existent risk that a strong military clique can take over a country even where there is no revolution at all. The degree to which this is regularly done is borne out in part by the ease with which normal freedoms are suspended when cold or hot wars are being waged. The democratic virtues of free discussion and dissent, being antithetical to the military ideal, are the first political casualties. When this occurs, most of the normal checks to tyranny vanish, and the hitherto most democratic of states become monolithic.

In American culture, for example, and even without a declared war, the military functions as a political lobby, makes its own appeals to Congress for funds, carries out its own research, promotes its own image by advertising, and can declare any facts to be "classified," hence unavailable to public inspection, if they might prove to be opposed to the military plan. In the modern era, Congress becomes secondary to the Pentagon, which can subvert any political programs by the simple device of secrecy. One of the few expressions of individuality which Congress has in fact offered has been to vote more money to military budgets than the military asked for. Thus, even the putatively most open of societies has come to exhibit the inverse of the old maxim of Clausewitz, which now reads that "peace is simply a time to wage war by other means." The existence of massive expenditures for current and future wars, with weapons which can do their damage in moments and conclude all hostilities in hours, makes it impossible for politicians to know whether their actions interfere with national security, and equally for military strategists to know whether their actions are making a democratic society impossible. As recently as a generation ago military and political activity seemed simply distinguishable. Now, affairs are so complex that we cannot tell whether we are at war or not, let alone whether we are being run by military or political strategists. It used to be possible to tell a state of war from a state of peace by the size of the soldier body and its budget. This cannot be done today. In fact, we are so caught in the consequences of commitment to military patriotism that we have no non-military authorities whose judgment we respect in times of international tension. Even as recently as World War I we could feel that we were opposing the kind of military state exemplified by the Kaiser as the real nemesis of a democratic society. Modern states, however, have granted more to kaiserism than appears to be its due, with the result that all states appear equally controlled by gladiators.

In a world in which advertising is a recognized means to stimulate trade it is, perhaps, natural that public relations specialists should have been hired for the purpose of selling war to the citizens. War propaganda is no haphazard affair, although there are always self-appointed entrepreneurs in the business. Obviously, no war can be palatable to the citizens unless the opponents can be portrayed as possessing an inordinate share of the human capacity for sin. The message about the enemy is carefully leaked to the public through the media of the press, radio, television, manuals for soldiers, and official accounts of enemy behavior. As in the case of the Vietnam war, much of this startling news turns out to be unavailable to the public, or false when it does become available. [35] The circumstances under which this publicity is disseminated are such as to make verification extremely difficult until the facts which were once claimed to exist are no longer accessible to any inspection at all. The espoused need for such official secrecy falls under the rubric of "national defense." Not only is the citizen quite incapable of knowing what is happening, but he is indoctrinated to suspect his motives for wanting to know. Gullibility and patriotism become identified, and doubt or dissent are branded as subversive. Men in high places share in the general ignorance. Newton D. Baker, Secretary of Defense during World War I, was able to write apodictically, "Certainly the occasion of the United States' entering the World War was the resumption of submarine warfare."[36] Yet, in scholarly retrospect, and far too late to make any appreciable difference to the subsequent decisions of state, the entrance of the United States was seen to be due far more to political ineptitude and statesmanly stubbornness than to German wickedness.

Some Americans still imagine that Pearl Harbor was the cause of World War II, or that the Tonkin Gulf incident was the cause of American bombing of North Vietnam. The differences between the American government White Paper and the Citizens' White Paper[37] on Vietnam suggest either official stupidity or cupidity. The American people may be no more misled by their government than people of other nations when they are told that American wars are always between freedom-loving peoples and oppressors of mankind. Citizens are taught to believe that their own country never enters a war for sordid reasons. This has produced what has been called "the myth of the good and the bad nations."[38] Upon this myth most American foreign policy mistakenly rests, and, doubtless, most nations of the world are in a no more enlightened position than we. We delude ourselves with the conviction that our cause is always some cosmically virtuous principle, while our enemies always wage war for icons of clay and for immediate and immoral ends. Our allies are called "peace-loving nations," in spite of the disparity between the term and the facts in the case of such countries as Korea, Taiwan, South Vietnam, the Philippines, not to mention France, Germany, or Japan. Our opponents are called "slaves of dictatorship," "victims of aggression," "monsters of inhumanity," or, more simply, "Huns," "Japs," or "Reds." That the Japanese and the West Germans, at least, are now our allies might prompt one to search for the radical change in character which their people must have experienced The Russians were once our noble allies, even if now they are mentioned as perfidious scoundrels. Even so sober a mind as Harold Laski simplified the issues of World War II into a conflict between human right and human degradation. This is not to say that there are no genuine and morally moving war aims, but only that it is unlikely that the virtue is concentrated on one side.

One of the casualties of war is good sense and a respect for the facts. The citizens, in a time of war, are susceptible to any argument which makes them appear virtuous, and which demeans the aims of their opponents. The claimed "atrocity stories" circulated by Lord Bryce concerning actions of the Germans in World War I were widely accepted as true because of his stature as a scholar. Although these tales were shown to be, for the most part, false some years later, they are still quoted as "evidence" of the iniquity of our enemies. During the same war Adolf Harnack, the distinguished German biblical scholar, accused England of having broken down the ramparts of European civilization. He saw Germany as the only cultural hope for the West. In like manner, Rudolf Eucken, a German philosopher, identified the German cause as possessing the soul of humanitarianism. In the same war, Paul Sabatier, the distinguished French religious biographer, asserted that his country was fighting for the salvation of all mankind. His histrionics reached the turgid limits of an appeal to the Crucified One of Calvary as the chief public relations agent for the French cause.

The line between education and propaganda is a narrow one in issues such as war, but there is, nonetheless, a clear line between truth and falsehood, and between valid and invalid inference. It would be antecedently odd if all the virtue should be on one side in any war, although it would certainly not be an impossibility. What is impossible, however, is that all the claims of all the nations claiming virtue should be true. Error, like atrocity, is not peculiar to any one national climate. Consider, for example, the execution of Edith Cavell, the British nurse, by the Germans in Brussels. This act was hailed as a prime instance of Germanic degradation, and was used as one of the major reasons for the U.S. entry into the war. Shortly after this event, the French executed two German nurses under about the same circumstances. When the German officer of propaganda was asked why he had not capitalized on this obvious sign of French depravity, his reply was that the French had a perfect right to shoot them.[39]

Unfortunately one of the major, if not the chief, propaganda institutions furthering the myth of the black and white nations, or the good and the bad nations, has been the Christian churches. This fact is especially crucial for religious institutions since they make cosmic claims about moral insights and divine sanctions. Perhaps this is one of the sad prices that must be paid for religious overconfidence, that the institution that claims the most will make the most universal errors. The fortunate aspect of this has been that Christian churches normally make very few practical commitments. But, even here, the failure to be committed may then entail a cosmic oversight. Churches, in general, do not appeal to the putative ethic of the Prince of Peace when they sanction their country in its war efforts. Perhaps this is just as well, since the image of a bayonet-wielding Jesus is a little offensive. On the other hand, what churches do as an alternative may be even worse. They may cringe at praising the Lord and passing the ammunition directly, but indirectly their associations still show a fantastic concession to the things that are Caesar's. It may make as good sense to have chaplains to soldiers as to prisoners. What may not make sense at all is the sanction by the chaplain of what is being done by the parishioners.

The foreign policy of nations has ends quite divorced from even fairly crass Christian messages, and it ought to be at least one of the functions of religion to identify those differences. We have failed in an elementary way when we categorize our wars as between the Swastika and the Cross, or between atheism and God belief. National policies toward the outside world are usually bellicose, militant, coercive, selfish, and wrong. The church which gets too closely aligned with the state very quickly finds itself in the metaphorical position of cheer-leader for a gas chamber. The alternative is not that religion retreat to the weary epigram, "our kingdom is not of this world," but that it make the elementary distinction between leaven and gunpowder, between salvation and damnation. The criterion by which to be judged is not that we render to Caesar because contingency demands it, but that we promote the right, however unrealistic it may be to do so.

THE CRITIQUE
OF WAR

V *The Attack on the War System*

WAR IS AN ANCIENT MEANS to certain political and social ends.
Since it has been an institution that tends to self-perpetuation,
criticisms have commonly been directed toward the rooting out
of the entire structure. Such criticisms made no effort to tidy up
what they thought to be an otherwise adequate procedure for
the solution of human problems. Instead, such antipathy as we
shall consider saw war to be ill-suited to its putative ends. Even
if war had ever been able to accomplish socially acceptable results, the criticisms would still indict it on the grounds that it
exacted a price incommensurate with its rewards. There are many
ways to bring about social stability, for example, and they range
all the way from slow education to the extermination of the population by a hydrogen bomb. The debate over war as a means
concerns, in part, the question whether war is a kind of gentle
persuasion or whether it is a form of destructive exasperation.

The most extreme moral criticism of war is that it is national
murder, even though the normal justifications for war carefully
separate the taking of life in war from certain other circumstances
under which it might be done. The defender of war considers it
to be a form of police action, and the deaths it produces are believed to be an aspect of capital punishment for political or
social crimes. Such an analogy, however, makes a fundamental
mistake. Police action is under law, while war is in a state of

anarchy. War is like the old West range battles, which were carried out by self-appointed vigilantes and without any legal sanction. War is like Ku Klux Klan activity, and the deaths that result are like Klan lynchings rather than like executions at San Quentin. War presumes a double standard, which is both atavistic and insolent, and this is part of the basis for the criticism that war is really a form of murder. What is banned for individuals outside of the context of war is blessed by the state when the individual performs them in wartime. What is banned for states within a federal union is blessed for states outside a federal union. Police, after all, are not expected to be praised for destroying the residents and their homes under the guise of rooting out local crime. A police force which was as careless and callous of human values as an army is, would be investigated and abolished.

Saint Cyprian (d. 258) had noted in the third century that "the whole world is wet with mutual blood; and murder, which in the case of an individual is admitted to be a crime, is called a virtue when it is committed wholesale. Impunity is claimed for the wicked deeds, not on the plea that they are guiltless, but because the cruelty is perpetrated on a grand scale."[1] Seneca (54 B.C.–39 A.D.) had made the same observation that what was prohibited in private life was, in war, commanded by public ordinance. We praise soldiers for doing by deceit and treachery what would meet with capital punishment among civilians. Even Thucydides (471–400 B.C.), with all of his concession to the common need for war, agreed that men would commit acts in war which they would never contemplate in peace. "As usually happens at such times, there was no length to which violence did not go; sons were killed by their fathers, and suppliants dragged from the altar or slain upon it."[2]

Thoreau (1817–1862) reflected on the moral callousness of war and on the peculiar inversion of values which it produced. War, after all, destroyed the very things from which living gained its meaning. By the time war had begun, action had lost its warrant, and could not be defended on any moral grounds. In December, 1839, he commented on the reason for this state of affairs:

"When the world is declared under martial law, every Esau retakes his birthright, and what there is in him does not fail to appear. He wipes off all old scores and commences a new account. The world is interested to know how any soul will demean itself in so novel a position. But when war too, like commerce and husbandry, gets to be a routine, and men go about it as indented apprentices, the hero degenerates into a marine, and the standing army into a jest."[3]

He reminisced several years later, March 16, 1842, "somehow, strangely, the vice of men gets well represented and protected, but their virtue has none to plead its cause."[4] He deplored that sensitive persons whose sentiments cried out at the slaughter of war remained quiet in their chambers. Only the military Napoleons ride boldly for their causes.[5] It is small wonder, then, that war has been praised as one of man's freedoms, while survival is ignored as unworthy of concern.

This peculiar distortion of values prompted Malinowski (1884–1942) to consider man to be a victim of an incredible deception. War entitles the participants to a human hunting license with no limits to the criminal acts the hunter may perform. The basest of deeds become the occasions for the awarding of medals, and the most undisciplined of emotions become the marks of good soldiery. "Indeed," Malinowski remarked, "some contemporary writers in Nazi Germany and elsewhere try to teach us that the freedom of war is one of the inalienable rights of man."[6] Paul Peeters, in a current work on the inhumanity of war, believed that war was "repugnant to the moral aspirations of the American people."[7] Yet the fact remains that these same American people are astoundingly indifferent to the entire enterprise. The warnings of scientists concerning the holocaust of atomic war find an unexpected number of Dr. Strangeloves. Men of otherwise sensitive reactions speak approvingly of war risks where only ten or twenty million lives might be lost. The warning that radioactive fallout from our own bomb tests could reach the unborn and persist in the race for generations is not seen as a sign of the unlimited madness of such testing, but is crowded into the subconscious, or wherever else we put unpleasant truths. Even David Starr Jordan (1851–1931), who saw some excuse for World War I, believed that "a just weighing of all this evidence, however, leaves a decided balance in favor of a grave racial hurt in consequence of war."[8] This comment was made twenty years before thermonuclear bombs had even been invented.

This whole diffidence of the human race to its own demise prompted Voltaire (1694–1778) to remark facetiously: "That is doubtless a very fine art which desolates countries, destroys habitations, and in a common year causes the death of from forty to a hundred thousand men. This invention was first cultivated by nations assembled for their common good."[9] Outsiders commonly see us more objectively than we see ourselves. Raymond Aron, a contemporary French writer, assessed American belligerence abroad and concluded that "the United States is planning, and will concentrate more on planning, the ultimate war, the war which no one will envisage launching in cold blood."[10] The general lack of reaction to or memory of the dropping of the bombs on Hiroshima and Nagasaki at a time when Japan was already defeated, and with the knowledge that neither city was a prime military target, may testify to the degree to which we become accustomed to whatever we have done. In a thinly veiled satire written in 1914 an anonymous French writer pseudonymously showed that the standard defenses for war and for cannibalism were identical.[11] The psychic defenses of man would permit no such analogy, even though valid, and we candidly insist that we are not like those barbaric head-hunters or flesh-eaters. After all we do not save the corpses, we incinerate them.

T. H. Green (1836–1882) studied this whole position with great care. He concluded that to call war "multitudinous murder" was incorrect. If murder entails that a person kill with malice and that he do so for personal gain, then soldiers do not commit murder. This fine semantic distinction was not intended, however, to cover a sanction of war killing. While war may not be properly called murder, it is still a violation of the individual's right to life.

Even the fact that a soldier knowingly accepts the possibility of his own death does not alter the fact that persons have a right to life. Men may give their lives, but not their right to life. The state, on its side, may escape culpability for the death of its soldiers on the grounds that the "life of the state" was at stake. Even when this bit of specious rhetoric has been appealed to, there is still an unresolved question of life. Green's conclusion was that the taking of life in war is always immoral.[12] Even if killing in war is not murder, properly speaking, there are other ways to sin while taking life. Some writers, like Leon Trotsky (1877–1940), thought that Green's semantic quibbles were evasive, and that to draw such terminological distinctions merely made war more palatable. War, under Green's analysis, simply becomes hypocritical murder, since war endorses what under any normal circumstance would be an infraction of the commandment not to kill.

> *"In so far as the state is concerned, in peaceful times it limits itself to legalized killings of individuals so that in time of war it may transform the 'obligatory' commandment 'Thou shalt not kill' into its opposite. The most 'humane' governments, which in peaceful times 'detest' war, proclaim during war that the highest duties of their armies is the extermination of the greatest possible number of people."*[13]

A second general criticism of war as a system has been that it destroys political and social stability. William Jay claimed, for example, that war had caused the ruin of almost every republic which has fallen.[14] The kind of organization which war preparation entails was basically disruptive of the kind of unity and permanence which stable societies need. As far back as the Chinese sage, Mencius (c. 372–289 B.C), it had been noted that only peace brings unity, and hence a wise people guides its prince in the way of peace. The criticisms of Norman Thomas are in this same tenor. He indicted war because, among other failings, it did not solve political problems. World War I did not make democracy any safer in the world, and even if in some sense it had, it was still the case that human beings weren't in any better shape. The line between democratic death and dictatorial death is pretty thin for the dead. Thomas also doubted that World War II would be able to make the world safe from fascism. In fact, quite to the contrary, he believed that World War I had spread the seeds of militarism and imperialism, and he predicted that the next war would spread a dark ages of tyranny of which fascism was an expression.[15]

R. G. Collingwood drew the same conclusions with regard to the effect of war upon political life, as well as the sense in which war is a sign of political sickness. War occurs when men who are faced with the task of making a decision of diplomacy simply do not know what to do. This led Collingwood to assert that "war is due, not to political strength, but to political weakness."[16] In spite of this general awareness that war is poor medicine, it is still *au courant* to say that a nation's stature and prestige, its honor and its strength, are all demonstrated by the posture of military victory. The archetypes of success are still Napoleon, Peter the Great, Hitler, Churchill, or Roosevelt; and the sites of this victory are still the beaches of Normandy, Belleau Wood, Iwo Jima, or Tonkin Gulf. Men have still not been able to think of U Thant as a symbol of political strength, or to picture the U.N. Security Council as a place where political strength may be found. It is still widely said, if not believed, that to back away from military battle is a sign of national decay, and, thus, bomb-power means political power. By a peculiar inference political power is then claimed to imply moral or spiritual superiority.

One of the current American aspects of the conviction that the war system can be tolerated alongside of a political state, or within its structure, is expressed in the existence of the Pentagon, the C.I.A., and all the complex of secret, undemocratic, and divisive instruments with which they work. In spite of a tradition in America to keep military leaders from political power, there has been a breakdown in the older distinctions between a time of peace and a time of war. The Pentagon operates as if perpetual war were the case, and hence as if perpetual military governance were always necessary. Military lobbies function perennially with peace-time lobbies, and they not only advertise their wares, but offer financial grants for military research. Massachusetts Institute of Technology, for example, has received over 328 million dollars in defense contracts in the space of five years. In fact, seventy percent of the scientific research done in America, 1966, was done directly or indirectly through the Pentagon.[17] It comes as no surprise, therefore, that the donors should call on these research persons to come to Washington, D.C., to testify that all is really very well with the foundering world community. For example, Herman Kahn[18] observed that while atomic fallout and nuclear war might cause a high level of pre-natal death, this would really be only a personal tragedy, and not a social one. The American parents are apparently so fecund that the added deaths would not be missed. It would be absurd to deny that when a nation is geared to military ends its social and political ends suffer significantly, and this turns out to be the case in cold war as well as in hot war.

The C.I.A., in particular, poses serious questions about the role of secret agencies in an otherwise open and democratic society. In a study of spy agencies in the nations of the world, Paul W. Blackstock concluded that they perform "a continuing disservice to the peace."[19] The job of the C.I.A. abroad is, among other things, to recruit illegal agents and to maintain contact with the forces subversive to the government within a country. Since they operate under the shelter of diplomatic stations around the world, their very presence undermines the credibility of any diplomacy at all. It was reported by the C.I.A. that at the middle rank of American diplomats about half the men in any American embassy or diplomatic station would be members of the C.I.A. These agents operate, of course, under cover names. In the A.I.D. mission in Saigon, for example, the C.I.A. are in charge of the "Rural Affairs Section." In Laos it was called the "Programs Evaluation Office." On Quemoy and Matsu it was called "Western Enterprises, Incorporated."[20] What kind of diplomatic posture can a nation hope to give when subversive provocateurs are part of the pretended peace agency? It is as if the International Red Cross should also be the agency for the distribution of germ warfare.

Communist criticisms of war have concentrated, in addition, on the thesis that war is a bourgeois weapon against the proletariat. Since war is a continuation of politics, according to Lenin (1870–1924), it is obvious that the class holding political power will wage the war for its private gain.[21] This seemed so obvious to Marx (1818–1883) that he proposed at the First International that the Party eschew war altogether, as long as the bourgeoisie held the political power. Marx, further, credited the French and English proletariat with blocking a campaign of French and English bourgeoisie to support the South during the American Civil War.[22] V. I. Lenin branded World War I as an imperialist war, and claimed, therefore, that "phrases about defense of the fatherland in the present war falsely suggest that the imperialist war of 1914–16, which is a war for the distribution of colonies, for the looting of foreign lands, etc., is a national war."[23] He did believe, nonetheless, that if the proletariat could be organized on one side of a war, and have the bourgeoisie on the other side, such a war might well be justified. Neither Lenin nor Marx was as worried about the principle of war as about the practice of it which pitted proletariat against proletariat. In order, therefore, to know whether any given war had worthy aims, it was first necessary to pay attention to the politics which preceded it. As a consequence of such a study Lenin affirmed in 1917, before the World War had ended, that "the government considers that it would be the greatest of crimes against humanity to continue this war,"[24] and he pledged the determination of Russia to sign immediately conditions of peace which would be just for all peoples without exception. In 1936 V. Molotov warned the world that crises in capitalist countries were accentuating the dangers of war, and that "imperialist wirepullers"[25] were already planning wars of annexation as an escape from their internal crises.

Thucydides called attention to a further criticism of the systematic pursuit of war. War destroyed civilized culture. He noted that it "brings most men's characters to a level with their fortunes."[26] The whole moral fiber of a society is lowered, and the conventional morals are, in wartime, sacrificed to expediency and ridiculed as unmanly. From the solitude of Walden, Henry Thoreau observed the newspaper talk of war with England. He wrote in his *Journal* for February 27, 1856:

> *"What asylum is there for nations to go to? Nations are thus ready to talk of wars and challenge one another, because they are made up to such an extent of poor, low-spirited, despairing men, in whose eyes the chance of shooting somebody else without being shot themselves exceeds their actual good fortune."*[27]

The expectation that war will save a culture survives even the bitterest of negative evidence, in spite of severe criticism. The illusion that German arms could save German culture was derided by Nietzsche. Not only was the culture of the defeated France still intact, but the culture of the victorious Germany played no part in the military success.[28] Herbert Spencer was so sure that culture and war were antithetical that he believed that when a nation arrived at the position where ethical considerations were entertained, it would then reject offensive war.[29]

Surely it should not take an advanced stage of intelligence, said Hobhouse (1864–1929), to see that pestilence, famine, and organized slaughter are not conditions for the advancement of culture.[30] War destroys, or at least blunts, the faculties which are distinctive to man and which make civilization possible. Wars result in the loss of personal liberties in precisely those areas where the creative side of man is most fruitful. Either a nation decides to work for those institutions that make peace possible, or it wages war with enthusiasm, and, as Nietzsche observed, pays the price by becoming insensitive, stupid, barbaric, and vengeful.[31] The army will always get along without culture, but no so-called civilized nation can. Herbert Spencer[32] and William Graham Sumner[33] both stressed the fact that, while armed might may have served a progressive end in the childhood of the race, we long since have reached the stage where war does not promote civilization.

War rarely accomplishes anything close to its presumed ends. We wage war for "humanity" and rally our military fire-power on behalf of the gentler virtues, but, as Voltaire pointed out:

> "What becomes of, and what signifies to me, humanity, beneficence, modesty, temperance, mildness, wisdom, and piety, while half a pound of lead, sent from the distance of a hundred steps, pierces my body, and I die at twenty years of age, in inexpressible torments, in the midst of five or six thousand dying men, while my eyes which open for the last time, see the town in which I was born destroyed by fire and sword, and the last sounds which reach my ears are the cries of women and children expiring under the ruins."[34]

It was, in part, this pragmatic failure of war to fulfill any of the ends it claimed to be fighting for that led Norman Thomas to title his book, *War: No Glory, No Profit, No Need*. War is supposed to promote patriotism, but the nationalistic chauvinism that ensues is better unlearned, since it is this which blocks hopes for world order and feeds the fires of new aggressiveness. War is claimed to bring about the redress of grievances, but in the end, we must all come to the conference table, and it is there that decisions are constructively made. Some have even made the claim that war purges the society of the weak and the dissolute. Here, too, war is a dismal failure, since it takes only the physically fit for cannon fodder. Even if war did bring about some eugenic end, the price should certainly be measured against the gain. Even where war enthusiasts claim that it awakens the virtues of courage and self-sacrifice, they ignore the fact that such attributes are virtues only when they are directed toward worthy ends and when they utilize worthy means. The war-system is so successfully self-perpetuating, however, that it commonly seems futile to oppose it. We arm ourselves against hypothetical enemies and, far sooner than an enemy arises, we find the occasion to use the arms, precisely because we left undone those things which make arms unnecessary.

Many writers have bemoaned what Melman called the "escalation of brutality."[35] War has never been seriously credited with promoting a reverence for life; however, the sheer magnitude of horror that is now possible with modern weapons has created a new and mindless kind of brutality. Now we are able to annihilate whole continents, a deed which should stagger a sensitive imagination more than it does. Now we have banished the distinction between the civilian and military people of a country, since our new bombs cannot discriminate any better than the users of them. Even to think about what some have called the unthinkable has involved a cosmic devaluation of human life. The concerns which seemed important at the turn of the century at the Hague Conferences related to the bombing of hospitals, civilians, unfortified cities, the use of gases or cruel explosives. Such peccadilloes no longer awaken moral indignation. We now comfort ourselves with the jesuitical maxim that modern wars are total wars in the sense that everyone is a belligerent. With this kind of conditioning of insensitivity utopian schemes to humanize war are seen to be hopelessly naïve.

Our ability to destroy has so far outstripped our ability to imagine the results that we have become uniquely insensitive and heartless. The mere admission that we might plan for thermonuclear war creates what Melman called "a crescendo of complaisance" in the face of the potential extermination of the human race. The simple fact that within a few years of the close of World War II modern leaders can now think of the acceptance of the death of fifty million persons would seem to confirm every jeremiad about the brutalization which the threat of thermonuclear war has produced. In a potential war where the first strike could well be the last strike, leaders still worry about the damage they might be able to inflict in a robot-directed second strike. In a nation which would be a mass of rubble, it is a stark tragedy to contemplate retaliation. Indeed, the sheer pragmatics of the situation would seem to entail to any thinking persons that war is the great unreason that destroys the most important values we cherish.

VI   *Conscientious Objection and Pacifism*

THERE IS A RADICAL division of the Christian scholars as to whether pacifism may be rooted in the New Testament, and specifically, whether Jesus endorsed the position. On the one side, John Bennett concluded that "Christian pacifism has been a minority voice during most of Christian history."[1] In a similar vein, Umphrey Lee drew the inference that "Jesus left no pronouncement on the question."[2] This position rests on the conclusions of biblical scholars like Adolf Harnack, A. C. McGiffert, and James Moffatt. They emphasize the supposed millennialism of Jesus and the disciples, and the consequent other-worldliness which this expectation of the imminent end of the world led to. From this point of view they are able to dismiss the mandate to turn the other cheek and to go the second mile as not intended for ordinary citizen relations. On the other hand, they note the number of Church Fathers of the second and third centuries who accepted Christian war as a natural practice. On their side they could mention Justin Martyr, Clement of Alexandria, Tertullian in his early period before his conversion to Montanism, Irenaeus, and Eusebius.

On the other side, however, Christian scholars have stoutly maintained that quite the opposite was the case. C. J. Cadoux insisted that Jesus' position can be understood only from the pacifist perspective.[3] He illustrates this conclusion by reference to passages such as Matthew 24:15–22, Matthew 26:52, and Matthew 4:8–10. In a study of pacifism, Leyton Richards summed up the case with the remark, "The authority of Christ and the nature of war are so diametrically opposed that the Christian apologist for war is of necessity involved in a fatal contradiction."[4] Carl David Soule[5] also concluded that Jesus never endorsed the sword in either rebellion or war. These men were able to cite Church Fathers of the next few centuries to illustrate their thesis that leaders of Christianity had drawn the same conclusion right from the beginning. Leaders such as Justin Martyr, Tertullian after his conversion, Tatian, Origen, Cyprian, Arnobius, Lactantius, and Athanasius all gave fairly clear statements of an anti-war position as derived from Jesus. There is, in any case, some evidence that both positions had been asserted by the Church Fathers. The ambiguities of scripture and the risks involved in Bible-quoting, however, suggest that it is as little fruitful to attempt to read the mind of Jesus by his words as it is to attempt to show that his general outlook and deeds were as alien to sword-thrusts as they would have been to flame-throwers today. If the leaders of the Christian Church in the first few centuries were divided on the matter of war, this would be no more surprising nor troublesome than the contemporary fact that this is so today.

The practice of resistance, by non-violent means, to the war system as a means of abolishing it appears to have entered the Western world through Protestantism and Socialism. For example, in 1632 the Mennonite Articles of Faith, known as the Dort Confession, asserted in Article XIV:

> "As regards revenge and defense, in whom men resist their enemies with the sword, we believe and confess that the Lord Jesus Christ forbade His disciples, His followers, all revenge and defense, and commanding them, besides, not to render evil for evil, nor railing for railing, but to sheath their swords."[6]

George Fox, the Quaker, wrote in his *Journal* in 1659 that any-one who claimed to fight for Christ was mistaken, since His kingdom was not of this world.[7] In 1661 he wrote that the weap-ons of Quakers were spiritual not carnal, and that their weapons were plowshares and pruning-hooks, as the prophet Micah had asserted.[8]

> *"Our principle is, and our practices have always been, to seek peace and ensue it and to follow after righteousness and the knowledge of God, seeking the good and welfare and doing that which tends to the peace of all. . . . All bloody principles and practices, we, as to our own particulars, do utterly deny, with all outward wars and strife and fightings with outward weapons, for any end or under any pretence whatsoever."*[9]

The varieties of pacifism are quite complex, and one of the problems in understanding it at all is the suspicion of some opponents that the position is really quite simple. John Bennett, for example, said that there were two kinds of pacifism to be distinguished. The first kind recognizes the conflict between Christian faith and the waging of war, but it does not claim to have an alternative program in place of war. This type of paci-fist may go to war, or may refrain from war as a matter of selec-tive withdrawal.[10] The second kind of pacifist, said Bennett, is convinced that modern war is so devastating that it is always the greater of two evils, and they refuse military participation. They may, however, distinguish between force used by an inter-national agency, and that used by warring nations. The line between these two kinds of pacifist is loosely drawn. Neither type is necessarily absolutist or perfectionist, and neither may in a given situation offer any alternative. The sole possible point of departure seems to be Bennett's inference that the second type eschews war as a means under any circumstances. But dis-tinctions such as these are not too helpful in separating, for example, the sensitive military general from the pacifists of the first type. Indeed, the first type appear to be simply those who think war is hell, and that is a position that has not historically been called pacifist. In fact, on these vague terms all but sadists are pacifists. But men who have refused to take up arms, or even to support by taxes any war effort, have done so for a variety of reasons and with a variety of expectations.

A first kind of war resister appears to have refused induction into the military simply as a witness to love of mankind. It was not imagined that such witness would end war, convert the aggressors, or solve the problems of nationalism. Even if national destruction were to occur, this first witness would believe that his act was morally approvable. If his gesture of defiance seemed quixotic, it must be remembered that he did not accept the premise that a nation deserved to survive. He would let the institution of the church perish in the same way rather than use killing to preserve it. Leo N. Tolstoy considered the protest of the Caucasian Dukhobors to be of this type. These persons testified to the conviction that a Christian cannot be a murderer in uniform.[11] Norman Thomas thought that this was the attitude of the early Christians.[12] One thing was clear, however: these protesters did not think they were solving the problem of war, any more than Telemachus was solving the problem of the Roman arena. This first kind of pacifism, motivated by a sense of universal brotherhood, and expecting no cure for war as a consequence, was typified in the pledge of the nineteenth-century New England clergyman, Elihu Burritt (1810–1879):

> *"Believing all war to be inconsistent with the spirit of Christianity, and destructive to the best interests of mankind, I do hereby pledge myself never to enlist or enter into any army or navy, or to yield any voluntary support or sanction to the preparation for or prosecution of any war, by whomsoever, for whatsoever proposed, declared, or waged."*[13]

A second pacifist option prompts men to resist war as conscientious objectors, and to be non-violent resisters in the belief that such non-destructive resistance works for the conversion of the enemy. A. J. Muste[14] held this position with regard to pacifism as an instrument in the labor struggle. Indeed, it would be hard to deny that arbitration, as a form of non-violent resistance, or picketing and demonstrating as further expressions of this method, are socially safer and more likely to succeed than armed violence on the picket line. Norman Thomas held a form of this same expectation, although he no longer considers himself a pacifist at present.[15] It was the late Mohandas K. Gandhi (1869–1948), however, who idealized this principle into a practice. He believed that non-violent resistance in the peculiar situation in which India found herself would function effectively. He did not hold the principle of non-violence as a universal panacea. Faced with a situation where he did not believe that non-violence would work, he said:

> *"I do believe that, where there is only a choice between cowardice and violence, I would advise violence. Thus when my eldest son asked me what he should have done, had he been present when I was almost fatally assaulted in 1908, whether he should have run away and seen me killed or whether he should have used physical force which he could and wanted to use, and defended me, I told him that it was his duty to defend me even by using violence."*[16]

Gandhi himself had taken part in the Boer War and in World War I. His advocacy of non-violent resistance in India rested on the belief that it would work while violence would surely fail. When the circumstances are right, then non-violence will alter the attitudes of the violent attackers, on the thesis that love and self-suffering are powerful psychic weapons. The distinction made by A. D. Lindsay between pacifism as a principle and pacifism as a dogma fails to take account of this second basis for pacifist action. The principle of pacifism, Lindsay said, holds that where there is a legal avenue of redress, then violence is banned, but

where there is no legal avenue, then, as in war, violence is permitted. While Gandhi granted the possibility of violence under
some circumstances, his distinction was not a function of the
existence or non-existence of legal recourse. Pacifism could be
used even in war in spite of the absence of legal safeguards,
provided it was persuasive.[17] Yet there is some point of contact
even here, since Lindsay's notion of dogmatic pacifism referred
to a position which asserted that non-resistance, rather than
non-violent resistance, was always proper. Yet what Lindsay is
concluding is that pacifism is always improper in war, and this
is clearly not the position of Gandhi or Muste.

A third pacifist position considers that war resistance may so
undermine the war system that nations will abandon its use in
favor of arbitration. As long as national leaders assume that they
can count on the citizens to go to war whenever arbitration is
inconvenient or risky to national ends, for so long will arbitration and conciliation really not be tried. Why should any nation
submit its case to such a board as the U.N., and run the risk of
a decision against it, when it can always bank on citizen support
for armed resolution? When Albert Einstein (1879–1955) was a
pacifist, he said at a meeting in New York City, December 14,
1930, that if two percent of those assigned to military service
refused to fight, the governments would be powerless, since they
would not dare to send so many to jail.[18] Three years later, however, Einstein asserted that the refusal to perform military service was no longer effective, and that if he were a Belgian,
he would enter the army.[19] The French Socialist, Gustave Hervé,
urged his fellow men to declare, in advance of a war, that they
will not fight. He proposed, further, that if war is declared, the
Socialist comrades should desert the army, or go on strike if
they are reservists.[20] He believed that this latter gesture would
win the sympathies of the fathers and mothers whose sons constitute the soldiery. He called this strike against the conscription
of men into the military a "mobilization of the Countryless."[21]

Most who have held this pacifist position probably did not expect to convert enemy soldiers by their actions, but they did

expect to contribute to a situation where soldiering could not occur, simply because mankind had rejected it as a dishonorable and outmoded profession. Norman Thomas urged a similar refusal, and, in part, for the same reasons. If it seems like a naïve proposal, to undermine war by draft refusal, one must remember that Socialists see war as a consequence of a political and economic system, rather than as a legitimate method of international arbitration. Just as they believed that gas chambers in Germany were part of a Fascist or Nazi plot, they believe that war is a capitalist or imperialist plot. Their protest, thus, is larger than merely against military service. It is a protest against a whole way of life which they believe to be wrong and destructive. Some have held a milder version of this general war refusal. William Ellery Channing, for example, rejected the principle of non-resistance, but he did believe that individuals should not participate in unjust wars, and we can imagine him behaving like a disciple of Hervé under the right conditions, even though he would do so for different reasons. Saint Thomas was aware that there could be, in theory if not in fact, unjust wars in which good Catholics might be expected to fight. Theoretically, he made allowances for conscientious objection in the case of an unjust war. In fact, however, the Catholic requirement to be obedient to the duly appointed heads of state took precedence over private conscience, so that Roman Catholic pacifists were few in number, and they functioned for years in a kind of theological limbo. The conclusions of Vatican II, however, give official recognition to conscientious objection, and there has been a growing Roman Catholic pacifist movement. The easy assurance that Saint Thomas spoke the definitive word on war has been replaced by a strong wave of Roman Catholic rejection of the whole notion of the Just War.

A fourth kind of pacifism emphasizes a sense of reverence for life based either on religious or secular grounds. Its opposition to war is like its opposition to capital punishment and its aim is to abolish programs which wilfully destroy life. Pacifists in this category do their work essentially in peace time through promoting campaigns in favor of the United Nations, some form of World Federalism, a World Court, or some such means to the adjudication of war. Pacifists in this category believe that nothing is more sacred than life, and they find the patriotic circumlocution, "Give me liberty or give me death," either to have no meaning at all, or to apply only to persons other than the speaker. Life and death constitute genuine alternatives, and suicides are those who prefer death to life. These pacifists insist that if we wish to endorse war, or defend killing, we should not confuse the issue by claiming that death is better than life in any except a fictitious sense. Many a spiritual Patrick Henry really means to state that the lives of soldiers are less important to him than some end which he wants the soldiers to defend. It would be psychologically absurd for the soldiers themselves to assert that their own death was better than their own life, unless they are suicidally inclined. The old quip about a fate worse than death belongs on the silent screen where it can be seen as absurd.

A fifth kind of pacifism is motivated by the religious concern that killing damages your immortal soul. This is basically an individualistic testimony, but is certainly not to be impugned on that account. During a period in the medieval history of the Christian Church it was believed that clergy who serve communion ought not to have blood on their hands, and that the souls of even laymen were in some danger if they had slain their fellows in battle. The religious objections of Mennonites, Dukhobors, and Shakers have emphasized this concern with the soul. If this seems to be a self-centered and moral luxury which individuals ought not to expect, it still remains that one could draw the line at lynching Negroes, burning churches, operating gas chambers in some Belsen or Buchenwald precisely because he believed that such acts damned his soul in addition to what such deeds do to the victims. The primary reason why government recognizes religious objection to war as conscientious stems doubtlessly from the religious claim that salvation is affected by the killing act.

A sixth kind of pacifism opposes war because our relatives are, literally or figuratively, on the other side. Certainly German-born

Mennonites had a double problem in World War II when they were called into the American army. This was the issue debated by Krishna and Arjuna in the *Bhagavad Gita*. What do we do when we are asked to slay our own brothers? An extension of this concept is rooted in the religious or moral maxim that all men are brothers, and hence it should be just as hard to shoot Russian or Japanese strangers as to shoot our blood brothers, uncles, or father. These pacifists suggest that we ought to feel at least the paradox of Abraham, who was asked to slay his son Isaac in the name of religion.

Much of the shock which persons may feel when confronted with the pacifist position is due not so much to the position itself as to the fact that some persons have such sensitive moral feelings as to be willing to stand against government or social criticism. It is the kind of embarrassment which many feel about public protest, picketing, or marching demonstrations, as if there were something uncouth about a public proclamation of principle. There are, however, objections to pacifism which have been much more specific than this. It is common, for example, to point to the ineffectuality of the pacifist protest to end war or to solve international problems, but if we were to withhold moral judgment except in cases where we were assured of success, most moral compunctions would never be expressed. We would, then, never say, "No," except when it is to be followed by victory. It is, however, the case that much pacifist protest does not aim to resolve man's problems so much as it aims to identify the root of the problems. There would seem to be some justification for pacifism as a diagnosis even if it is not effective as a cure.

John C. Bennett suggests that he gave up the pacifist position when he discovered that it was not a pragmatically effective solution to totalitarian military aggression. But to admit that pacifism cannot stop a Hitler from his deeds does not commit us to the position that war is a solution to the problems which created a Hitler. If Bennett[22] felt that the United States government ought not to expose its people to nuclear attack without some power to retaliate, this position does not show that pacifism is wrong, since retaliation in a nuclear war is not so much a matter of national defense as of national pique. What rationale can there be for a nation which has just lost multi-millions of its citizens in a first-strike in feeling justified in a reciprocal strike? Is there some issue so important that the annihilation of two nations is preferable to the survival of either? Enough question has been raised concerning the defensive properties of nuclear weapons in a world where many nations have them to warrant the observation that nuclear deterrence may be as futile as pacifist protest, if the object is to provide national security.

A good bit of the opposition to pacifism as a general movement rests on the somewhat shaky premise that willingness to fight is a datum which deters would-be aggressors. It is this thesis that prompts some to brand pacifism as weakening the image of strength of the nation among the world of nations. This whole thesis assumes that nations of the world are all like Hobbesian wolves, simply waiting for the first sign of military weakness before they pounce on their weaker neighbors. If this were indeed true, the smaller nations of the world would feel far more anxious, surrounded as they are by nations they can never hope to match in strength, than they actually are. It is this type of illicit inference that has led some to accuse advocates of the United Nations of exhibiting weakness to the world, since this willingness to arbitrate could be interpreted as unwillingness to fight. Even Albert Einstein shared something of this fear, and, as a consequence, recommended that pacifists spend their efforts toward the establishment of some form of world government, rather than in objecting to war.[23]

A variety of so-called "test case" questions commonly confront the putative conscientious objector to war. He may be asked what he would do if men came to his door threatening his wife and children. Would he use force against them? There are begging presumptions in such a question that should be made explicit. To be sure one could hold the pacifist position as a principle of life, and maintain that what holds for international relations holds for husband-wife relations, that what holds for our treatment of the innocent bystander in war (cf. obliteration napalm bombing) also holds for guilty murderers (cf. capital punishment). This, however, would make a virtue of the most abstract kind of "consistency," and would insist that every stand of conscience be independent of what the facts are. Suppose we were to take the same camel-swallowing position with regard to those who conscientiously support war. Would we expect them to hold the same bomb-dropping reaction in labor-management issues, inter-neighborly factions, inter-church quarrels? Would the military man who refused to bomb Negroes marching in Atlanta be accused of faulty logic? Military men choose their wars, and governments choose the conflicts in which they propose to be involved. This being so, it is extremely indefensible to expect a pacifist to translate his international stand to his front doorstep, although, to be sure, he may wish to do so. There are after all Minutemen in the U.S. who propose to use trench warfare to solve our national economic and political differences of opinion.

The desperate problem facing the world today is not what to do with gunmen on our front steps. The problem is, rather: Do we propose to continue warfare, nuclear or otherwise, as a way of eliminating our opponents, or are we ready to accept international law, international courts, or international government? War has long since proved itself incapable of solving any economic, political, or social problem. Indeed, war now seems unable to solve any problem at all, unless it be the psychic one of providing an outlet for sadism, masochism, or simple exasperation. Human problems are all solved after the cessation of the killing. Surely no one would imagine that the capital execution of criminals in the United States solves any basic problem of removing the causes of crime. This is so even though in capital punishment we have the guilty person separate from the innocent.

In war, however, it is impossible to see how saturation bombing of men, women, and children who have committed no crime known to man, and are obliterated only because of the political accident of birth, could even be considered as "crime deterrence." War is obsolete, and from this fact, conscientious objection to it gains credence. A politician who was so obtuse and bellicose as to recommend solving the problem of the Negro demand for equality by well-placed atom bombs would be considered both socially dangerous and psychically sick. The current myopia, however, permits these same persons to propose a similar step in Russia, China, Cuba, or Vietnam without much of a response of revulsion from otherwise sensitive persons. As some military men have insisted, the death of the enemy is mere statistics, the death of our own soldiers is a tragedy.

The history of conscientious objection to war in the United States provides an insight into both the nature of the pacifist protests and the reactions of the country to them. As early as June 8, 1789, James Madison introduced a proposal for a federal bill of rights which would include the statement: "No person religiously scrupulous of bearing arms shall be compelled to render military service in person." This was not, however, included in the final version. Nonetheless several states did provide for religious objection to war. Maryland's early constitution provided that Mennonites, Quakers, Dunkers, and the like would not have to swear oaths in court. Many states had similar provisions. Maryland provided in 1864 for exemption from militia service for religious objectors. The constitution of 1819 of Maine had said that Quakers and Shakers may be exempted from military duty.

It was the Civil War which prompted the traditional peace churches to come to terms with the matter of war service. Some Quakers felt that they could not even support an anti-slavery president for fear that the president might have to endorse war. The Friends sent many delegations to Secretary Stanton in an effort to secure some written statement granting religious objectors release from military service. The sympathy they did receive is borne out in part by a statement made by Stanton to such a delegation of Friends in June 1, 1865: "He (Lincoln) and myself felt that unless we recognized conscientious religious scruples, we could not expect the blessing of Heaven."[24] On February 17, 1864, the Confederate Government passed an Act which provided that persons "heretofore exempted on religious grounds, and who have paid the appropriate tax, will still be exempted from military service."[25] Indiana, Iowa, Illinois, Kansas, Kentucky, and Pennsylvania allowed exemption for religious objectors provided they paid a fee. Michigan, Minnesota, New York, Ohio, and Vermont gave their legislators power to grant such exemption if they chose to do so. Connecticut, Massachusetts, Missouri, New Hampshire, New Jersey, Rhode Island, and Wisconsin had no statements on exemptions, but it was assumed that the possibility was there.

On April 6, 1917, when the United States declared war against Germany, the position of conscientious objectors was about the same as it had been at the end of the Civil War. Twenty-one states had constitutional provisions for exemption from militia duty for persons with religious scruples, provided that they paid an appropriate fee. When the Selective Service Act was passed on May 18, 1917, it contained, in section 4, the announcement that persons with religious scruples would not be compelled to serve in the military, but they would not be exempted from such alternative service as the President might declare to be non-combatant.[26] The Act contained, however, no interpretation of what constituted religious scruples or statement as to which sects fulfilled the condition. This decision was left to the local or district enrollment boards, with the result that a sect would be recognized in one part of the country and not in another. Most objectors, in any case, came under the jurisdiction of military authorities and their treatment of the pacifists varied widely. At Camp Funston, commanded by Major General Leonard Wood, pacifists were treated with such brutality that, after an investigation, five officers were dismissed from the service.[27] Five hundred and three objectors were given prison sentences ranging from the death sentence for seventeen to less than one year for three. The actual sentences as finally executed ranged from twenty-five years for one hundred and sixty-six to less than one year for two persons.

While the death sentence was assigned to pacifists in both the Civil War and World War I, the sentences were not carried out in either case. In World War I, unlike the Civil War, there were a number of non-religious objectors, and these posed a problem for Selective Service. An executive order of President Wilson, issued March 20, 1918, recognized only two groups: religious and non-religious. Major Walter G. Kellogg, a member of the Board of Examiners appointed by the War Department, distinguished three kinds of objectors: (a) members of a well-recognized peace sect, (b) those who based their views on the Bible but who belonged to no church, and (c) Socialists and similar political objectors. The Mennonite Churches supplied the majority of the objectors, although other denominations were also in evidence. The Jehovah's Witnesses were particularly in the public eye, in part because they were objectors even to alternative service, and because every member considered himself to be a clergyman, and hence entitled to clerical exemption. The degree to which war hysteria blinded otherwise normally accepted religious appeals was exemplified in the case of seven Russellites, or Jehovah's Witnesses, who were sentenced to twenty years in the Atlanta penitentiary, June 21, 1918, on grounds that their doctrines violated the Espionage Act of the previous year. The passage singled out for being especially subversive read as follows:

> *"Nowhere in the New Testament is patriotism (a narrowly minded hatred of other peoples) encouraged. Everywhere and always murder in its every form is forbidden. And yet under the guise of patriotism civil governments of the earth demand of peace-loving men the sacrifice of themselves and their loved ones and their butchery of their fellows, and hail it as a duty demanded by the laws of heaven."*[28]

Much of the pressure to punish Jehovah's Witnesses came from other protestant clergy whose periodicals praised the sentence. The difficulties of the Witnesses, however, do not stem from any pacifist convictions. They came into conflict with patriotic enthusiasts during World War II, for example, because they would not salute the flag, and because every Witness considered himself a clergyman entitled to draft exemption. The release of the Witnesses one year later prompted no feast of the fatted calf from other Christian churches.

Pacifism among the clergy in World War I was apparently a rare position, although the major problem in determining whether there were any pacifist ministers at all was the absence of much public information. In a study reported by R. H. Abrams,[29] only seventy pacifist ministers were known to exist, and none of these came from the South. There were sixteen Unitarians, thirteen Congregationalists, eight Universalists, eight Baptists, seven Episcopalians, seven Presbyterians, four Methodists, three Hebrew, three Reformed, and one non-denominational. Of the fifty-nine ministers occupying pulpits only thirty-two remained in their pulpits by 1918. Those who resigned were either compelled to do so, or voluntarily left rather than split their churches over the issue.

World War II saw far more acceptance of the pacifist position. Many churches recognized that pacifists had been trained by Christian teaching during the twenties and thirties. The World Council of Churches was being formed during the War and this seemed to symbolize the sense of world community among Christians, enemy and ally, in a way that was not evident during World War I. There was far more concern to keep the church free of military symbolism, and even the Archbishop of Canterbury, William Temple, criticized prayers for victory. In spite of this, however, the number of conscientious objectors is estimated to have been no more than about one million. Many of these were women or men over draft age. In any case, in the United States by the end of the War in August, 1945, 5,500 Conscientious Objectors had served or were serving prison sentences, and about 300 of these were non-religious objectors. By December, 1946, there were still 502 in prison, and of these, 455 were Jehovah's Witnesses. Objectors of draftable age were estimated to number about 50,000, most of whom obviously took some form of alternative service rather than prison.[30]

But if there was more awareness of the pacifist position in World War II there were signs that tolerance was still a long way from adequate. Those objectors who served in Civilian Public Service camps, as an alternative to military service, worked without pay, compensation for injury or death, allowance for dependents, or any of the demobilization benefits accorded to G.I. recruits. This lack of payment and protection was initiated by the peace churches that operated the camps, rather than because of any government decree. These peace churches did not want government direction in the camps to be stimulated by the fact that they were governmentally subsidized. When the war was over, their demobilization was considerably deferred, and they commonly found that they had lost the franchise or the right to be employed. While most churches probably did not function as recruitment agencies, there were few which aided and comforted the pacifists in their midst. Young men who had been inspired with the pacifist commitment found themselves, for the most part, without local comfort or concern. Nationally, however, some denominations did assist in supporting the CPS camps, since they were not subsidized by government funds. While financial support was given to pacifists in CPS camps, most Christians were unaware that there were Christian conscientious objectors and that their national church was assisting them. The vocal support given to objectors by clergy was a pallid contrast to the vehemence of the attack on pacifists made by Veteran's groups.

In the 1937 Oxford Conference there was a division of the participants over pacifism. Some advocated conscientious objection to all war, others recommended that objectors choose the war they opposed, some recommended that Christians support just wars, and still others supported all governmentally sanctioned wars (which really meant all wars in which one's country was engaged). Again in 1960 at the National Christian Council of India the peace advocates were divided. Some said the Christians should never consent to the use of nuclear weapons in an all-out war, while others eschewed nuclear weapons even in a limited war. Some advocated acceptance of military service as the duty of all citizens, while others chose objection to all war as the obligation of all Christians.

If religious conferences have been equivocal on the proper

posture for Christians in times of war, this same equivocation has been expressed by the major theologians. In general, theologians have exhibited suspicion of any thoroughgoing moral commitment of any kind, let alone on the question of pacifism. On the one hand Emil Brunner conceded that force is opposed to the spirit of Christian love, and on the other hand he insisted that the nature of the modern state required force, and that, unless Christians are to be anarchists, they must endorse, however sadly, the use of military force. A state which is not ready to use its armies might just as well give itself to the enemy. This is an odd inference, however, since it suggests that there are no alternatives to military force, and that, therefore, willingness to use an army entails using it in fact. One of the standard commitments of pacifists has been to the thesis that until nations are willing to relinquish force of a military kind in favor of political, economic, or moral force there will be little chance of avoiding the easy and premature recourse to war.

John Bennett concluded that "it may be our duty to do that which morally repels us."[31] It may well be that it is our political duty to do so, but it is not apparent why it should also be our religious duty. Bennett suggests that one reason why religious persons must wage war is to understand the depth of the meaning of original sin and the evil that lurks in the heart of man. Unless we commit evil we shall never understand evil seems to be the inference, although it is not apparent why ignorance of evil might not be the better part of wisdom if universal war is the price for the information. Reinhold Niebuhr believed that in an immoral society Christians must commit evil.[32] While he accepted pacifism as a form of Christian perfectionism, he insisted that such perfection was never meant to be an alternative to solving world problems by war. Niebuhr, however, fought a straw-man version of pacifism, and his easy victory against pacifist commitment rested primarily on a misunderstanding of some of the basic positions. Niebuhr recognized only non-resistance as being a genuine pacifist position. Passivity was the characteristic of pacifists, and he saw them in their authentic role as simply dragging their feet. The other options of pacifists which entailed non-violent resistance to evil he considered to be naïve and unrealistic. Either Christians passively resist doing anything, or else they should support the political need for military power. Niebuhr further complicated his own criticism of the objector by his assumption that the Gospels taught non-resistance rather than non-violent resistance. In part because of this, he concluded that Christian morals won't work in this secular world, and hence that our only recourse is to exert brute power against brute power. But from what mandate did the defense of this recourse come?

Nels Ferré recognized a partial concession at this point to secularism in a study on the Christian perspective on war. On the one hand he noted that "there is value in the process of strife and war. . . . God has made a process full of strife."[33] This strife is proper as long as it is constructive. The fact is, however, that "war is no longer constructive, even to the maintaining of necessary sovereign states."[34] Christianity, thus, rejects modern war as not fulfilling the spiritual requirement of being a constructive force.

Conscientious objection confronts the modern world as a spiritual gadfly. Partially supported by religion and partially by secularism, this movement compels rethinking of the whole issue of power, and particularly of the medieval notions by which we have traditionally understood power. In the contemporary world warfare has become so cosmically destructive that it is no longer a viable kind of power, and it is to this fact that pacifism so cogently witnesses when it objects totally to the notion of war. Where pacifists stand on issues of labor-management relations, family relations, or of crime within a state is not really germane to the war matter. The commonplace query directed to pacifists, "What would you do if a man came to your house and threatened to kill your family?" misunderstands both pacifism and war. The destructiveness of war surpasses in both quantity and quality the chaos of domestic battles between criminals and the police. It is no accident that pacifist protests against domestic police, or indeed against other uses of force short of war, are virtually non-existent.

War is a unique problem with a radical difference. It is not simply a big battle between criminals and police, since it is precisely the forces of law and order who do battle with each other in war. In addition, the havoc wrought to the general populace makes it indefensible as a means of preserving the political state. At such a price as war exacts, the contemporary sovereign states cannot defend their own survival, and the sooner they relinquish power to international government, the sooner the very option of war will disappear.

It is precisely the Christian rejection of the world as outside Christian healing which has prompted the revolt of secularism against the other-worldliness of religion. If Christians must acquiesce to the status quo of military power, then their kingdom is indeed not of this world, and the sooner mankind accepts its responsibility to provide its own humanistic healing, the sooner war's ills will be healed. When our theologians speak like our generals, one of the two groups must be confused, or else Christianity has indeed demonstrated its final capitulation to the impotence of its own message to alter human behavior. Conscientious objection confronts religion as a gadfly, for religion must then either rise up to be counted with the pacifists, make public confession that it is on the side of militarists, or retreat to its sacramental sanctuary as aliens in a weary and sinful world.

VII *Humane and Inhumane War Practices*

THERE ARE FEW AREAS OF the war-peace discussions which exhibit more of the confusion, naïveté, and paradox with which man confronts his dilemmas than those historic attempts to humanize war. The sanctity with which much of the discussion is cloaked may easily hide the suspicion that in some instances we are attending a meeting of gas-chamber operators who are trying to find quicker, more efficient, and more "humane" ways of exterminating their customers. There comes a point when it must seem anomalous to talk about Christianizing or humanizing a method with which neither Christianity nor humanitarianism ought to have any consort. The main presumption of the war-humanizing talk is that the method of war is acceptable provided that it is carried out in the right way. The thesis further assumes that selective killing is more beneficent than indiscriminate killing, that sudden killing is kinder than slow killing, and that bullets are more moral than biological warfare.

Strange as this position may appear to be, there is an apparent effort through the ages to set limits beyond which warlike action ought not to go. While there were men, like Bynkerschoek,[1] who claimed that war justified every method necessary to destroy the enemy, there were also, at the other extreme, contentions like that of Rousseau[2] that there were clear limits to what should be sanctioned in war. In an elementary sense the former considered the ends to warrant any means, while the latter was concerned that the means be such as to sanctify the ends. Those who believe in humanizing war, while still retaining it, commonly wish to show that wars have been getting more humane as a consequence of efforts like theirs. Those who see the war method itself as the problem, rather than the rules of war, see little improvement from the medieval forays of the Vandals to the contemporary flame-throwing and napalm-scorching expeditions of modern warfare. It is not merely that brutality seems unchanged throughout the history of warfare, but that it makes little sense to speak of humane ways of extermination. In spite of the contradictions implicit in the whole enterprise, the hope to make war more kindly has prompted a considerable amount of soul-searching on the part of persons with moral or religious commitments, who are still unwilling to abandon war to the sadists. Still the nagging suspicion remains that a loving bayonet-thrust is a contradiction in terms, and that a painting of a kindly and affectionate operator of a Belsen or a Buchenwald confuses some rather basic distinctions.

One of the earliest attempts to limit the destructiveness of war, and hence to humanize it, was that entailed in setting limits to the proper scope of war in terms of times, persons, or places, and with regard to weapons appropriate to such limits. In 1041 A.D. the Bishop of Arles and the Abbot of Cluny established the "truce of God," which limited the times when war should be carried out. Initially, war was permitted only between Monday morning and Wednesday evening. In addition, there was to be no fighting between Advent and Epiphany, from Septuagesima until the eighth day after Pentecost, and on Sundays, Fridays, and all holy days. Such a "truce" was probably never followed with any consistency and it never became established custom, nor was it institutionalized in spite of some modest influence. The "Peace of God" decreed at the Council of Narbonne in 1054 limited the kinds of persons who could properly be attacked in war. The "Peace" asserted, for example, that there should be no attack on monks, nuns, pilgrims, merchants, peasants, visitors to councils or churches, and to the surrounding grounds to a limit of thirty feet (provided that the visitors did not carry weapons), cemeteries, cloisters for an area of sixty feet around, clerical lands, shepherds of flocks, agricultural animals, wagons in the fields, and olive trees. This "Peace" endeavored to make a distinction between combatants and non-combatants, a distinction that enjoyed some support until contemporary times. But if the current concept of total war has done nothing else, it has shown the chimera of this medieval dream to limit war. Guglielmo Ferrero (1871–1942), a contemporary writer on the subject, asserted that limits must be set to war, once again, or else annihilation will be the ultimate result. This would be the right solution, he affirmed, if reason ruled the world,[3] and if war were fought in the relatively simple fashion of hand-to-hand combat. At the present stage of war skills the hope to limit or to humanize war is a fatuous dream. Indeed, the mystical belief of the leaders and citizens that their causes are sanctified by cosmic underpinnings makes it impossible to speak about the rights of opponents in armed conflict. The public relations campaigns which accompany modern war picture all evil to be residing with the enemy, and portray him as having relinquished all claim to any moral right. It seems, therefore, nonsense to speak of humanizing war in the twentieth century.

Lest we suppose, however, that medieval war was fought under more conscientious terms than was actually the case, let us note that even the recommendation that holy days should not be killing days was a contingent one. Saint Thomas,[4] while urging proper behavior on sacred days, allowed that if there was need for doing so, war could be waged at any time. The reference to holy days became, therefore, a weapon with which to shame the enemy, who might find it necessary to attack on the sabbath day. At the same time, it was the loophole by which military prudence could be permitted to one's own forces. In spite of this casuistry in the justification of military action, there were valiant efforts to keep war an affair of armed soldiers alone. Pierino Belli[5] re-affirmed the canonical mandate urging the protection of monks, nuns, pilgrims, merchants, shepherds, and farmers, although he admitted that these restrictions were rarely obeyed by anyone. In reference to the canon law concerning war on holy days, however, he conceded that such laws may safely be ignored. J. G. Fichte[6] urged in the eighteenth century that only the armed citizens should be considered as the enemy, and that unarmed citizens should be spared. Earlier in the century Benjamin Franklin (1706–1790) had endorsed the right to non-violent involvement of farmers, fishermen, merchants, artists, and mechanics.[7] But in spite of the long history of listing non-combatants, William Ladd (1778–1841) commented in his *Congress of Nations* that until the present there had been no attempts to guard the safety of the innocent, and that what current efforts there were should be credited to the Christians.[8]

In the days of kingly wars, everyone assumed that the civilian population stood outside the quarrels, and, as a result, it made some general sense to speak of certain persons as being innocent. Modern total war, with modern total weapons, makes it impractical to recognize any innocence in civilians. R. E. Osgood could observe that to the American people "the limitation of war is morally and emotionally repugnant."[9] His hope was, however, that the American people would see, on political grounds, that the limitation of the military aspects of war constitutes a rational national policy, quite apart from the simple fact that limited war is more compatible with respect for human life. Modern discussion, however, contains the expression "limited war" in a peculiarly esoteric and egregious fashion. In the Pentagon today, any war is limited if it does not involve both the United States and the U.S.S.R. Consequently the Korean War, with its loss of thirty thousand American lives, was a limited war. Military men explained that the bombing of Hiroshima and Nagasaki was a limited bombing, since, obviously, there were some Japanese cities left.[10] Osgood stated that limited wars could be fought with weapons ranging from atom bombs to daggers.[11]

On these terms, however, the notion of limited war has lost any significant meaning. It is not apparent what inferences one is intended to draw from the semantic distinction which notes that most wars are less than total, or that all wars to date have been limited. Even the medieval dream of sparing non-combatants was rejected by the theologians, whom one might expect would be the first to endorse the idea. Dietrich Bonhoeffer, the Christian theologian martyred by the Nazis, could assert on "ethical" grounds that "the killing of civilians in war, so long as it is not directly intended but is only an unfortunate consequence of a measure which is necessary on military grounds," [12] is perfectly permissible. It is strange that a Protestant should have reverted to this casuistic Catholic doctrine at a time when the Catholic theologians have found it wanting in Christian charity. It is even more peculiar that Bonhoeffer abhorred euthanasia, while he endorsed obliteration bombing. It is hard to reconcile the thesis of humanitarianism with the notion that the side effects of bombing are more humane than the direct effects of euthanasia. Surely it would be even more difficult to explain this distinction to the relatives of those who have been eliminated by these two procedures.

Saint Augustine was convinced that Christianity had contributed to the humanizing of war through the abolition of unnecessary killing. While he did admit that slaughtering, looting, plundering, and the general misery to which Rome had been exposed during the invasions from the north were the natural results of the customs of war, he did expect that Christian influence would diminish the scope of this havoc. The fact that even barbarians had spared the lives of people in Christian churches he attributed to the spread of the Christian temper. He remarked with more assurance than the facts would ever warrant, "far be it from any prudent man to impute this clemency to the barbarians." [13] In spite of Saint Augustine's expectations, clergy have demonstrated a remarkable inability to distinguish between the smell of temple incense and cordite. The comments of Harold Bell Wright (1872–1944), one-time clergyman in the Disciples church and the author of popular novels, were not unique when he affirmed in World War I, "A thirty-centimeter gun may voice the edict of God as truly as the notes of a cooing dove. . . . The sword of America is the sword of Jesus." [14] It is difficult to imagine much of a humane influence stemming from such a source of Christian charity. Edward Increase Bosworth, Congregational minister and dean of Oberlin College, added his words of disconsolation to the men in uniform: "The Christian soldier in friendship wounds the enemy. In friendship he kills the enemy. In friendship he receives the wounds of the enemy." [15] It was not immediately evident what difference this Christian friendship made to the enemy that he was slain with Christian compassion rather than with barbarian hate.

Both Saint Augustine and Saint Thomas thought seriously about the problem of humanizing war and, in particular, they were concerned to understand the relation of the Christian conscience to war. Their respective analyses of the nature of a just war make it clear that they accepted war as part of the Christian's duty. While in theory the citizen was not obligated to his country in the case of an unjust war, in fact there have never been any unjust wars. This has meant, among other conclusions, that the position of a Catholic conscientious objector has never had much theological support. It has been the contemporary rejection by some Catholics of the doctrine of the just war that has provided the impetus to a viable Catholic conscientious objection. Clerics were forbidden, according to Saint Thomas, to carry weapons, but the reasons for this mandate bore little reference to any humanizing sentiments.[16] The cleric was to refrain from war because it made it hard for him to think of holy matters, a reason which applied equally to forbid them from business and politics. In addition, it was believed that the priest of the altar ought not to have blood on his hands. If this appears, at first sight, to constitute a faint ray of Christian compassion, the thought is banished by Thomas's thesis that it is the duty of clerics to urge their laymen to war.

The chapter of history written by moral and religious prophets in the attempts to humanize war by some limitation on the kinds of weapons is both long and tortuous. Clerics were slow to show any concern at all over the practice of war killing. Saint Augustine was a major obstacle to any humanizing concern primarily because of his effective defense of unlimited war. "Provided the war be just, it is no concern of justice whether it be carried on openly or by ambushes."[17] As late as the Council of Trent, religious leaders were still deploring the use of swords in private dueling, while praising their use in wars. William Godwin, at the end of the eighteenth century, urged that the operations of war be as limited as possible so as not to generate further evils. Consequently he proposed the proscription of naval war as being clearly too inhumane. Contrary to most of his contemporaries' opinion, he expected that the humanizing of war would lead to its abolition while denying that the horror of war would ever be a factor in its removal. Horror begets horror, rather than revulsion. Men will abandon war when they discover the positive benefits of peace.[18] William Paley, one of his contemporaries, advocated the abolition of poison and assassination in wartime.[19] Kant also spoke disparagingly of poisoners, assassins, and liars as making war too horrible.[20] J. G. Fichte, however, found that only one thing was "downright illegal,"[21] and that was the use of snipers. A twentieth-century spokesman hoped "for the honor of the white race" that talk of developing bombs, poison gases, and aeroplanes was exaggerated.[22] Pope Pius XII added his anathema to poison gas.[23] By the time Adolf Hitler declaimed against air attack as too inhumane to be tolerated[24] it should have occurred to all that the whole discussion left something to be desired. Men may eschew old weapons of destruction, but new ones of even greater scope continue to arise, and the old ones become palatable by familiarity and use. Men of concern, however, met periodically to condemn the latest engines of destruction, while at the same time financing their development.

The instances of this are overwhelming. Nobel is neither the first nor the last to award peace and war efforts both. The Hague Declarations of 1899 and 1907 made "prohibited" the discharge of projectiles from balloons, the use of asphyxiating gases, expanding bullets, and contact mines or torpedoes which remain dangerous even after they have missed their mark.[25] Little remained for soldiers to do save to joust in the knightly fashion of the middle ages. The absurdity of this entire exercise was sharpened by the remarks of a doctor to the Berlin Military Medical Society in 1885 on the discovery of a high-speed, non-expanding bullet. "I welcome the new bullet with great joy and believe that if it were generally adopted by international consent, all humanity would have cause to rejoice."[26] He called this new type of bullet "humane." In the face of such comments we can visualize some modern Torquemada announcing to his Christian helpers the discovery or invention of a "humane" rack and thumb-screw. We have lost all sense of meaning of the term humane if we can talk seriously in this fashion. Yet the mandate against expanding bullets so impressed Hiram Maxim (1840–1916) that he considered his quick-firing gun to be "the greatest life-saving instrument ever invented."[27]

The latest weapons to join the hit-parade of banned instruments are the fusion and fission bombs. In spite of the abysmal failure to curb any weapon in the past on the grounds that its use would be inhumane, contemporary discussion still continues on the presumption that if we can show that the American use of atomic bombs on Hiroshima and Nagasaki was too barbaric, or too inhumane, then we will be able to persuade men to forswear their use. The proliferation of such weapons, in spite of all the talk about curbing them, suggests that everybody is fooling everybody. Humanitarian sentiments apply to the abolition of war, not to rules of propriety for the killing of the enemy. Albert Einstein believed that the potential radioactive poisoning of the entire human race was a fact that all men of sensitivity should deplore.[28] It was not mere charity that prompted this concern, but that the magnitude of new weapons makes old notions of retaliation and defense useless. The entire idea of limited nuclear war is a contradiction in terms.[29] The idea of limitation has no nuclear meaning.[30] Emil Brunner, who thought war could serve a useful end when conventional weapons were used, believed that with thermonuclear weapons war had outlived its usefulness.[31]

Paul Ramsay raised the ultimate question of strategy in a thermonuclear context when he asked, "Against a nation known to possess the H-bomb, and believed to be willing to use it all-out, would we be justified in mounting every reasonable and moral defense?"[32] His answer entailed the recognition that megaton weapons are no longer weapons, and that, hence, nuclear war is no longer war, and that resort to it is the *ultima irratio*. To press the atomic button in the face of one's own annihilation, only to be sure that the enemy perishes also, is both morally repugnant and pragmatically futile. He commented: "I had rather be a pagan suckled in a creed outworn, terrified at the sight of hands made impure by any shedding of blood, than a skilful artisan of technical reason devising plans to carry out such a deed."[33] P. M. S. Blackett agreed that the retaliatory slaughter entailed in a nuclear war would "complete the collapse of professed American moral standards."[34] Christians, above all, should be able to appreciate the possibility that occasions may arise where crucifixion is preferable to the millennium.

Over and against these expressions of concern that nuclear war would mark the end of civilization, and that to entertain such a war would be morally and physically suicidal, are the candid remarks of military realists, who state that we must learn to live with the destructiveness of the new weapons. Herman Kahn proposed the "thinkability" of the death of up to 90 million Americans, not to mention, of course, the valueless lives of a greater number of our putative enemy. The report of the RAND corporation that it seemed unlikely, in the next decade, that there would be world annihilation gave Kahn assurance that some American ends were still so important, though it was not clear to whom, that the possibility of all these deaths was not too great a price to pay. He summed this up with the sordid and empty cliché that there were, after all, fates worse than death.[35] Thomas E. Murray proposed to avert the dangers implicit in Kahn's approach by a program of what he called "rational nuclear armaments." This program involved limiting the size of bombs, a gesture which he considered to be rational in two senses. "It is consistent with the moral principles of the civilized tradition, and it is adapted to the military necessities of the nuclear age."[36]

It is difficult to know what is the more incredible: that a religious thinker should imagine that death by any kind of war was consistent with the moral principles of civilization, or that a hard-headed realist should have misread history so cosmically as to find meaning in the notion of a limitation of weapons. No nation, committed to its own survival, and believing that war is a legal way to protect itself, would ever limit its own weapons if the alternative were defeat. John R. Connery, S.J., weighed these issues and found the use of ultimate violence distasteful but necessary.[37] This is what one would expect from military and political leaders whether they had moral ends or not. In fact, it is not very helpful to indict as distasteful in one breath what one plans to call necessary in the next breath. The level of this oddly Frankensteinian discussion of the necessity of the immoral is not raised by the observation, commonly made, that actually more persons die yearly in auto accidents than in wars. While this may be so for the Korean war, and for the Vietnam war, 1966, it is blatantly false for World War I with its eight and a half million dead, and World War II and its sixteen and a half million dead. These figures include only battle deaths. It has also been noted that the potential estimates for radioactive damage to subsequent generations is less than that for all peace-time casualties. But surely the question we face is more complex than whether we kill more persons by war than are accidentally killed in peace. If numbers of deaths were the only datum, then the Korean war would have been better than normal American living during the same period, since fewer died in the war than at home. It is this kind of Alice in Wonderland logic that could lead to the dismissal of the tragedy of Nazi extermination camps since, after all, everybody will die eventually.

It is little wonder in the face of such disregard for human life and spirit that such difficulty was encountered in attempting to justify the War Crimes Trials of the Nazis after World War II. In a culture which finds human deaths so acceptable, it is hard to arouse concern. In the initial defenses of the Trials, appeal was made to the notion of offenses against law and the customs of war, whatever these might be. The Moscow Declaration of

November 1, 1943, announced that at the cessation of hostilities the responsible German officers would be tried for criminal offenses. One of the key debates in the whole matter centered around the question of responsibility. If a German soldier was merely obeying orders of a superior, then was he responsible for what he did? The *British Manual of Military Law* of 1914 answered this question in the negative. The same year this notion of absolute non-liability was incorporated into the *American Rules of Land Warfare*. In an attempt to atone for the obvious inability to judge any but a few officers of the Nazi regime on the basis of this interpretation, Sheldon Glueck proposed that soldiers be considered culpable only if they know, or should have known, that their actions in obedience to orders were unlawful by the customs of warfare or by criminal law generally.[38] This sounds much clearer than it actually is, since everything is actually sanctioned in war today, and there are no international bodies of law speaking to the question of war criminality. Surely, much of the revulsion against the Nazi death camps arose because the enemy was the offender. What is surprising, however, is the general lack of any comparable revulsion over an event as extraordinary as the bombing of Nagasaki and Hiroshima, or an ordinary event such as the napalm bombing of a Vietnam village. Every nation has a way of explaining its own military acts as justified by strategy. There is something macabre, in any case, in an enterprise which has rules for the conditions under which men may incinerate each other properly.

Dietrich Bonhoeffer called the Nazi extermination process "arbitrary killing," and considered it to be vastly more offensive to sensitive persons than so-called normal war killing. How does one explain to the descendents of the Hiroshima victims that the nuclear oven which obliterated their relatives was on a higher moral plane than that which obliterated the helpless Jews in Nazi Germany? How does one explain that the former perpetrators are within their rights, while the latter have committed acts of inhumane cruelty? If we note that the proscriptions of the Hague Congresses of 1899 and 1907 are now standard war practice, might it not be the case in the near future that all nations will operate their extermination camps to handle the enemy? Time has a way of making ancient uncouths good, and there is thus little reason to hope that we have finally reached the intellectual limit of the morally unthinkable. Once we have granted the legitimacy of war and the necessity of weapons which kill, there is no clear basis, save private pique or humanitarian sentiment, on which to draw the moral line against a weapon merely because it kills in a new way or to a new degree. While we may wish that all not be fair in war, humanitarian considerations seem incapable of giving us the criteria by which to judge such fairness or unfairness.

In the last analysis, the discussion of "humane" war practices is so casuistic, question-begging, and insular that it should lie beyond the domain of religious predicates. Practicing administrators might beat their breasts with the claim that the guillotine was more humane than the rack, and that electrocution was more humane than hanging, but neither ordinary morals nor religious revelations give bases for such distinctions. While hydrogen bombs are not radically different from bayonets from the perspective of the ones who are killed, since they are dead either way, they are different in the fact that such bombs cannot be used with any discrimination. We either kill everybody in an area, or we leave the area unbombed. This is the choice with thermonuclear weapons. Yet what military tactician could be expected to recommend losing a war through considerations of humanitarianism or politeness? Religious leaders are wasting their words and misplacing their emphases by engaging in debates over which weapons are the most humane. The problem of man is with war itself, and not with the sadism of war policies. The rate at which America has developed its nuclear power many "over-kills" beyond the power needed to wipe out the human race would indicate that there is no general anxiety about nuclear extermination, and even less about the morality of the issues involved. The threat supposed to exist by virtue of the purported plot of world communism is a pallid affair compared with what we conscientiously contemplate. Indeed, as John C. Ford, S.J., concluded, if our dilemma is really to wipe out the communists or be wiped out by them, then, he said, "I would consider that we had arrived at the point where absolute moral imperatives were at stake, and the followers of Christ should abandon themselves totally to divine Providence rather than forsake these imperatives."[39]

WAR AND RELIGION

VIII   *Religion and War*

A FEW ISOLATED PROPHETS of early Judaism and Christianity predicted that with the rise of their respective religions, swords would be beaten into plowshares and ultimate peace would prevail. The history of warfare portrays, however, the improbability of this expectation. William Lecky (1838–1903) concluded his long history of European morals with the sad observation that, with the exception of Islam, no religion has produced as much war in the short space of a few centuries as has Christianity.[1] Instead of decreasing war, the influence of ecclesiastics has been far more on the side of multiplying the occasions for its use. We look in vain for any striking instances in which clergy, as a body, exerted itself on behalf of peace. If Christianity takes pride in having played so large a role in the elimination of dueling, it must also be granted that it invented such dueling in the first place through its endorsement of and sanctification of the knightly jousts. If there are cases where the organized clergy have aided in the critique of war, let alone in preventing armed conflict, such cases have been lost in the misty past. During a long period of early Judaism all wars fought by the righteous were religious wars, in the minimum sense of having divine sanction, and not in the extreme sense of aiming at the spiritual conversion of the enemy. The sanguinary battles of the twelve tribes were fought with the aid of Jehovah. He marched with the battle wagons and his sword arm aided the armies of Joshua and Gideon in a most bloodthirsty annihilation of soldiers and civilians alike.

If we were to count only those wars to be religious which had as their aim the conversion of the opponent, then it would have to be admitted that so-called pagan religions fought very few wars. Their gods were too culture-bound, and they had no power beyond the national boundaries, so that it made no sense to speak of any kind of missionary activity, verbal or violent. Rousseau commented on this fact as being one of the marks of pagan religion. It did not wage wars to sell itself to foreigners.[2] In fact the Romans always left the vanquished with their own gods, whatever else they might have demanded of them. Rousseau thought that since Christianity set up no national religion, it could never reasonably fight a religious war. Since this is obviously false, several alternatives present themselves as a resolution. Either Christianity did set up a national religion, as in the case of the Roman empire after Constantine, or in the many cases of European states under Calvinistic influence, or they intended no state religion, in spite of what happened, but usually found it possible to endorse political doctrines as religiously worthy of the support of the sword.

This kind of semantic legerdemain, however, does not absolve religion from complicity in the promotion of wars. Even the Jihad, or holy war of the Moslems, aimed at the establishment of a world political state as well as of a universal religion. Indeed, no religion is free from the accusation that it has sounded the war trumpets. In polytheistic cultures all wars were religious at least in the sense that the gods endorsed the wars, and few religions, in practice, seem to have raised any serious anti-military questions about the religious sanction of military ambition. The discussion of dharma in the *Bhagavad Gita* concluded that a man must always do what his caste requires in order to attain eternal blessedness. Krishna's advice to Arjuna was that if he killed his ancestors in war as a result of a caste duty, he would not be guilty of any sin. Thus early Hindu thought made the most conventional of immoral acts, namely the taking of life, religiously palatable.

During a long period of the middle ages the Catholic Church had its own armies and its own military tacticians. It could scarcely be expected that this church find any problem with war. Ever since 383 A.D. it had been too easy for the Christian church to make a religious sanction for political ambition, and states have found that wars are most easily justified by claiming religious support. It was Pope Urban II who inaugurated the crusades at the Council of Clermont in 1095, and by this act formally instituted wars organized and administered by religion. It was this fact that prompted Marsilius of Padua (1290–1343) to speak of the popes as worming their way throughout the world for the purpose of universal political domination.[3] Marsilius, however, was not objecting to the principle of churchly wars but, rather, to the simple fact that church prelates undermined the power of secular princes. This was part of what John Calvin hoped to avoid when he asserted that war was to be condemned for religious use, while at the same time permitted for state use. In spite of this warning, Calvin did expect that if there were political sanction for any war, then the church should be expected to add its blessing.[4] Furthermore, Calvin's discussion of war presupposed that it was a chastisement from God for human sin, and thus to be accepted as from God for our good,[5] even though war was not to be thought of as a lasting institution in the divine plan. Christ's kingdom, said Calvin, was to be furthered by spiritual means alone, but the political alliance that churches had made with the powers of Caesar led them, in fact, to be a major support for all wars. The renunciation in spirit when coupled with the embracing in fact of war is, as Ernst Troeltsch remarked, "where sophistry begins."[6]

Whether people believe that religion is to be promoted by war or not, they still tend to believe that their secular wars have the support of God. The clergy of most denominations rarely let the laymen down in this expectation. The laymen still have a problem, however, since in any war there are usually victors and vanquished, and there are usually religious people on both sides. The losing side must be fighting against God. This is all very easy for Americans who have never lost a war, but how difficult it must be for German religious persons to reconcile their defeats. The presumption is that just wars must be victorious wars, and victorious wars must be just.[7] Even Shailer Matthews, who saw some merit in the interrelations of patriotism and religion, conceded that if religions are ever to aid in banishing war, they will have to undergo a radical transformation and root the war out of their own hearts.[8] L. T. Hobhouse attributed this state of affairs to the unprincipled compromise with which churches identify with the aims of their respective countries, and the ease with which they accommodate the gospel of peace to the stern realities of power politics.[9] Indeed, the limits of most church concern with war have been characterized by attempts to "humanize" not to eliminate war.

One of the more obvious expressions of the religious sanctification of war is the existence of the chaplaincy in the branches of the military. While the priestly blessing of armed conflict goes back to the middle ages and especially to the period of chivalry, the formal function of the chaplaincy is fairly recent in origin. The office of chaplain was first introduced into the United States military service during the Revolutionary War when clergy were first appointed to the Continental Army. The Act of March 3, 1791, fixed the strength of the army at 2,232 officers and men and provided for one chaplain. The Reverend Benjamin Balch, who fought at Lexington with the famous Minute Men, was the first known navy chaplain. He was appointed in 1778 and served aboard the frigates *Boston* and *Alliance*. With the exception of a few denominations there have been no official disavowals of the role of clergy in the military service.

Some of the contemporary assessments of the chaplain's role, however, have indicated that there have been some pious misgivings. One World War II chaplain noted that "they contribute greatly to morale if given a chance,"[10] but indicated that chaplains commonly had no such chance, and even where they did, contributing to morale would scarcely count as an end of lasting religious significance. Chaplains commonly reported that the role of morale-building was unrelated to their putative function as ministers of God. As ministers it was not clear what they were supposed to bless, nor whether they had any religious liberty distinct from the secular commands that came down to them from their commanding officers. As one chaplain explained his concern, "it may not be the church's function and duty to teach and to encourage men to kill; but it is the church's function and duty to undergird a man with such a faith and with such an understanding of the issues involved that he will be able to accomplish what is expected of him by his God and by his country." [11] How difficult it must have been for any chaplain to separate the two functions in battle!

It would be interesting to hear the discussions among German, British, and American chaplains gathered after some war to compare their relative successes in undergirding their men without encouraging them to kill. It would seem undeniable that some soldiers were comforted and relieved by the sanction which the mere presence of the chaplains offered. Surely if there were any doubt as to the legitimacy of a claim that a war was religiously approvable, then the chaplains would not have been in the military at all. Since the chaplains are there, then whatever the men are commanded to do must, at the same time, be religiously commanded. The state sets the context for patriotic obedience, and in the case of military obedience, the chaplaincy gives religious sanction to it. In principle, a clergyman might be expected to give some healing word, and to lend some spirit of forgiveness toward the enemies. In principle, the men might be led in prayer by the chaplain for the souls of the enemy, and hear from his lips that the men on the other side were their brothers. In practice, however, there seems to be ample evidence that the chaplain would not boost morale by mentioning these issues at such a time. It would scarcely be considered morale-building to disturb the conscience of men about to kill. As a means of guarding against the likelihood of pacifist chaplains, known pacifist ministers were rejected unless they agreed to sign a statement testifying that they no longer held the pacifist view.[12] Men in the military who at the same time have religious compunctions about killing are in a very ambiguous position, and this position is not made any easier by officers wearing crosses. From a position conveniently remote from the battlefield Pope Pius XII announced that "while defending faithfully and courageously his country, a Christian must, however, abstain from hating those whom he is obliged to combat."[13] If we assume that such an attitude is possible, do we also expect that the men on both sides should be able to express it, and that if they do so, then each side can kill the other with religious sanction?

There is, however, another side to the question of the relation of religion to war, although it must be admitted that it is a small minority of religious leaders who express it. At the International Congress of Anti-Militarist Clergymen, August 13–15, 1928, the members announced that one of their aims was "to declare the office of military chaplain inconsistent with the Gospel."[14] They asserted that war and Christianity were incompatible, and that it was a special task of Christianity to declare war to be sinful as well as secularly criminal. The clergy at the Congress agreed that they should oppose all armament races, and that they should support disarmament possibilities. Such a protest was, however, a feeble voice crying in a wilderness of general clerical diffidence, resignation, or positive approval of the whole war enterprise. Catholic writers might assert that if Pope Benedict XV had not been excluded from the proceedings of the Peace of Paris after World War I, the tragedy of ineptness of the Treaty of Versailles would never have occurred.[15] Pope Leo XIII might also claim that the sources of war and enmity stem from disregard of the authority of the church.[16] But the fact remains that the church still sanctions all national wars once they have begun. What is even more significant, the sanction is given independently of whether the war was avoidable or whether it was the fault of the erring Christians themselves. Unlike most other areas of sin, religion blesses the sin of killing after it has been committed, even though it normally condemns the act before the fact.

There are some signs that religious leaders are becoming uneasy with their long alliance with Mars. In 1964 the Catholic Peace Fellowship was organized to encourage Catholic laymen and clergy to become aware of the anti-war traditions. While the specific support for Catholic opposition to war comes from twentieth-century statements, and is relatively unassisted by the earlier eighteen hundred years, the fact is that some clergy and laity now speak against the church-war alliance. The human devastation in Nagasaki, for example, was equated with abortion by some Catholic thinkers, and hence officially to be condemned. In Section 79 of the *Constitution on the Church in the Modern World,* produced by the Second Vatican Council, Roman Catholic conscientious objection is officially condoned. Pope John XXIII stated in *Pacem in Terris* that modern war cannot be considered as an acceptable means of vindicating human rights. It is now not uncommon to find statements by Catholic leaders which denounce the older distinctions between offensive and defensive war, and which reject any modern application of the concept of the just war.

Protestant statements, however, antedate these Catholic pronouncements by a long time. Between the two World Wars the major Protestant denominations spoke explicitly and firmly against war, and most of them defended the position of conscientious objection. A few, such as the Christadelphians, Dunkard Brethren, Church of the Brethren, Assemblies of God, Christ's Church of the Golden Rule, Christ's Sanctified Holy Church, Church of God (Anderson and Oklahoma), Church of the Gospel, and Emmanuel Association, forbid participation in war of its members. These, however, are small sects and do not contain more than a fraction of the Christian membership of the United States. In the 1963 edition of *Statements of Religious Bodies on the Conscientious Objector* there are fifty-nine statements. While the editor noted that failure to be included does not mean that the denomination has no stand on conscientious objection, the fact does remain that only fifty-nine bodies replied. Of these groups, 21 were what would be classed as "major" denominations, 32 were "minor" sects, and 6 were federated bodies such as the National Council of Churches. The problem that Protestant groups face is the lack of central authority to speak on an issue such as this. Where a national position is put forth, there is, in general, little indication that the local churches share the stand. If pacifism entails a genuine boycott of war, then only the so-called minor sects qualify. Further, the elaborate machinery by which churches meet the religious needs of their men in the armed forces is not matched by anything comparable whereby they minister to the needs of the conscientious objectors in their ranks. Where is the religious prototype of the chaplain to whom conscientious objectors can turn for counsel? Religious objectors who endeavor to find some alternative service to fulfill their draft obligations commonly have to turn to secular institutions for such jobs.

Habit is a hard opponent of human conscience, and there have been centuries of religiously sanctioned havoc to overcome. In 700 B.C. the armies of Ashurbanipal invoked the sanctity of religion and presumed that the great war god, Ashur, took his share of plunder and human heads. In his discussion of the Aztecs, Prescott noted that "the soldier who fell in battle was transported at once to the region of ineffable bliss in the bright mansions of the Sun." [17] The religious support given to war by any religion partakes of this crusading contempt for human life. It is easily forgotten that the Vandals were Christians who committed depredations out of piety. The history of the Saracens and the Crusaders is the same. Each slew the other under the guise of religious devotion. Some anomalies occurred. For instance, Peter the Great assigned corporal punishment and even death to soldiers apprehended using unchristian oaths, while at the same time he and his armies enjoyed the reputation for unexcelled butchery. After Menéndez, the Spanish leader, had massacred the men, women, and children of Fort Caroline because they were of the Reformed faith, he piously concluded that their deaths were necessary for the proper service of God. In France during the latter half of the sixteenth century there were nine consecutive religious wars. Thus war and religion have not been strangers, and though religions may speak of princes of peace, their war-lords seem to have the greater following.

Religion has been a convenient weapon for a variety of causes. In its organizational and institutional manifestations it serves commonly as a holy medal to ward off twinges of conscience. Most of the social, political, and economic institutions of culture have known the value of religious sanction, and most of them have called upon religion in time of need to bless what would otherwise have been repellent as too inhumane to deserve to be supported. From the point of view of "political realism" many unpleasant acts may have to be performed, if a culture is to survive. In a world of colonialism, colonies may have to be won or saved by war. In a world of economic enterprise, foreign factories may have to be defended by invasion. In a world of ardent nationalism, national pride, honor, face, or prestige may have to be preferred to human life. There remains, however, the undemonstrated religious conviction that religion is obligated to support whatever nations undertake. In the subsequent chapters we will explore two options for religion. Either Christians can be soldiers, or else war is unchristian. If the practical resolutions to these choices are far more complex than the options seem to suggest, it yet remains that we cannot consistently be on both sides at once. If war is indeed the only alternative to national obliteration, or if war is required for the survival of what we call culture, then it may be that, faced with thermonuclear devastation, we would choose the better part to cast our fate with Providence and to die gracefully. If eschatology is the correct metaphysics, then self-abnegation may be the noblest ethics.

IX   *War Is Unchristian*

ANY ATTEMPT TO show that the Christian churches, since Constantine, have exhibited any widespread opposition to war will be refuted by the facts. Any claim that many Christians, since the fourth century, have cringed at killing by virtue of their religion will be falsified by the paucity of exceptions.

In spite of this dismal prediction, there were from the earliest period of the first-century churches some spokesmen who felt that the Prince of Peace denounced war in any form. While no clear statement to this effect appeared until the end of the second century, this may have been due in part to the preoccupation of the founders of Christianity with religious institutional matters. Perhaps, as Celsus (2nd Century A.D.) claimed, early Christians were simply so uninvolved in any worldly matters that the question of military service did not occur to them. Celsus had accused Christians of permitting civilization to perish by virtue of their unwillingness to fight in the Roman army. The ease with which armies have destroyed cultures throughout human history may make Celsus's concern somewhat misplaced, but the fact that he raised the criticism indicates that Christians were not taking part in soldiery to any degree. The fact that the Roman legions did not have to conscript soldiers surely must have had some bearing on the Christian silence on war. There always seemed to have been enough men willing to serve so that both Christians and Jews, like slaves who were forbidden to serve in the army, could absent themselves without causing any social problem. In addition to these facts, the Roman legions were essentially policemen rather than soldiers in the modern sense of the term. The legions kept internal order far more than they functioned as invading mercenaries or as protectors against foreign invasion. When police forces behave themselves within the political and legal framework of the society few, save criminals, find anything to object to. Perhaps, further, Christians were preoccupied with millennialism, and there is some evidence that a great deal of political escapism was practiced by millennial Christians. After all, if the world is going to end any moment, there is little reason to be concerned about the things that armies putatively protect. It may have been the obvious failure of millennialism that served as a factor in the rise of third-century Christian concern with the whole issue of Christian obligation to the world in which they now seemed doomed to live. At the end of his careful study of early Christianity and war C. J. Cadoux concluded that "there is no trace of the existence of any Christian soldiers between these cases mentioned in *Acts* and, say, 170 A.D."[1] There is some evidence that this state of affairs was due to Christian compunctions about killing rather than to simple political diffidence.

Saint Justin Martyr (100–165) wrote in his first apology that conversion to Christianity entailed giving up some former practices, and that among these altered actions were those associated with hating and killing.[2] Christians, he claimed, no longer waged war against their enemies,[3] and they have converted their weapons of war into instruments of agriculture. One could get the impression that vast armies of Christians had mustered themselves out of killing and into farming were it not for the fact that we know there were virtually no Christians in the armed service. The remarks of Justin Martyr are probably intended in the spirit of aiming at a general beating of swords into plowshares in the secular society, rather than as a sign of a Christian about-face.

He reaffirmed this position in his dialogue with Trypho, and claimed that, as Christians, they no longer waged any kind of violent war.[4]

It is not clear, however, that this renunciation of war really attacks it on the grounds that killing is wrong so much as that involvement in the affairs of this world is wrong. Tatian (110–180), a disciple of Justin Martyr, asserted that he declined military command, but then he declined political and economic leadership also.[5] Clement of Alexandria (160–215) deplored the sacrifice of lives in the stadia, and condemned those who took pleasure in killing others, even in wars, but such an attitude does not confirm, let alone assert, that warring is unchristian.[6] Prior to his conversion to Montanism, Tertullian (160–230) had written that Christians were essentially like any other group of citizens: "We sail with you and fight with you, and till the ground with you."[7] After his conversion he saw Christians as persons set apart. Indeed, if a man was converted to Christianity, he ought not to become a soldier. On the other hand, if a soldier was converted to Christianity, it was not clear whether he had to give up his soldiering. The counsel of perfection was unambiguous to Tertullian, however, for "the Lord afterward, in disarming Peter, unbelted every soldier."[8] The case of the soldier who becomes a Christian is different from the Christian who is planning to become a soldier. Consider, for example, Tertullian noted, that Jesus did speak favorably of the centurion, and did not intimate that he ought to give up his profession. Nonetheless, Tertullian reported approvingly the case of the young soldier who gave up the military crown and sword.[9] By this time, however, Tertullian had clearer answers to the knotty question of soldiering Christians. "I think," he vowed, "we must first inquire whether warfare is proper at all for Christians. . . . Shall it be held lawful to make an occupation of the sword?"[10] His answer, now, is an indisputable negative. In addition to military service Tertullian ruled out many other professions for Christians, such as icon-makers, silversmiths, teachers, and politicians. He doubted that Christians would be able to function consistently in any role of political or social leadership. The addition of these other professions, however, dulls the edge of his antipathy to the military life. The attitude now appears to be that of a man who does not intend to be involved in worldly affairs at all, rather than that of a man who conscientiously opposes the Christian taking of life. There are two issues involved here. On the one hand it seems to have been the case that early Christians did subsume the earthly matters under the more important issue of salvation in eternity. This commitment by itself would explain why they appeared to have understressed social and political action. On the other hand, the literature supports the thesis that Christians had a conscience on killing, and that the taking of human life was never part of the counsels of perfection. It would be an oversimplification, therefore, to imagine that the millennialist belief alone influenced social and political disinterestedness. Once the second century was past, and the world had not ended, millennialists tended to think in longer stretches of time before the end was to come. This meant that millennialism and social action did not need to be incompatible.

With the early general rejection of participation in the social and political milieu it was natural for Celsus to accuse Christians of failing to be good citizens. Some Christians refused to accept the normal civic responsibilities. In response to this accusation, Origen (185–254) explained that Christians were forbidden by their religious convictions to take any life.[11] While he recognized the need for soldiers in a militant society, he considered that Christians performed an equally important function in their role of peaceful leaveners. By their priestly and prayerful ministrations, and by their noble example, they did their patriotic part in aiding the king.[12] While this may sound presumptive, it would ordinarily be conceded that there are many functions other than military which good citizens need to fulfill. What may not be apparent is that there is any pacific function which states need to have fulfilled. It would be both naïve and false to imagine that the military performs any very pervasive, lasting, or constructive tasks, particularly when compared with the peaceful efforts of the professions like medicine, education, and law. The survival of culture in the world has not paralleled the escalation of armies. Indeed, the common claim that if all Christians were pacifists, or at least conscientious objectors, then societies would collapse rests on no systematic data. Where societies do not take recourse to their armies to solve their international relations, they commonly invent far more viable means of human interaction. The militant programs of Genghis Khan, Peter the Great, Napoleon, Hitler, MacNamara, or Johnson are not what save culture. American military action in Vietnam saves no culture at all, nor did German action in France, Poland, or Czechoslovakia. Perhaps those first- and second-century Christians saw this fact, and took their stance for diplomacy against the Horatio-at-the-bridge type of coercion.

Although Origen admitted that states had a right and duty to defend themselves militarily, he may still be classed with the so-called vocational pacifists, for whom non-killing is commanded, while still conceding that others may not be so required. When, for example, the Jews had a national homeland, then it was right for them to wage wars on their invaders. Indeed, to take away this right from them would be to subject them to political annihilation.[13] Christians, on the other hand, had no state, and hence no such military pressures are upon them. It is not that they shirk all civic obligations, but rather that they have a more divine role to play in the cosmic and mundane plans.[14] It was probably assumed that there would always be enough non-Christians to take care of military national defense and, equally important, that there would be enough Christians to take care of the spiritual health of the nation. This idea is not so preposterous as it may at first appear. Even in modern militant states we do not draft the members of the President's cabinet, the Supreme Court, or the Congress—on the grounds that they make their contribution to the political health of the nation. Nor is there any formal draft of the clergy, although they are expected to volunteer in sufficient numbers. In the unlikely event that every citizen in a country embraced Christianity, and there were thus no soldiers, Origen expected that the sheer weight of prayer alone would be sufficient to overcome any enemy.[15]

Saint Cyprian (200–258) saw a similar healing role for the committed Christian, who was urged not to permit communion to be administered to anyone who had the blood of his fellows on his hands. He vowed, further, that "the hand that has held the Eucharist will not be sullied by the blood-stained sword."[16] Obviously it would not be necessary to mention this were it not for the number of failures to live up to the ideal. The contests in the arenas were specially condemned for their blood-letting, and for their glorification of the art of killing. What would be called homicide when committed by ordinary citizens was considered to be a virtuous skill when done in war or the arena.[17] Some of the pacific edge may be taken off this eschewing of war and the gladitorial combats by his expectation that divine vengeance would take care of the unjust since Christians were not permitted to do so. This, of course, debased the morals of God, but it did, at least, do something to save the morals of man.[18] The abhorrence of blood was generally shared by all Christians, and Minucius Felix (210) declared that Christians did not even use the blood of eatable animals in their food.[19] Arnobius (300) asserted that Christians would sooner shed their own blood than have the blood of another on their hands.[20] After a long diatribe against the contests in the arenas, which he called "public homicide," Lactantius (313) stated that Christians were forbidden to kill even in war, and to this mandate he found no exceptions.[21] Saint Athanasius (296–373) pictured barbarians giving up their arms as soon as they were converted to Christianity and as substituting matins for swordplay.[22]

Since the same men who forbade Christian military service also forbade Christian political service, men like Tertullian, Origen, Justin Martyr, and Athenagoras laid the foundations for a Christian monasticism. By the beginning of the third century there was at least one monastic refuge in Egypt for any who wished to pursue his ideals in isolation. This was the group that held the ideal of Christian pacifism unsullied after the conversion of Constantine (313), and the later adoption of Christianity as the official religion of the Roman Empire (383). Even the monks, however, were not united on this question. In 376 the emperor Valens forced monks into the military service, not as chaplains but as soldiers. For the next 1,000 years the councils of the churches endeavored to lure the clergy back out of the army. From the middle of the third century, and on, military metaphors for the Christian life became common. Christians were called soldiers. Christ was an imperator. The church was a camp, baptism was a sacramentum (a military oath of allegiance), and heretics were rebels and deserters from the camp.[23] While the metaphorical usage of military terms should not be interpreted to mean an absolute capitulation of the religious to the military, the use of such terms at all is a concession. Some hymns still bear a familiar military stamp in many of their lines. Pope Leo Magnus (440–461) insisted that it was against the rules of the church to return to military service after having done penance. Yet the Council of Chalcedon in 451 found it necessary to note that "a cleric or monk who enters the military service or accepts a secular dignity and does not repent shall be anathematized."[24] But by this time the objection was not against war in general for Christians, but only against war in general for priests.

In 383 Christianity became the official religion of the Roman Empire, and under this new liaison the church found itself confronted with the necessity of interpreting its position on war to the empire which had so graciously befriended it. When the church had been more in the position of a neutral observer, it could judge war independently of the nations that were involved. Under this new arrangement the church took on the view that the nations waging war may make a difference as to the moral status of the war. In particular, the Roman Empire took on virtues which the earlier Christian church had not recognized that it might possess. The failure of the Roman church ever to condemn its own empire made this position clear. Not only did the Church now sanction the wars of the state, but it did so independently of the aims of the wars. Since the state was always good, the wars it fought were always right. Both the Councils of Toulouse in 633 and Meaus in 845 condemned the clergy to demotion in rank for bearing arms. Apparently such attempts to limit the militancy of the clergy were largely ineffective. In 990 ordinances were directed by several bishops in southern France against the practice of clerical private war. The bishops agreed to exclude from Christian privileges those who took part in war in violation of the bishop's commands, and to deny these clergy Christian burial. But too many bishops were capitalizing on warfare for these gestures to have any serious effect. Even the Truce of God[25] was generally ignored and violated in spite of threats of excommunication.

In 1076, at a council at Winchester, England, the cases were considered of men who had fought with William the Conqueror at the battle of Hastings. Many of these men were troubled by memories of the people they had slain in battle. The council decided that penance should be assessed in proportion to the number of men each penitent had killed. Distinctions were made for those who had struck down opponents but did not know whether they had died of their wounds, a situation commonly the case with archers. In these instances the men were assigned the penance of prayers one day a week for the rest of their lives. Such moral niceties were a far cry from the positive position of Saint Tertullian. By these distinctions killing had become a permissible sin, for which adequate penance could be performed. If this seems to be a rather casual way to handle killing, it should be remembered that not even this much is required in the twentieth century. In 1139 the Second Lateran Council, in Canon 12, warned belatedly that anyone fighting on holy days faced possible, though not probable, excommunication; and in Canon 14 the Council ruled that anyone losing his life in a knightly joust would be denied Christian burial. In spite of this verbal censure, and with the general blessings of the clergy, the tournaments were popular for another four centuries. The lack of progress in the whole area was marked by the need at the Third Lateran Council in 1179 to repeat the threat of denial of Christian burial to tournament casualties. These protests, however seriously offered, were ineffectual, for by 1311 at the Council of Vienne bishops were urged to punish ministers who were engaged in the trade of butcher, bartender, or paid assassin.[26] As late as the seventeenth century, Grotius observed that some church councils were still recommending that men who had served in the army after baptism not be permitted to become ordained ministers. But if these strictures went largely unpracticed, they are still more of an expression of opinion on war than contemporary churches tend to make.

The voice of Christian compassion was not extinguished in spite of this obvious transition from the non-combatant thesis of Tertullian and the general absence of Christians from the armies to the prevailing clerical bellicoseness and militancy of a John of Salisbury (d. 1180). Erasmus (1467–1536), the Dutch Catholic scholar, deplored the militancy of his age, and the general clerical diffidence in the face of war. He rejected the position that Christians could be warriors, especially against other Christians, but also against infidels. After all, did the angels blow war trumpets at Christ's birth? Far from such martial music, these angels heralded peace and denounced murders and wars. Consequently, he concluded, "Is it not a monstrous thing if a Christian shall fight with a Christian?"[27] Yet the fact remained that few were embarrassed by this state of affairs, whether they were professors, priests, or cardinals. After all, he continued, "What hath a crozier or a sheephook to do with a sword? What hath the Gospel book to do with a shield? . . . Dost thou with the selfsame mouth wherewith thou preachest peaceable Christ laud and praise war? . . . Dost thou, covered with a cowl, incite at the holy sermon the simple unto murder, the which of thy mouth looked for the evangelical doctrine?"[28] The profession of the soldier cannot be made compatible with the Christian message; and even on secular grounds, the worst peace is still better than the most just war.[29]

A similar strong distinction between being a Christian and being a soldier marked the statements of George Fox, the Quaker. In 1650 he turned down a captaincy in the Commonwealth Army on the grounds that the way of Jesus prohibited holding such an office. The sight of erstwhile Christian nations drenching the soil with human gore was an obvious contradiction. What, after all, could the Prince of Peace have to do with such an occupation? But George Fox spoke in a vacuum of diffidence and to a world which had by then become inured to religious inhumanity. His clerical contemporaries did not understand him, and his pacific sentiments were branded as unpatriotic by the generally bellicose Christian constituency. The blood of Abel cried from the ground, but few Christians heard its voice or responded to it with anything like charitable concern.

By the turn of the twentieth century the pleas of Leo Tolstoy were almost without religious reception, and this was not because of any ambiguity on his part.

> *"You are surprised that soldiers are taught that it is right to kill people in certain cases and in war, while in the books admitted to be holy by those who so teach, there is nothing like such a permission, but, on the contrary, not only is all murder forbidden, but all insulting of others is forbidden also, and we are told not to do to others what we would not wish done to us. And you ask, is not this fraud? . . . Yes, it is a fraud, committed for the sake of those accustomed to live on the sweat and blood of other men, and who have therefore perverted, and still pervert, Christ's teaching. . . ."*[30]

A man would have to be either a fool or a charlatan to insist that Christian killing be praised. Christian militarism, like Christian sadism, or Christian torture, is a mistake of a radical dimension. Tolstoy believed that the Dukhobors were consistent Christians in their rejection of all military service. He found it hard to understand why he stood almost alone in his support of their witness. Whatever else war may be, there should be no confusion among Christians, at least, that war must be rejected as immoral. Such assurance, however, must be tempered by almost fifteen centuries of a lack of churchly conscience on the subject of war.

Six centuries ago Dante (1265–1321) commented on the failure of the Christian churches to have promoted peace on earth and good will toward men. Since then very few major voices expressed any concern over war. Men like Wyclif, Waldo, Fox, Penn, Garrison, Whittier, and Tolstoy did rise to the occasion and testified to the minority opinion that war was unchristian. The most vocal spokesmen for the separation of Christianity and war in the early twentieth century were considered too radical, too unorthodox, and basically too secular both by many of their colleagues of the cloth and by the laymen. This was true for Norman Thomas, Harry Ward, Jerome Davis, and Kirby Page, as well as for laymen like Eugene Debs and Scott Nearing. It has always seemed easy for some clerics and laymen to dismiss these kinds of protest on the grounds that they were offered by socialists rather than by Christians. The gap between leaders and laity, like that between national pronouncements and the commitments of the local churches, has never been more pronounced than in this area of war and peace. It is because of this that any attempt to classify Christians as pacific or pro-war is bound to prompt data to the contrary. Debs may have caricatured the army chaplain, but he certainly made the issue clear.

> *"The army chaplain is one of the interesting by-products of war. He is a shining example of Christian patriotism—praying for war, shouting for war, thirsting for blood and 'ministering' to the soldier boy with his legs shot off. . . . The Christian army chaplain prays to his Christian God to bless and prosper the killing business on his side of the line, and to have no mercy on his Christian brothers on the other side, whose Christian army chaplain is praying to the same Christian God at the same time to bless and prosper them in the same infernal business."*[31]

Perhaps chaplains do not thirst for blood or shout for war, as Debs intimated, but it is certainly incumbent on them to make clear precisely that to which they think they are witnessing. The wearing of the uniform is itself a support of the extensive military program, and the aim of the military is, after all, not the conversion of the enemy but the death of the enemy. If the determination that war is unchristian were to be determined by calling the roll of Christian pacifists, the statistics would not support the position. It is not merely the existence of the whole apparatus of the chaplaincy that supports this, but the fact that churches now, as in the past, function as a major sanction for military recruitment, and perhaps as the major rock of strength for those whose conscience may bother them about the killing business. In the twentieth century we may not only come to the altar with blood on our hands, but we may be blessed for doing so. Men and women may not only consistently join the military ranks as Christians, but we may pin Calvary crosses on their lapels to sanctify the decision.

A current pamphlet containing statements from religious bodies in the United States on the matter of conscientious objection includes general endorsements of the religious permission to be a war-objector from fifty-four out of two-hundred-seventy-six denominations.[32] Since many of the denominations included have no central authority which can speak for the church, some of the pronouncements reflect only a narrow segment of the church. While all of the fifty-four permit a member to be a conscientious objector, and almost all of them permit their members to be soldiers, there is a careful avoidance of aligning Jesus with either side. Church organizations differ radically in what responses are expected to such manifestos. The so-called sects, for example, tend to demand a particularly rigid obedience to certain behavior, and it may be assumed, therefore, that the statements from the Brethren, Christadelphians, Church of God, and the Plymouth Brethren are matched by lay approval. In the case of Protestant denominations like the Methodist, Presbyterian, and Baptist this is not the case. Not only do these denominations not require obedience to national credos, they would be unable to implement such a requirement. The Roman Catholic church, which is in a position to command universal obedience, has generally been reluctant to issue mandates that would pose a test of such obedience. Until the Vatican II Council, no Pope had praised conscientious objection as a Christian option, but, as we noted earlier, there do exist Roman Catholic groups which issue anti-war and pacifist pronouncements. This has meant that if the question of Christian pacifism were raised in the right circles, support could be found from both Protestant and Catholic authorities. Christians, in most churches, may do whatever their consciences dictate and still be considered to be members in good standing. While this state of affairs constitutes a good basis for existential moral responsibility, it does leave the significance of the word "Christian" in considerable ambiguity.

It is not inappropriate to raise some related questions about whether Christians have reservations about other types of groups to which they might belong. Denominations are silent on whether their members may remain in good standing if they join the Ku Klux Klan, the American Nazi Party, the John Birch Society, the Silver Shirts, or the American Sons of the Golden West. The reorganized Ku Klux Klan was revived by some Protestant clergy in the South, and its platform stipulates that it is a Protestant and, hence, Christian movement. Most clergy were probably embarrassed by this alignment, but what laymen need is a positive statement to this effect. In the absence of such a clear word, many infer silence to mean consent. One of the sad commentaries on the supposed role of the churches as the defenders of culture is the general lack of religious pronouncements proscribing any activity at all, and an almost equal lack of affirmative endorsements. Occasionally the local church may attack some straw issue like prohibition or gambling, or support some platitudinous position on health or flood relief, but the major history of the major churches is a great wasteland of indecision on the problems of life and death. Religion is not, thus, believed to entail any practical consequences, since as a matter of fact everything seems to be permitted. If war is unchristian, uncharitable, or at least unpleasant, this datum does not seem to be of sufficient Christian concern.

In spite of this notable miasma with which religion confronts us on the issue of war, it is still the case that, throughout the history of Christian churches, men and women have spoken against war. Some still insist that the expression "Prince of Peace" is not a mere metaphor, and that the term "Christian" cannot consistently be linked with any noun or any verb. Indeed, when we consider the various reasons churchmen gave for supporting war, none was so compelling that any necessity attached to it. Christians have supported war, but no theological principles necessitated this support. Most religious arguments make this plausibly clear. It was not piety, per se, that required Christian citizens to kill. It was, rather, the supposed obligations of citizenship which required the war. Even the claim that God chastises his children has not been generally observed to entail that man may, thus, napalm his enemies.

Christians need to reconsider the question whether Christian duties are culture-bound and whether they are secondary to political or national duties. If Christians do merely what the laws of their respective lands require, then it is not clear whether it means anything more to be a Christian than to be a law-abiding citizen. No question arises, normally, in times of relatively humane inter-personal relations. War, however, poses the problem: Does being a Christian occasionally involve the believer in civil disobedience? Or, are Christians always obedient to the political powers that be? As long as the Christian church remained a middle-class club of respectable citizens, there seemed little reason to expect that it would offer any leaven of radical charity to the evils that were built into the culture. The first-century church was not respectable in the social and political milieu, and that may be why it could offer revolutionary advice. C. J. Cadoux believed that the first-century Christians took Jesus to be an advocate of non-violence and gentleness in the literal senses of the terms. "They closely identified their religion with peace. They strongly condemned war for the bloodshed which it involved."[33] When the church achieved respectability in the Roman Empire, it fell victim to a moral bondage from which it has yet to be freed. Perhaps the variety of meanings to which Christianity has been attached is so discordant that the issue of war will have to be settled independently of the Christian movements. If the thesis that war is unchristian has so little Christian support, modern man had better base his actions on secular morals untarnished by piety, and consider that the Christian church is simply one more of the atavisms that need to be rooted out if man is to survive at all.

X *Can Christians Be Soldiers?*

IN EVERY AGE, Christians have had to grapple with the question as to whether there were moral limits to proper Christian behavior. In determining what was moral, Christians tended to appeal to the supposed testimony of scripture and, in particular, to seek from the words attributed to Jesus some support for their stand. This whole procedure of Bible quoting tends to a spurious kind of defense. Passages are appealed to out of context, and may be given meanings that a first-century Jew would not likely have intended. On the assumption that scripture should be studied with the tools of historical analysis, the movement called Modernism developed some minimal words of caution. Albert Schweitzer's *The Quest of the Historical Jesus* summed up the whole matter of appeal to scripture in the conclusion that the quest was a lost cause. Scripture is too much a blend of the views of the authors, later emenders, and of the reactions of Christians years after the death of Jesus for us to be able to have much assurance that the "letter" of Jesus's remarks has been preserved. It takes some effort to be confident that even the "spirit" of Jesus's comments is preserved in printed scripture. In general, attempts to justify Christian soldiering by New Testament quotations run aground on the very obstacles that Modernism so ably identified.

The problems of showing, therefore, that Jesus and the Christians of his age either endorsed warfare, rejected warfare, or were silent on the whole issue are problems that no analysis has quite been able to avoid. C. J. Cadoux in *The Early Christian Attitude to War* and G. M. C. MacGregor in *The New Testament Basis of Pacifism* make very plausible cases for the view that the New Testament supports the pacifist position. Jesus's comments and the actions of both him and his disciples may be mustered in support of this thesis. In order to make the argument coherent, however, each must determine plausibly which passages are to be read literally and which are to be read metaphorically. The care with which both of these scholars make their cases leave one with the clear impression that Christians could not consistently be soldiers. Jesus's apparent rejection of involvement in Zealot uprisings, his advice to Peter to put away the sword, and his own non-violent pursuit of a project that led him to a cross all seemed to make it obvious that the Christian enterprise did not depend upon the military enterprise. Roland H. Bainton supported this contention in his observation that the anti-militarism of the early Christians did not come from any explicit New Testament prohibitions but, rather, from an attempt on their part to read the mind of Jesus.[1]

On the other hand, Umphrey Lee in *The Historic Church and Modern Pacifism* believed that he had shown that Jesus actually endorsed the war option or, at worst, was silent on the matter of Christian involvement. He emphasized the supposed millennialism of Jesus and presented him as basically an ascetic recluse who did not care about worldly matters. If we accept his thesis that Jesus's kingdom was not of this world, then the entire case of Cadoux and MacGregor is cast into some doubt.

The question does not need to hinge on the resolution of this debate, however, since for whatever reasons may be imagined, the early Christians, at least until the end of the second century, did refrain from war. Both the language of scripture and the actions of New Testament Christians support the position that Christianity and the military were incompatible. The Church Fathers of the second and third centuries, as we noted in the previous chapter, supported this peace-tradition. It really does not matter what the reasons were that led the Roman leaders to exempt both Christians and Jews from military service. The fact is that this exemption was accepted by Christians as a compatible alternative. In a day of wars and rumors of wars the New Testament is remarkably unmilitant.

The end of the second century, however, marked the beginning of a separation in attitude toward the responsibilities of Christian citizens to the state. Apparently soldiers had been converted to the Christian faith, and this in itself raised the question in a new light. It was one thing to refrain from soldiering because one was a Christian, and another matter to refrain from being a Christian because one was a soldier. In a letter traditionally attached to the *Apology* of Saint Justin Martyr, reference was made to the *Legio Fulminata,* whose Christian members prayed successfully for rain for themselves, while hail and lightning descended on their enemies. Thus there were Christian soldiers. A few years later Tertullian referred to the *beneficiarii,* which were troops assigned to the governors of the provinces for non-military tasks.[2] Christians who had compunctions about killing might have been able to take this non-militant alternative.

Clement of Alexandria recognized military service as a profession into which Christians could and did go. Indeed, the preparation for the military life was one of the messages of Christ, the Educator, which he offered to believers for their edification.[3] Nonetheless, Clement affirmed that Christians were ultimately educated by Christ for peace, rather than for war. While the life of a soldier was encumbered by material possessions and concerns, the life of a Christian, by contrast, was simple.[4] In general, while soldiers could become Christians, Christians were not expected to become soldiers.

Between the founding of the Christian movement and 325 A.D. a number of events occurred that changed the whole context of this problem. By 325 A.D. Christianity had become an acceptable and respected movement. If in the first century or so Christians tended to be in the minority and to be in a relatively outcast position, this had changed by the fourth century. Political, military, and economic leaders had embraced the new religion, and far from being merely a minor religion of a few socially unimportant persons, Christianity was now a major movement. As the Christian church received its structure from Saint Augustine, patterned after the Roman Empire, it now had to face the problem of war and soldiery in a way that it had not previously. In part, a prophetic movement does not tend to identify with the status quo powers, and the early church was thus more of a social gadfly stinging the conscience of the members of the society. A priestly church, however, as the fourth-century church had become, assumes social responsibilities in a much more conventional way, and thus becomes more vulnerable to compromises.

Some rather atypical behavior was noted, especially by members of the clergy. In 245, for example, Bishop Jacob of Nisibis inspired a war against Sapor. In 410 Bishop Synesius of Cyrene personally organized the military defense of his island. In contrast to these isolated instances, Canon XII of the Council of Nicaea in 325 criticized Christians who, having given up the belt of the soldier, later returned to it.[5] But it was becoming increasingly difficult to maintain this early Christian antipathy to war. In 295 a young Christian named Maximilianus was executed for refusing to offer incense to the emperor and to take part in the shedding of human blood. Here, however, his fellow-Christians approved of his actions and demonstrated their favor by making him a saint of the church.[6] This Christian praise of non-killing became increasingly hard to express as Christianity became the religion of leaders of state, who, by virtue of their office, felt dedicated to the promotion of the military defense of that state. Bishop Eusebius (260–340), for example, portrayed Constantine as a savior of the world,[7] and this commendation left the Maximilianus position in some doubt.

The adoption in 383 of Christianity as the official religion of the Roman Empire confronted Christians with a new context for their decisions on the issue of war. Their official political status thrust upon them a new kind of responsibility. During the period when Christianity was a permitted, though not favored, alternative for the religiously inclined, the individual could be far more radical in his consistency. Prior to its elevation to political privilege, Christianity could develop monastic outlets for those who, in addition to rejecting war, rejected also the other worldly concerns. Now even monasticism needed a new look. If Christians were going to assume the care of the political affairs of the world, then the problem of military service could not be so easily condemned. Prior to Constantine the issues of God versus Caesar might result in the rejection of Caesar in favor of God. Now the situation required that the boundaries of responsibilities be delineated so that each power be rendered its due homage. In spite of the distinction which monasticism enjoyed, most Christians chose to be citizens in the world, and hence they faced the genuine problem of potential conflict of allegiance.

Jerome (340–420), Ambrose (334–397), Chrysostom (345–407), and Prudentius (348–410) all praised the empire of Rome as the bearer of culture, and in so doing they set the standards of chauvinism for centuries to come. Ambrose replied to a magistrate named Studius, who was troubled by the question of Christian killing, with the comment that he who wields the sword serves as God's avenger against those who do evil. Once this became clear, the issue of serving communion to men with blood on their hands was resolved. While it may seem difficult to be in love and charity with one's neighbor while holding a bloody sword against him, political responsibility was a duty which justified anything that seemed to be required.[8] Saint Augustine claimed that no person should doubt that God was pleased with military service.[9] If the biblical David could be in God's favor, surely there could be nothing wrong with the military life. The fact was that the affairs of God require both the sword of the flesh and of the spirit for their success. The new Christian kingdom was engulfed by the world and indistinguishable from it. When some of his contemporaries were troubled by the Sermon on the Mount mandate with regard to turning the other cheek, Saint Augustine assured them that such precepts referred only to the interior disposition of the heart and not to exterior actions.[10] It followed, therefore, that a man could thrust his sword into his enemy while subjectively turning the other cheek. Christians slew their opponents with humble sword thrusts. The political state that honored the Sermon on the Mount would thus wage its wars with kindness and slay its enemies with compassion. The Christian churches had become so well integrated into the military program that under Theodosius II, whose pagan rites were excluded from the army, only Christians could serve as soldiers. Although pious historians could claim that Clovis and other barbarians had militarized Christianity, there seemed to be sufficient evidence that the move was made without pagan assistance.

When the Crusades became a standard of religious excellence, and participation in them a sign of religious devotion, there was no question about the possibility of Christians being soldiers. From the first Crusade in 1095 to the seventh Crusade in 1270 the church was in an unquestioned militant phase. Clergy fought in battles with the rest of the people, and even nuns put on military garb and fought, occasionally even against their bishops. In 1180 John of Salisbury sanctified the soldier's role as the secular complement of the clergy. Soldiers were inducted with a sacred oath, a sacramentum, by which they swore to fight with courage in the name of God, Christ, and the Holy Ghost.[11]

> *"Turn over in your mind the words of the oath itself, and you will find that the soldiery of arms not less than the spiritual soldiery is bound by the requirements of its official duties to the sacred service and worship of God. . . . But what is the office of the duly ordained soldiery? To defend the Church, to assail infidelity, to venerate the priesthood, to protect the poor from injuries, to pacify the province, to pour out their blood for their brothers. . . . The high praises of God are in their throat and two-edged swords are in their hands."*[12]

The profession of soldier achieved such an intrinsic status that it made no difference whether it was dedicated to the service of a king who was a believer or to an infidel. Soldiers were Christian independently of the ends for which they fought. This was precisely the kind of moral vacuum to which the position was doomed to arrive.

Once it had been determined that being a Christian was an affair of inner attitude, apart from both ends and means, then it was a simple and natural step to consider both methods and goals as of no Christian import. With almost five hundred years of application of the doctrine of military piety it was not difficult for Martin Luther (1483–1546) to resolve Christian conscience compatibly with war. His contemporaries were perplexed with the Gospel advocacy of non-resistance to evil and, specifically, they could not comprehend the Sermon on the Mount approval of turning the other cheek. The solution Luther proposed entailed the recognition of two spheres in which the Christian lived: the secular and the spiritual. In the spiritual sphere swords are not needed, while in the secular area swords are divinely ordained.[13] We are counseled to turn the other cheek in church, but we are commanded to use the sword outside of church. Indeed, Luther remarked, if God had not intended the sword to be used for secular ends he would have said so. Since he did not prohibit soldiery, he must approve of the profession. The sophistry to which this argument from negative data leads is matched only by the ease with which religious people have been able to accept the inference. Among the practices not prohibited by scripture, and thus presumed to be permitted, if not commanded, are slavery, economic inequality, racial discrimination, poverty, and disease. In any case, God honors the sword, and the soldier who uses it is acting in God's name. In an essay titled "That Soldiers, Too, Can Be Saved" Luther remarked with an unequivocal affirmative that it would be no more difficult for God to do this for them than for clergy. With remarkable candor he noted that "although slaying and robbing do not seem to be the work of love . . . yet in truth even this is a work of love,"[14] and the hand that wields the sword is not really man's but God's. It is God who really "hangs, tortures, beheads, slays, and fights."[15] Franciscus de Victoria summed the matter up simply: "Christians may serve in war and make war."[16]

Luther had a long scholastic tradition in his favor, so that it came naturally to him to view war as universal, rational, and in accord with the spiritual life. The notion of the just war as developed by Saint Thomas and his followers presupposes that war is a legitimate function of the state. While war was not indiscriminately endorsed in principle, nor indiscriminately forbidden in principle, it was in fact the case that all wars enjoyed the divine sanction of the priests of the countries at war. This fact implies that either there was cosmic confusion in the godhead, or that the discussion of the just war was merely a bit of ad hoc rationalization. Saint Thomas had claimed that the killing which is involved in the war business is never intended by the Christian, and thus Christians are not morally culpable for it. After all, it is morally natural for states to defend themselves by actions which unintentionally result in the death of others. The self-defense of the state is all that is intended, while the death of the enemy always comes as an unintended contingency. This entails the so-called principle of the double-effect, which played a major role in Roman Catholic doctrine justifying killing in war. This is precisely the kind of casuistry which every nation uses to explain why the bombs it drops intend the death of no person. Persons who are killed by bombs are at fault for being where the bombs fall. Some of the persons at the war crimes trials in Germany appealed to this same time-honored principle and claimed innocence for the same reasons. The double-effect theory has some significance in separating accident from intention, but it would appear to make no sense at all in warfare where the death of the enemy is intended in general. The accident applies only to which of the generally intended victims are the actually slain ones. If this were a viable distinction, then it should hold as well for the man who dropped the bomb on Nagasaki as for the one who turned on the gas at Belsen.

If war can be sanctioned with such a religious dogma, it must still be noted that some Caesars had their secular doubts. Yet during the medieval period the commitment to war was so religiously oriented that the majority of jurists favored the position that religious unbelief was a sufficient reason to go to war against an enemy. In a series of decrees of the Fourth Lateran Council in 1215 priests and bishops were urged to recruit their parishioners for the crusades and to go themselves. Clergy who did so would still receive the benefices normally due to them for a period up to three years while they were absent on a crusade. Anyone who fell in battle against heathen, or indeed against anyone who opposed even Roman liturgy, could be assured of heavenly bliss. Few voices spoke against this trend, and Christian soldiery seemed to be the noblest profession a Christian could enter. While all this was part of Luther's inheritance, he did attack the principle of religious crusades, and did not agree that priests and bishops should take the sword in person. Christian laymen, however, lived in both worlds, and they must wield the sword whenever the earthly prince commanded it.

The historian Lecky reported that it had been claimed in some parts of Ireland that in baptism by immersion the right arms of the male babies were carefully held above the water so that, untouched by the sacred water, they might strike more deadly blows in battle.[17] In England an assembly of high churchmen in 1530 listed as one of the heretical errors the belief that Christians should not use the sword. The 1552 version of the 42 Articles of Religion of the Church of England stated that it was lawful for the Christian, at the command of the magistrate, to wear weapons and to serve in lawful wars. The 1571 version, with 39 Articles, deleted the requirement that the war even had to be lawful. A form of recantation from an Oxford document of 1575, which identified four Anabaptist errors, listed as one of these errors the notion that a Christian should not wear a sword.

From Hugo Grotius to William Paley war was affirmed to be consonant with divine law, and the profession of soldier was claimed to be nowhere forbidden in scripture. John Calvin was assured that nowhere in the New Testament was war ever condemned. This typified the ease with which Christians, generally, were able to endorse any act not explicitly forsworn.[18] Francisco Suarez concluded that war was not intrinsically evil nor was it forbidden to Christians, and he claimed to derive his conclusion from the scripture itself.[19] Somehow Calvin and Suarez never had to reconcile the contradictions their views posed. There were, however, some war problems that Christians of the most bellicose variety still found to be thorny ones. What would a priest do if he is attacked by assassins while he is baptizing a child? Should he finish the baptism to assure the child eternal security and risk his own temporal death? Ideally he was encouraged to accomplish both ends, but if he really had to choose between the eternal salvation of the child and his own mortal life, he should lose the latter to save the former.[20] As late as William Paley[21] the sanctity of war was still being defended by the appeal to Jesus's supposed commendation of the centurion. In spite of the problems of biblical interpretation, however, Jesus appears to have praised only the faith of the centurion and not the profession which he practiced. Clearly it would take an inference of cosmic proportions to translate this approval of the faith of the centurion into a Christly endorsement of the whole military complex. For a leader who held no military post, and whose disciples were not soldiers, it would be contradictory to credit him with such a sweeping praise for the profession of soldier.

In the nineteenth century the French socialist, Pierre Joseph Proudhon (1809–1865), praised war as the most sublime phenomenon of man's moral life, and he considered war as more authoritative than the Gospels. War was a sign of religiosity and dignity, while peace was a sign of moral decay. Proudhon, however, would scarcely be considered as an authority on either the doctrine or the practice of Christianity. On the other hand, some clergy seemed to reflect this point of view. As a Boston minister of the mid-nineteenth century so bluntly put it, war tends "to rectify and exalt the popular conception of God," since "there is nothing like the smell of gunpowder for making a nation perceive the fragrance of divinity in truth."[22] As he portrayed the Christian history it was one long support for warfare. From the bloody battles of the twelve tribes of Israel, through the Crusades and to the modern era, warfare had been an expression of divine administration, and every raid and ambush, every slain civilian and soldier were facts approved by the all-accommodating Lord of Hosts. This is the picture which has prompted some historians to maintain that, with rare exceptions, the major effort for peace and against war has come from persons professing little sympathy with historic Christianity.[23]

If all through the period of the Holy Roman Empire Christians had faced the issue of war with mixed feelings, the problem was no less keen in America when the Revolution for Independence was fought. Ray H. Abrams[24] observed that one of the factors contributing to the American revolution was the doctrine preached in New England churches which favored the public acceptance of the revolt. The support of major churches, such as the Congregational, made recruitment relatively easy, and ministers of the Gospel served as agents for enlistment. One enthusiastic minister of Ipswich, John Cleveland, was said to have preached his whole congregation into the army and then to have gone himself. Many from the Presbyterian, Baptist, Lutheran, and German Reformed saw the Revolution as in defense of the wish for liberty that had first brought them to America. Denominations like the Methodist and Episcopal, however, had their roots in England, and their clergy tended to urge the end of the war. John Wesley called John Hancock a criminal and urged the colonists to lay down their arms. Mennonites and Quakers, however, maintained their traditional stand against war even though they were sympathetic to the idea of independence.

During the Civil War most Christian denominations avowed allegiance to their respective sides in the conflict, although, again, the Quakers and Mennonites kept the anti-war position alive. The prevailing position, however, found most churches convinced that North or South, as the case was, was engaged in a struggle to maintain home, property, and religion. When the war was over, many northern clergy came south and took over the churches, justifying the confiscation by an appeal to Jesus's mandate to spread the gospel to the heathen. Religion generally came to the support of the country in the Mexican and Spanish-American Wars as well.

By the time of World War I clergy had developed a fine talent for sanctifying soldiering and finding holiness in national wars. In this war, above all preceding wars, churches promoted the theology of the good and the bad nations. This war was between the forces of light and those of darkness, virtue was pitted against vice, humanity was beleaguered by bestiality, and the choice facing man was civilization or chaos. World War I was a genuine holy war, and many Christian churches made it so. The antipathy to the League of Nations at the end of the war demonstrated, however, the callowness of this entire pretension. Samuel McCrea Cavert, then assistant secretary of the General War-Time Commission of the Churches, saw the ultimate issues of the war as moral and spiritual survival. World War I was a missionary enterprise,[25] in which all good soldiers of Christ should be happy to serve. Sending soldiers to Germany was equated with sending missionaries to the heathen. The American Board of the Congregationalists declared the aims of the war and of the missionary activity of the Board to be identical! Frank Mason North, president of the Federal Council of Churches of Christ in America, felt that the breath of God enlivened the American cause.

Even Jesus Christ was not exempt from the draft, and the Methodist bishop, Edwin Holt Hughes, announced that it would be a pity if Christ were not enlisted to march in the front lines with the soldiers. Albert C. Dieffenbach, editor of the Unitarian magazine, *The Christian Register,* was even confident that Jesus would be uniformed and taking grenades in hand would bomb the enemy with the rest of the soldiers. Jesus would wield the bayonet without compunction. Written under the sponsorship of the Y.M.C.A., a masterpiece of Christian sadism was composed on the Christian use of the bayonet. To any young man pardonably troubled by the thought of killing his brothers, the authors, Henry B. Wright and George Stewart, Jr., gave the following Christly comfort:

> *"At first I shrank from associating Jesus with the bayonet and essayed to place in His hands the sword the use of which*

He himself sanctioned. But soon I reflected that the sword,
which is today only an article of adornment, was in His day
the most terrible weapon of mutilation and destruction known
and that the modern bayonet is no more dreadful an imple-
ment since it is simply the sword attached to the rifle."[26]

Through the clouds of glory he saw Jesus, blood-spattered and
weary, shoving his bayonet into German soldiers. Jesus was, of
course, dressed in an American uniform and he blessed the American cause. Jesus thus took his place with other religious soldiers
like Moses, Joshua, David, George Washington, Robert E. Lee,
and General Pershing. If the analogy made Christians a mite
squeamish, their churches discouraged them from voicing their
doubts. With religious administration on the side of political administration, it was not surprising that individual conscience was
almost stamped out.

There were, nonetheless, clergy who opposed this war fever
during World War I and who kept alive the conviction that the
Prince of Peace could not consistently be aligned with military
effort. After the War there was a relatively widespread revulsion
of clergy against the degree to which the churches had sanctified
that War. Virtually every major denomination of Protestantism
issued strong peace stands, and pacifism in one form or another
was openly endorsed and praised. The position of the Quakers
received formal endorsement from the large Protestant bodies,
and conscientious objection was viewed with wide favor. When
the Federal Council of Churches proclaimed in 1932 that the
Christian Church should not bless or sanction war, there were
only one or two dissenting votes among the four hundred delegates who represented the twenty-five denominations of the
Council.[27] Much of the isolationism of the inter-war period tended
to rub off on religious attitudes, and some pacifism was less concerned to make wars obsolete than to keep Christian hands clean
from the shedding of blood. Some pacifists, notably in the Fellowship of Reconciliation, made pacifism into a method for handling disputes of every kind, from those involving essentially

inter-personal problems of what to do when you are about to be raped to the resolution of labor aspirations. This tendency to reject force in any violent form, quite apart from war, prompted Reinhold Niebuhr to withdraw from the F.O.R.[28] He appreciated non-resistance as a possible Christian position, but he rejected non-violent resistance as naïve. Yet Niebuhr was not claiming that Christians should be soldiers, but rather that in a world such as this violence may on occasion be required for political, if not for religious, reasons.

The mood of Christian churches immediately prior to the outbreak of the United States participation in World War II was overwhelmingly anti-war. George H. Buttrick, then the president of the Federal Council of Churches of Christ in America, pleaded in 1939 against the United States intervention in the conflict. In October of that same year the Council unanimously passed a resolution calling upon the fifty member denominations to denounce war as contrary to the mind of Christian thought.[29] Pearl Harbor, and the formal entry of the United States into the War, brought about a rapid change in religious perspective. Even the most outspoken of the non-interventionist journals, *The Christian Century*, announced in the first editorial after December 7, 1941, that it would stand behind the government decision in what it called "an unnecessary necessity."

If World War I roused excesses of religious oratory in favor of a "holy war," World War II found the clergy much more cautious in their endorsement. R. H. Abrams noted that, by contrast with their brothers in World War I, the clergy in the second World War took it as a grim necessity.[30] While the chaplaincy flourished, this was not a sign of a callow capitulation to the gods of war. During this War pacifist clergy were outspoken, more numerous, and less persecuted than during the former World War. About 12,000 conscientious objectors served in Civilian Public Service Camps or in some form of alternative service, and an additional 6,500 served an average of thirty months in prison for violation of the Selective Service Act of 1940. While most churches displayed service flags with stars for each member in the armed services, some displayed comparable flags for the conscientious objectors from their congregations. Henry Hitt Crane reported that his Methodist Church in Detroit at one time had a military and a pacifist flag with fifty stars on each. The Churches during World War II were sharply divided. Even those clergy most sympathetic with the United States' involvement in the war, like Reinhold Niebuhr, did not consider the war as much a Christian obligation as a civic one.

But if World War II still had some religious sanction, neither the Korean War nor the Vietnamese War has given rise to any comparable religious approval. The active participation of the government in Vietnam through the sending of troops has not been received by any general enthusiasm on the part of American clergy, whether Protestant, Catholic, or Jew. While the dilemmas discussed in *The Deputy* were not unique to Roman Catholicism, they were fairly typical of the kinds of inferences which clerical silence have tended to prompt. Like most wars, once they have begun, the one in Vietnam tends to be discussed from the perspective of how it ought to be conducted, rather than whether it ought to be fought at all. If religion has a contribution here it would seem, from its tradition, that it should be in the role of spiritual gadfly. It is not that Christians should absent themselves from the affairs of this world, but rather that of all the institutions, the Christian church should remain sufficiently aloof to be in a position to lend a cosmic outlook to the essentially internecine business of war. Religion ought not to be a matter of prudentialism, and the failure of war, even on secular grounds, makes this much more essential.

The difficulty in giving an unambiguous answer to the original question, "Can Christians be soldiers?" is compounded by the varieties of church structure and by the differences in attitude toward central authority. The Roman Catholic church, on the one hand, has the central power for a clear and united answer, but its use of that power does not provide us with what we need To be sure Church Councils have legislated against soldiering, and Vatican Council II, while conceding that wars of defense may be permissible, still branded war as alien to Christian counsels of perfection. Protestant churches, however, with their traditions of decentralization, have always had trouble in presenting a united front. There is rarely anyone who is entitled to speak for the group. Protestant federations have attempted to bridge this gap. In 1932 the strong anti-war statement of the Federal Council of Churches of Christ in America represented spokesmen from only 25 denominations. A similar statement by the group in 1939 had endorsement from 50 denominational representatives. It would be naïve to suppose that the millions of churchmen and the thousands of clergy responded with anything like general enthusiasm to these peace commitments of their delegates.

Yet, even granting all of this, the fact remains that opposition to war has been a persistent thesis in Christian traditions. Even so, in the modern world the overwhelming number of Christians do serve as soldiers when they are drafted to do so. Only about 18,500 men served in alternative service or in prison as conscientious objectors in America during World War II, and not all of these objected on Christian grounds. Still the participation in military service of the lay Christian is not commended so much on Christian as on secular patriotic grounds. John C. Bennett, who concedes that there is a pacifist tradition in the Christian church, and that such a position is perhaps closest to the counsel of perfection, still believes that there are moral grounds for military force, and these grounds derive apparently from secular responsibilities rather than from religious doctrine.[31] If most Christians act incompatibly with this peace tradition, however, there are genuine reasons for doubting that the traditions are very significant. Chaplains are, after all, clergymen and their presence in the military indicates, at the very least, that war and Christian duty may coincide. Whatever may have been the sentiment of the early Christians, modern armies do not lack for Christian soldiers, nor are they without clerical support for the soldiering profession.

In perspective, then, the post-Constantine Church has been of two minds. On the one hand, it has kept alive the conviction that Christians ought not to be soldiers; and on the other, it has agreed with Luther that Christians should be soldiers. If mankind wishes ever to reverse its fraternity with war, it will first of all need to see clearly the incompatibility of war with religion. If, on the one hand, the Christian churches propose to continue the elaborate chaplaincy ministry, they will need, in addition, to invent some comparable ministry to conscientious objectors. If, as a concession to a basically evil world, Christians take up arms against their fellows, they also need to recognize the degree to which such a concession is in contradiction to their oldest traditions. Notwithstanding all of this, the abysmal failure of war to resolve international relations, even on secular grounds, may lead men to reject it for reasons quite unrelated to their moral hopes.

THE CAUSES OF WAR

XI *Psychological Causes of War*

IN THE SEVENTEENTH CENTURY Thomas Hobbes observed that "all men in the state of nature have a desire and will to hurt."[1] Hobbes, of course, was referring to a condition antecedent to political organization, and not to any supposed psychological brute which primitive man might be supposed to have been. It is this psychological thesis, however, which is our concern, and it is the so-called warlike nature of man which is under consideration. The assessment of such a claim required a science of human behavior, and until comparatively recent times this was not available. For the past sixty years psychologists have endeavored to structure experiments and to define man so that his "human nature" could be known, understood, and manipulated. It now seems generally conceded that man's basic psychic drives do contribute toward the likelihood of war as well as toward the possibility of peace. In order that this be brought about we will need to understand the sadistic impulses, the defense-mechanisms whereby we hide our sadistic impulses, and the entire complex of motivations whereby we can be spurred to action. We will need to go back to the ancient Abraham-Isaac motif, whereby even a father can be led to slay his son provided the motivation be adequate. Indeed, people who can think of Abraham as noble in the face of his willingness to commit such a deed will doubtless be amenable to almost any act, however cruel it may be. With such a long tradition of biblical fratricide, we ought not to be surprised at the ease with which the elder statesmen send the youth to war, and in effect sacrifice their sons. Let us look first of all at the old suspicion that the root of the trouble lies in human nature itself in an ineradicable way, before we turn to whatever word of help modern psychology can offer.

In the context of personal struggle with sin the author of the New Testament book of *James* asked, "Whence come wars and whence come fightings?"[2] His answer was that they come from lust, coveting, aggression, and man's irrational nature. *James,* of course, was not speaking of war but, rather, of the obstacles to personal purity. Nonetheless, the inner cravings of human nature that prompt men to come in conflict with whoever stands in the way of fulfilling these cravings became an explanation for conflict at all levels on the part of later interpreters of human nature. It really makes little difference whether the author had in mind spiritual or physical warfare, since the subsequent interpretation that has survived for twenty centuries has been that war is derived from human nature and that any effort to eliminate war must founder on this irremediable human fact.

Most of the ancient and medieval religious writing moved easily between this spiritual and physical analysis of war as being rooted in our own contradictory natures. Legnano could speak of an opposition between reason and appetite[3] as the efficient cause of wars of all kinds. Men are thus naturally inclined to do battle. If we simply noted the ease with which men go to war, on slight or non-existent pretexts, and in the process risk the material and cultural things that ordinarily matter most, it would seem natural to conclude that there is some inner surd which blinds man's reason and hurls him off the precipice of self-annihilation. There seems no doubt but that men love war with a profound passion, while at the same time they fill their books with sentimental nostalgia about love of man, build hospitals for the cure of ills that wars maximize, and worry about the fate of starving peoples in far corners of the globe while yet planning to exterminate these same people with the most modern, efficient, and clean bombs that technology can produce. If there is such a thing as the civilian's natural repugnance at the unaccustomed sight of the gore of warfare, experience, with the help of psychologists, has shown that such resistance to killing is rooted in one's whole psychic history, and is part of a long environmental conditioning process. It is one thing to train soldiers to fire weapons, and something quite different to get them to shoot other persons. In his book, *Men Against Fire*, S. L. A. Marshall observed that in the Korean conflict only 15 to 20% of the men in any unit actually fired against the enemy. Even where this resistance can be overcome, and it must be somehow or else no persons would be killed in war save by accident, it is still the case that hatred of the enemy is difficult to inculcate. In a study made after World War II it was noted that vindictiveness played almost no role at all as a combat incentive. The major spur was simply the desire to get the job over with.[4] In the same vein, the study reported the resistance shown by the soldiers to indoctrination about the value of the war.[5] Indeed, most of the mind-set toward the war seemed to have been created by factors long antecedent to military training.

In a publication for the infantry in 1943, military leaders were assured by psychologists that:

> *"The cure for the anxiety that results from this kind of conflict between conscience and reason is to understand it. Once a man realizes that the feeling is natural in men brought up, as the average American is, to respect human life, this particular worry won't haunt him so much. He may have a few bad dreams, but they won't interfere with doing the job ahead, disagreeable though it may be."*[6]

One does not know whether to be depressed that such a human manipulation is possible, or filled with consternation that any psychologist would be willing to conduct an experiment to see how it might be accomplished. Surely the German psychologists must have faced this same problem in getting operators for their extermination camps, and obviously it was possible to manipulate human beings so that they could perform these tasks. In a study of war neuroses in World War I it was considered to be a sad fact that the qualities that make for good peace-time citizenship do not prepare soldiers to endure the strains of war.[7] The peaceful attributes of independence of judgment and concern for the sufferings of others unfit men for obedience to military orders and to kill. The author concluded that the ideal soldier must be more or less a "natural butcher." A soldier cannot afford to be sensitive to pain in others nor offended by the sight of dismembered human bodies. This would seem to suggest, however, that war is not so natural or so psychologically grounded in human nature as we have been led to believe.

One of the early psychological explanations of the naturalness of the drive to war was contained in the expression "the instinct for pugnacity."[8] If some persons did not seem to be strongly led to overt war, this could be explained as a sign that the innate strength of the instinct differed from person to person. In case we should wonder why an instinct with such destructive consequences should ever have survived, we are told that war has really not been injurious. In fact it has been one of the most civilizing of processes, and is basically a survival response rather than a death wish in disguise. Sigmund Freud (1856–1939), while not lauding war as a bestower of blessings, did not think that it signified human decay. Men were simply creatures with libidinal capacities, and whenever society removed the restrictions to the expressions of these capacities, as is done in wartime, then this absence of community rebuke leads men to cruelty, treachery, and barbarity.[9]

"From the foregoing observations we may already derive this consolation—that our mortification and our grievous disillusionment regarding the uncivilized behavior of our world-compatriots in this war are shown to be unjustified. They were based on an illusion to which we have abandoned ourselves. In reality our fellow-citizens have not sunk so low

*as we feared, because they had never risen so high as we
believed.*"[10]

Freud believed that brief forays of killing and carnage, as long
as they were carried out under the conditions of social approval,
did not cause any particular lowering of relative morality within
the national boundaries.

On almost every level of society personal violence and killing
have become channeled into other avenues. These institutionaliza-
tions of killing in media such as boxing, football, and body-
contact sports generally, are well-covered by the press and apparently widely appreciated by the readers. The sports of hunting
animals are engaged in with some enthusiasm by a sizable portion
of the population. In spite of this, however, there is also generally
antipathy to the violence ingrained in American culture. Literal
warfare is not so natural nor so appreciated but what conscription is required to get enough men to make even the pretense of
aggressive behavior toward their fellow men. Still, some human
beings do get satisfaction out of slaughter, whether interpersonally
as in a boxing ring, or impersonally through dropping bombs on
persons whom they never see and whose cries they never hear.
The emptiness of the reasons men verbalize for war suggests that
war really does not rest on any rationale. If we go to war to make
democracy safe or to protect the American way of life, it turns
out to be irrelevant that neither democracy nor this way of life
is helped by war. Indeed, it turns out to be irrelevant that war
destroys these very ends rather than protects them. People who
want to go to war are not generally concerned with whether
war is a means that actually accomplishes its espoused ends. As
one writer put it, "They are concerned with what they call right
and wrong, and they want to do something about their feeling
of concern, and the thing they feel like doing is fighting."[11]

After all, if people didn't like to fight, there are no good reasons
why they should do so much of it. Bertrand Russell spoke to
this matter when he stated that men fight because of desire on
the one hand, and from sheer impulse on the other. Just as chil-

dren run and shout from impulse, and dogs bay at the moon, so
grown men quarrel, boast, beat each other, and murder.[12] Gordon
Allport spoke of an expectancy of war which made it easy for
leaders to provoke their citizens to fight. He believed that if
persons were left to themselves, they would never go to war.[13]
As he developed it, most people hate war, but they expect it to
happen, and this expectancy determines that they will bring wars
about. Part of the problem we face is to determine whether this
expectancy rests on some ineradicable warlike urges, as George
Santayana believed,[14] or whether the brain of man has developed through ages of killing a "phylogenetic action pattern of
killing."[15] Perhaps, on the other hand, man's aggressiveness has
a more direct and immediate cause. There have been studies to
show that there is a close relation between militant nationalism
and attitudes toward out-groups, with the result that aggressive
patriotism, anti-Semitism, anti-Negro, and anti-Oriental sentiment
are correlated. This bears a relation to a thesis offered by Carl G.
Jung that the greater our awareness of our own defects, the
quicker we are likely to see these faults in others, and to take
aggressive action to curb them.[16] Thus it would follow that the
greater our feelings of personal inadequacy, the more likely we
will act aggressively toward others.

What psychological evidence is there that the native hate and
aggression in the heart of man make for a kind of psychological
necessity for war? There is one helpful bit of information referred
to by Gardner Murphy[17] that should at least curb the excessive
presumptions that there are so-called aggressive nations. There
are no national characteristics such that one could speak of
German warlikeness or Japanese belligerence as if these were
peculiar to a special race or culture. What we do find, however,
is that societies may be made warlike or pacific with relatively
little effort. Germany, Russia, Japan, and the United States are
excellent examples of how cultures with traditions of gentility can
be converted into war machines and back to culture lovers
within the same generation. Any nation, or any society, where
there are major frustrations may easily be led into war. It is not

that there are warlike peoples so much as that when persons are frustrated long enough, they take recourse to war. Satisfied peoples do not go to war. Dissatisfied peoples do go to war.

Is there any evidence for the contention that aggressive behavior in one area tends to carry over into all areas? H. J. Eysenck concluded that aggressive attitudes tend to be general[18] and, further, that attempts to sublimate such aggressiveness by moral equivalents of war fail to drain off the aggressive urges. If a society is teeming with frustrations, no amount of sublimation can calm the aggressiveness which has been produced. Yet if there is no substitute for aggression, then William James's hope for a moral equivalent for war rests on a mistake. J. C. Flugel was not sure whether international competition in sports served as a release for energies, or whether it simply fostered war by promoting competitiveness.[19] In spite of what appears to be psychological lack of unanimity in accounting for aggressive behavior, there is still general agreement that conditions which breed suspicion and a sense of being deprived do tend to generate war.[20] Conditions in pre-war Germany were of such a kind as to bring about the attitudes which feed war-mindedness. It makes no sense, therefore, to talk about means of keeping the warlike nations in line, since any nation, given the conditions, can change from pacific to warlike and back again with no profound alteration in what might be called national character.

Whenever man's culture rewards warlike behavior, it is reasonable to expect that war will be welcomed and endorsed. There are, after all, values which war produces. There is an excitement to relieve the tedium of assembly-line jobs and meaningless activity; there is a luster which uniforms and medals can give to men who have achieved no recognition; there is a security and comfort which military life can give to persons who have lived in abject poverty and who have known no sense of dignity. For millions of men and women war is a great relief, and the direction and certitude which military commands offer to the indecisive is a vast comfort. Many writers have called attention to the sense in which war provides a return to the womb, and to the fact that the security of professional military service is one of its great attractions.[21] But if this is true, it follows also that this kind of security is precisely what young men and women ought not to have if they are to develop initiative, imagination, self-direction, and maturity. Military authorities, from the sergeant to the general, function psychologically like alter-fathers, who, though they may deal with us harshly, always do so for our own good. The military belt serves, therefore, as an umbilical with the parent figure, and as long as young people are thwarted from maturity, the military life, even with war, will appear as a haven of solace.

What shall we make of this morass of conflicting psychological theories and predictions with regard to the future of war? Was Freud correct, when, in a letter to Albert Einstein,[22] he concluded that there is no likelihood of ever curbing mankind's aggressive tendencies. Is the hope for unwarlike men a vain dream? Even if Freud were right in this dismal prognosis, it would still have to be shown that wars are caused by warlike persons, rather than the other way around. Since there is far more likelihood that wars are declared by the stupidity or cupidity of our diplomats than as a consequence of their choleric temperaments, Freud's thesis, even if true, may have far less significance than it has been credited with. In a study of personal aggressiveness and war published just before World War II[23] some very interesting psychological insights were summarized. There are, it was maintained, unconscious aggressive impulses which influence us without our being aware of the fact. These impulses create an ambivalence in us between love and hate. Since we do not wish to remain in ambivalence, we tend to develop ways of repressing the unwanted impulses or of displacing them by hurting a stranger when we really feel like hurting a friend. When we harbor these impulses to destruction long enough we feel such shame and guilt, such self-condemnation and self-hatred, that we alleviate our tension by seeking a scapegoat. We project, therefore, and attribute to others the evil wishes which we possess, and we then see the world as full of wicked monsters, imaginary enemies, malevolent fiends who must be exterminated if we are to survive. The German persecution of the Jews is a case of such projection, and the blind fear which Nazis expressed toward Jews and the blind hate with which they treated them, demonstrate that there must be some deeper psychic meaning to an action which has no cognitive rationale. The fear of communism, which moves so many Americans, must stem from a similar inner and inverted anxiety. Recent studies of the relation of religious commitment and fears of Jews, Communists, and minority racial groups support the suspicion that fundamentalists in religion have the strongest fears of "subversion" by "alien" groups.[24] These studies suggest that the preoccupation of religion with sin, predestination, Devil, Hell, and dire divine punishment contributes to the likelihood that such religion will promote paranoia. The ease with which we assign to China, for example, all the aggressiveness which we primarily exhibit must have some non-rational source. It is as elementary as the projection which has prompted historians to speak of every Indian attack on a white village as a massacre, and every white attack on an Indian village as a battle. We can smile at the behavior of primitive tribes which exhibit this chauvinism, while not recognizing the phenomenon when we exhibit it.

Edward Glover noted in 1931 that no country in the world has ever spent a penny on investigating the psychological aspects of war motivation.[25] The accusation was, in his case, no idle complaint, for he outlined, then, a rather model pattern for psychologic research into the relevant issues of war and peace. While much of the research that has been conducted since then has been of the order of showing military leaders how to make warriors out of former farmers, there have been serious practical and theoretical attempts to understand the psychic factors that keep war such a viable human option. In a study carried out just prior to World War II, a clinical psychologist found that war was rooted in sadism, on the one hand, and the Oedipal conflict on the other.[26] He noted, also, that war fever, race-hatred, and cruelty were all closely linked.[27] While there may be argument over the Oedipal account, or even over whether sadism is an operationally clear concept, it is at least significant that the author considered war to be a sign of sickness rather than of normality. And in addition, whatever the causes of war might be, it appeared psychologically obvious that the fact of war depended upon man's willingness to fight.[28]

One of the more hopeful signs coming from UNESCO is a study project undertaken to explore the tensions that affect international understanding. If wars do indeed begin in the minds of men, then any insights into the psychological states of mind of peoples of different nations which could assist in alleviating tensions would directly contribute to the promotion of peace. Since there are good reasons for doubting that wars are actually fought for the reasons that are publicized, knowledge of man's psychic tensions can add immeasurably to our understanding of the reasons we do go to war. There are, for example, psychoanalytic reasons for suspecting that the moral breast-beating which usually precedes a nation's entry into war is a case of rationalization. Such expressions as "the free world," the "Iron Curtain," or "slave societies" may well conceal our own paranoia beneath a veneer of putative moral concern. Perhaps psychologists will be able to explain the phenomenon of clergy of the Prince of Peace rushing to preach vengeance, pillage, and the annihilation of the enemy on the eve of any war in which their nation happens to be involved. Though the fact remains that clergy did not do this in World War II in any fashion comparable to what occurred in World War I, and neither the Korean nor the Vietnam conflicts have produced any general clerical flag-waving. Many clergy have confronted the American leaders in Washington, D.C., in organized protest against American bombing in Vietnam in 1965, 1966, and 1967. While they are few in number, whatever clerical approval the Vietnam war may have remains unexpressed in any organized fashion.

Psychological studies have been made of war-time phenomena from the World War II period which could be helpful to any group interested in running a war efficiently or to any group seeking to understand how to avoid the need for war at all. In an experiment in mass communication, tests were conducted to determine whether soldiers could be persuaded of the war aims better when two sides were presented or when only the one side was presented. It was discovered that persons who opposed the government policy were influenced more when two sides were presented. On the other hand, for men who were convinced that the government was right, the presentation of two sides was not effective. The better educated men were more favorably influenced by the two-sided presentation, while the poorly educated men were better influenced when only the government position was given.[29] Such information is, of course, morally neutral in the sense that whatever attitude one was trying to sell, there was a shrewd way in which to go about doing it. The experimenters were not raising the question as to whether the government position deserved to be distributed, but only that if it was to be distributed, then there were efficient ways to do it. The variety of studies of this kind, the results of which are to be used for some propaganda aim, may explain in part the emergence of *The Journal of Conflict Resolution,* one of whose aims is to encourage scientists to sell their talents only for peaceful ends. The efforts of Charles E. Osgood are notable in this regard. He coined the word GRIT, by which he meant "graduated and reciprocal initiatives in tension-reduction."[30] His thesis is that American foreign policy, like that of every other nation, is not currently designed to make either understanding or peace possible.

What is called "diplomacy" is carried out with a chip-on-the-shoulder approach which makes it virtually impossible for any nation to win or lose without losing what is euphemistically called its "face." American foreign policy, for example, is carried out with an implied nuclear threat if our enemies do not comply with our wishes. Since no nation could reasonably intend to carry out its threat of nuclear annihilation, our opponents must either assume we are bluffing or that we are inhumane. For any nation to succeed in this kind of dialogue, the losing nation must be crushed, psychically if not physically. Common sense, if not sound psychology, could see that the means of normal international correspondence are a mistake.

It is incredible that any adult could imagine that we would achieve anything by a policy whose aim is to show to the enemy that America is not a "paper tiger." What do people do when they discover that the enemy they face is real and not paper? Do they, as a matter of fact, swoon in terror or capitulate in resignation? American diplomats make it vocally clear what our attitude is toward real opponents, thus why should anyone imagine that Chinese diplomats do not respond in accordance with the same psychological principles? Aggression begets aggression, and any nation which feels that it has been offered no genuinely friendly overtures may resort to war. Based on data as to personal responses in tension-reducing situations, Osgood reasons that nations should react under the same circumstances in the same way. This view seems so obvious that it is quite incredible that so little attention has been paid to it. Either we believe that nations respond in accordance with different laws from those discussed by Osgood, or we doubt that national actions can be understood at all. If the former is the case, then psychologists ought to leap to fill this breach of knowledge, for no problem stands in greater need of resolution than international understanding. If the latter is genuinely the case, then we might do better to abandon ourselves to Providence than to play the risky game of nuclear "chicken."

After the cessation of hostilities in World War II our country faced the difficult task of readjusting soldiers to civilian life. Psychologists were extremely helpful in helping to bring about the adjustments. Many of the problems which actually occurred were anticipated by the experts. For example, it was predicted that upon cessation of the war there would be a general revulsion against the destruction that had ensued and a feeling that it had not been worth the effort; the people would blame their politicians for having got them into the war; there would be cynicism about our putative peace aims, and increased hostility toward Jews, Negroes, labor, and big-business. All of these took place more or less as predicted.[31] One of the surprising facts was the speed with which attitudes of hostility could change to attitudes of friendliness. In a survey of Allied soldiers in the European theater on the question: "Do you have strong hate of the German soldiers?" in April, 1945, 41% said that they did, while in August, 1945, only 21% said that they felt strong hate.[32] In July, 1943, about one-fifth of the troops sampled said that they sometimes or very often felt that the war was not worth the effort. By January, 1944, five months before D-day, about one-third of the troops in the British Isles gave the same answer. By four months after VE-day the proportion had jumped to about one-half. Yet only a small minority of the soldiers felt at any time that another war could be avoided in the next twenty-five years.

Independently of the cause for which these surveys were made, there are grounds for considerably more optimism than early psychology and medieval religion had given us reason to believe. Men are, after all, not so much victims of innate drives, warlike instincts, or aggressive tendencies as they are the pawns of national psychological warfare or chauvinistic brain-washing. The human animal is a malleable creature, and there seem to be substantial reasons for assuming that if we ever put our psychological talents to the end of educating men to live in peace with each other, we could accomplish this goal with no violence to the human psyche. If psychological theory may occasionally tend to stress the subconscious or genetic conditioning to which men have been exposed, it also offers hope that new conditioning may alter the old responses. Perhaps we shall some day evolve an economic order and a social system which make it possible for us to identify meaningfully with each other without mutual destruction. Perhaps we will evolve an economic security that will abolish the too great biological frustrations. Psychology also offers hope that if we did create an international or supranational state, individuals could be taught to be just as loyal to it as they are to their present narrow national groups.[33] The problem is not that we do not know how to develop man's peaceful drives, but that we have not yet decided that we want to live under these circumstances. Race riots, for example, are not necessary, but as long as cities will not do those things that need to be done to avoid the riots, then for just that long they will continue.

The psychological observation is perhaps correct that we simply like war too much to give it up easily. But to imagine that this is grounds for pessimism is to forget that previously imagined human pleasures which were supposed to be ineradicable, such as the Roman arena or the medieval jousts, have been educated out of the social fabric without having to alter any human nature in the process. While it would be naïve to imagine that a staff of psychologists could, by some shrewd campaign, educate war out of the human picture quite apart from additional economic, political, social, and cultural alterations, there are no apparent reasons, short of unwillingness, why men cannot learn to live with each other as sufficient brothers without recourse to the scourge of war.

XII *Military Causes of War*

It was recognized as far back as Plato (427–347 B.C.) that the military class possesses peculiar virtues for which it is selected and conditioned. Courage and aggressiveness, as well as diffidence to personal pain, were all required and, hence, cultivated. Plato realized, then, that talents such as these were not preparation for political leadership, nor were they likely to produce insights into the nature of the good society. Soldiers were trained for a specific task, and the Spartan virtues which they exemplify were not conducive to Athenian culture. Aristophanes (448–380 B.C.) called attention to the armament makers of the time whose business it was to prolong the constant warfare between Athens and her neighbors. For over a millennium professional mercenaries sold their services to the highest bidders, and political states showed their appreciation through religious and secular honors bestowed on those who had distinguished themselves in battle. The imperishable crown of military martyrdom was extolled and knighthood given as a reward for martial prowess. The economic advantages of military life were sufficiently attractive so that the middle classes, who were normally peace-loving, flocked to it in large numbers. Through centuries of exposure to the prizes of the gods of war an acceptance of the role of the military as personally rewarding and socially useful became the general rule. Ancient Sparta still stands as a symbol of a single-minded effort to train citizens in a warlike psychology. All desires except those of the battlefield were frowned upon, and so thoroughly had this training been given that the Hellenes faced the Peloponnesian wars as though they were a festival, and battles were begun on the flimsiest of pretexts.

Military preparedness is an ancient institution, whose theoretical excuse for existence was to serve as a defensive bulwark against invaders. The obvious practical impact, however, has been to offer military battle as a convenient excuse whenever discussion was undesirable or the aims of a country were improper. In modern societies there is even a military lobby, a facsimile of our own Pentagon, whose chief concern is to multiply its own excuse for existence. With the rise of modern business, the private arms industry appeared, and free-lance entrepreneurs engaged in the manufacture and sale of the tools without which no wars could be fought. The virtues which capitalism endorsed led business men to claim the right to promote war as they claimed the right to promote heroin, tobacco, quack medicines, and unsafe machines. A committee investigating munitions after World War I called them the "merchants of death." We shall look at the two basic theses on which most effort gets its justification: that armed readiness is an effective deterrent to would-be aggressors, and that armament sales are one of the capitalist rights to free enterprise.

Adam Smith theorized that there were only two ways of maintaining defense in a civilized society.[1] Either we require all able-bodied citizens, or a portion of them, to put in military service, or we have a standing army of professional soldiers. In either case, however, the myth is maintained that defense means armaments. The international anarchy that prevailed in the time of Adam Smith may have been an excuse pardoning him for neglecting the obvious political and social defenses on which the culture of nations has always genuinely rested internally. Nations discovered early in their histories that internal affairs state are best defended by almost everything except armed power: by education, cultural attractions, economic security, and free expression.

The shibboleth of the military as the defenders of the "security" of a nation has had a hardy life, and, even in the twentieth century, it stands as an almost impregnable icon. What has been called the Prussian policy has been surrounded with a mythos of justification. Military preparedness is considered to be a sign of humanitarian solicitude and of genuine concern for international peace. The aura of plausibility is furthered by accounting for all armaments as defense rather than as offense, so that the reason for weapons is to "keep the peace." What we may call an era of armed peace, aggressive defense, or armed persuasion became the accepted mode under which men lived, and the deception was so complete that they never accepted the clear fact that peace-breaking and peace-making now meant the same state of affairs. Thorstein Veblen spoke specifically to this memorable bit of national self-deception:

> *"It has long been a commonplace among observers of public events that these professedly defensive warlike preparations have in effect been preparations for breaking the peace; against which, at least ostensibly, a remedy had been sought in the preparation of still heavier armaments, with full realization that more armaments would unfailingly entail a more unsparing and more disastrous war,—which sums up the statecraft of the past half century."*[2]

George Santayana saw military establishments as no part of the life of a reasonable society. Commonly the price a nation pays, in both money and culture, for possessing a large military is far greater than the havoc it is intended to avoid. Commonly the evils an army claims to hold at bay are little more than patriotic cant, such as a purported invasion by another nation. There are ample instances from every major nation of the world where just such invasion has been advocated in the name of progress or the defense of liberty. If this is a live possibility, that a nation may gain by invasion of its own boundaries, then it would seem the better part of valor to permit the invasion with a minimum of bloodshed and material destruction, much as we would admit the physician without feeling obliged first of all to hold him at bay with guns. Even if invasion of one's land by another country were a genuine evil, it would take far more explanation than ordinarily offered to prove that even a successful defense, not to mention an unsuccessful one, is more preserving of the values than a simply permitted invasion. It is a moot question whether the American Indians were really better off attempting to defend their homeland from the invading hordes of English, French, and Spanish than they would have been by bowing to brute power in the first place.

Surely every country which loses a war must face this issue in retrospect. Germany aimed to save its culture by military defense in World War II. The destruction of life, property, and values that they suffered ought in retrospect to raise serious question as to the worth of the whole enterprise. What about England and the price she paid? It takes a kind of omniscience to assess whether the protection is more disastrous than the disease. If nations had foresight, and knew when they were going to lose before the fact, they would doubtless be able to do a more credible job of showing when and whether military protection was the lesser of two evils. The case made for aggressive action is, of course, different from that made for defensive action. It was surely easier for Americans to pay the price of havoc as they were dropping the bombs on Dresden than it would be for the citizens of Dresden to see the destruction in terms of their own military protection.

It is not obvious that Korean life is better for having had a blood-bath, and surely the Vietnamese who defend their country against the western power of America might have been better counseled to let the behemoth in and resolve the dilemma later by more constructive means. Santayana suspected that even such dread possibilities as foreign invasion might be less horrible than military, taxes, service, and arrogance.[3] He accused military men of having inherited a love for war, irrational combat, senseless jealousy, and a penchant for precipitating their nation into war.

He called military institutions "adventitious and ill-adapted excrescences,"[4] whose acts are stained with needless blood.

On the other hand, military spokesmen have come to their own defense with disavowals of the tendency to promote or encourage war as a consequence of a military machine. Homer Lea commented on this matter: "It is strange a belief should prevail that standing armies are a menace to the world's quietude, while it has only been due to the formation of permanent military forces that intervals of peace have been lengthened."[5] He referred to the invention and spread of gunpowder as the scattering of little seeds which grew into oaks of national strength. Prior to the invention of gunpowder, and of standing armies, he claimed, there was no peace. One struggles to envision the bloody periods of human conflict prior to gunpowder, and the idyllic periods of peaceful living since gunpowder. What is incomprehensible, however, is where the data for such a chimera ever arose. Wars have increased in scope, seriousness, and frequency in proportion as weapons have improved and the recourse to them has been made simple by the sheer convenience of armament stockpiles. In spite of this, many military defenders have claimed that the growth of civilization and the growth of armaments have developed in a one-to-one correlation. Friedrich von Bernhardi[6] made no claim that military preparedness minimized the chances of war, but only that it increased the chances of success, provided that no nation, or alliance of nations, could muster greater might. It is a part of the peculiar military mentality to suppose that wars come to the nations which want and expect them least. What this means, in simple terms, is that militarily armed states do not have war forced upon them. Apart from the falseness of the statement, there is an odd locution entailed in the words "forced upon them." Obviously a nation with no arms would not willingly go to war, while one with the arms, we presume, leaps gladly and voluntarily into the fray. It is not clear, however, where the moral lies unless it is that it is better for nations to enter wars of their own volition than to do so involuntarily.

In an address given to the Fourth Conference on Cause and

Cure of War, 1929, Captain Thomas Schneider insisted that

> *"Our army has never been the cause of a war; nor has the Navy. The members of our regular forces are practically without voice in political and diplomatic affairs. . . . In our country war, in every case, has been demanded by a public opinion aroused by grievances, and our armies have always been raised after the people, through their representatives in Congress, had recognized a state of war forced upon us by an enemy."*[7]

Such cant does not touch the issue at stake. He who fills the liquor cabinet so that a chronic alcoholic can use it in times of stress can scarcely disclaim responsibility. There was, to be sure, a difference between the military role in America in the period between the World Wars and that played since World War II. The difference, however, is not so much one of aim as it is of ability. If the military was a relatively minor factor in political decisions in 1930, it was not so much genuine political disinterestedness as it was actual political powerlessness that prompted this state of affairs. The more basic question relates to the advisability of war as an instrument of policy and the likelihood of peaceful diplomacy if massive armaments are available. Nor is it true that wars are demanded by public opinion against a passive military establishment. The Pentagon is involved in political decisions, and the military leaders are consulted for their advice on diplomacy. The people are the last ones to be consulted, and their diffidence is so great that a massive educational campaign is required to persuade them to go to war at all. In addition, two wars, Korea and Vietnam, have been carried out without benefit of a declaration of war so that the Congress could be bypassed and the ultimate decision to engage in undeclared war could rest on a small group.

A similar kind of stale advice is popularly given as justification for massive deterrents. General Curtis LeMay[8] admitted that in an all-out nuclear war the whole affair could be over in a matter of minutes. Common sense would tell us, therefore, that the path to take is the rejection of a nuclear arms race and the impending threat of a massive nuclear retaliation. But General LeMay was made of sterner stuff and his recommendation was to arm to the teeth now with nuclear devices so that we can wipe out our enemies posthumously if necessary. This kind of pique may be understandable on the playground but it is unspeakably atavistic in international relations. Thomas K. Finletter, former Special Assistant to the United States Secretary of State, on the other hand saw that some arms control was essential, and some form of disarmament must be begun. He saw that the greatest cause of international tension consists in the massive and destructive arms stockpiles.[9] Both he and Leo Szilard have restated this position with authority and simplicity, and have insisted that partial disarmament is far too weak a proposal for the magnitude of the problem. Nothing short of total disarmament can save us from nuclear suicide. But such admonitions were more than balanced by the commitment of the United States by Secretary of State Dulles in 1954 to a policy of massive nuclear deterrence. The decision was to "deter aggression" by building up our capacity to retaliate instantly with thermonuclear weapons.[10] That no one in his right mind intended using such weapons soon became obvious to the strategists in high places, and there emerged a credibility problem. How could we sell the Russians on the idea that we were not merely involved in a massive economic boondoggle? A first effort to make the missile race credible was the monstrous fall-out shelter hoax, by which the Americans in power hoped to frighten the Russians into believing that we really intended to eliminate their whole continent unless they showed us the respect proper to our status.[11] It was this commitment to double-think that has plagued most international diplomatic discussion ever since. We are always willing to talk with other nations, but the understanding is that if they do not listen sympathetically, we are ready to obliterate them. As Norman Cousins has pointed out, "The possibility of war increases in direct proportion to the effectiveness of the instruments of war. Far from banishing war, the atomic bomb may in itself constitute a cause of war."[12]

Such behavior among nations has been a current topic for psychological analysis. Gregory Bateson noted a custom among the Iatmul tribe of New Guinea whereby at a ceremonial meeting two men would alternately boast and provoke each other with increasingly bolder movements until battle ensued. He called this process "schizogenesis," meaning "the manner of the formation of cleavages." When both men reacted with aggression he called their behavior "symmetrical schizogenesis," and when one was submissive in the presence of the domineering of the other he called the situation "complementary schizogenesis." Ordinary arms races are "symmetrical" rather than "complementary," and thus the claims of militarists are false, since aggression begets aggression ordinarily. It is, on the face of it, an incredible bit of self-deception that any nation imagines that it could protect itself by arms, unless all other nations would cease arming. One might prolong the outbreak of war since each nation would wait to attack until the strategic moment. Only on the grounds that such a strategic moment never arrives for nations engaged in an arms race could we suppose that armaments build for peace.

This splendidly apprehensive foreign policy by which nations have chosen to operate has produced a business which both feeds on the fear generated and contributes to the generation of the fear. I refer here to the private-enterprise arms industries, which, like any other respectable business, advertise discreetly, pander for contracts, and lobby in high places for consideration. In his survey of the role of the armament industry, Philip Noel-Baker concluded that it exerts tremendous influence over the news media, controls news favorable to war-scares, influences congressmen to see threats to national security, and generally incites war hysteria.[13] In a League of Nations questionnaire circulated in 1925 concerning private manufacture of arms, nations were solicited for opinions as to how to handle this delicate free-enterprise right. Czechoslovakia proposed national legislation to provide for the confiscation of newspapers which printed false information on armaments, and Poland proposed that persons who incite war through escalation of international tensions should be liable to imprisonment. They advocated further that there be a tribunal to hear the cases of journalists accused of undermining peace. In the generation of such a breakdown of international diplomacy, the arms industries appear to have played a dominant role. War was, after all, their business, and peace signaled an international boycott of customers. In discussing the events leading up to World War I, Lord Grey of Fallodon saw that the increase of armaments produced fear in the one nation and belligerence in the other. The war was made inevitable by the enormous growth of weapons.[14] Yet at the annual meeting of the Vickers Ltd. arms firm, the Honorable Sir Herbert Lawrence, chairman of the board, found the suggestion that wars are fomented by arms to be groundless. Further, he saw the discussion of the morality of armaments firms prejudiced by a "mistaken ideal respecting the sanctity of life."[15] On December 15, 1915, the Honorable Clyde H. Tavenner spoke to the House of Representatives of the United States on "the Navy League unmasked." The substance of his report showed that the Navy League was a general sales-promotion scheme for the sale of United States arms to every nation in World War I, enemy and ally alike. In 1917 Mr. Tavenner reported the successful milking of the American treasury in 1893 by the major steel corporations, Midvale, Bethlehem, and Carnegie, by selling to the government armor-plate at $439.95 per ton which was sold elsewhere at $251 per ton. President Cleveland had imposed damages against the Carnegie company which were paid without demur. It was this same Navy League which circulated the statement that "strong armaments by pacific nations prevent war." When President Hoover proposed a reduction of naval expenditure in 1931, the Navy League accused him of serving the Japanese interests to the peril of the U.S.[16]

From 1793 to 1917, with but a few exceptions, the United States government insisted that private arms manufacturers had the right to sell wherever they could. On May 15, 1793, Thomas

Jefferson, then the Secretary of State, in a famous note to the British minister at Washington, supported the right of munitions manufacturers to earn a livelihood through the sale of war weapons. This private right was later extended to apply to weapons from machine guns to warships. By 1934 President Roosevelt stated that the arms race then occurring was due in no small measure to the business salesmanship of munitions makers. During the war between Bolivia and Paraguay in the 1930's, the English munitions firms sold most of the weapons to Paraguay, while American firms supplied the Bolivians. In 1934 an embargo on the shipment of arms was introduced, and on the strength of this the Curtiss-Wright Export Corporation was indicted by a federal grand jury in New York for smuggling machine guns into Bolivia. In the war over Leticia between Colombia and Peru, American arms firms sold weapons to both sides. Federal Laboratories supplied bombs to both countries, DuPont supplied TNT, and Colt Firearms supplied the handguns.[17] In Cuba in 1933 Federal Laboratories was reported to have sold weapons both to the government and to the revolutionaries trying to overthrow the government. The same evidence of financial salesmanship was reported in the Chinese wars of the 1920's and in the Japanese war in Manchuria in 1931–1932. Weapons were sold to both China and Japan by English, French, German, and American firms. At the height of the war in 1932 DuPont sold the Japanese a secret process for munitions manufacture. Obviously the publicity received by the DuPont Company, for example, was not accepted with diffidence. In 1934, L. DuPont published a pamphlet to answer the charges. He observed in the introduction that "disregarding all humanitarian motives, and from the very narrowest viewpoint of financial self-interest, the DuPont Company does not want war and has vastly more to gain from peace."[18] Early in the document he assured the reader that there was no prospect of extraordinary profit for manufacturers of munitions.[19] Twenty pages farther in the book he noted that the company's profits during World War I increased tenfold over the pre-war sales.[20]

At the Peace Conference after World War I, in the League of

Nations Covenant, and in the earliest discussions of the League of Nations in Geneva the whole question of the private sales of arms was discussed, but the United States refused to enter at all or even to answer inquiries from Geneva. Article VIII, paragraph 5 of the League Convenant stated that the private manufacture of arms was open to grave objection. In Article XIII the members advocated that the League supervise all trade in arms. The United States was not a party to either attempt to control the "merchants of death," and the record from 1925–1932 shows a dismal failure generally to implement either Article. In November, 1939, Congress repealed the arms embargo, primarily so that America could sell arms to the Allies, but shortly before the outbreak of American participation scrap iron was still being sold to Japan.

Ever since the most ancient times there were spokesmen for the maxim that to prepare for war was to prepare for peace. Part of the basis for the claim was a belief that weapons served as deterrents. Since every country operated on this assumption, the thesis reduced to a claim that the horror of war would deter any nation, or all nations, from resorting to it. The ubiquity of both war and aggression toward war vitiates this presumption, and the lack of hesitancy modern nations show in going to war, in spite of their fantastically more cosmic weapons, causes the whole thesis to vanish as a chimera. The other part of the claim that preparation for war is preparation for peace is the almost universal bit of self-deception practiced by nations that each of them is really a peace-loving nation surrounded by war-loving nations. Armaments do not make for peace, but they do make it possible for peaceful nations to be as efficient as warlike nations. Armaments made it possible for peace-loving nations to make their way of life mandatory for their opponents. This kind of sophistry, however, is a far cry from the literal meaning intended by the armaments promoters when they affirm that the more a nation builds its military power, the less chance there is for war to occur. This Maginot-Line mentality leads to arms races, and arms races lead to war.

It is the crassest casuistry to speak of one's own weapons as defensive, while those of one's neighbors are offensive. Since every nation practices this bit of chauvinism, some of them must be either lying or deceived. And yet the deception continues, and every new weapon is claimed to produce a counter weapon, a claim admitted to be false even by some of its proponents. Herman Kahn, in spite of his commitment to a massive retaliation policy, admitted that it was virtually impossible to give any degree of protection to populations in any all-out surprise nuclear attack.[21] Here again, where one would expect that common sense would demand that we alter our suicidal race toward annihilation, Kahn proposes that we learn instead to live with the possibility of mega-deaths. In Kahn's book *On Escalation* there is an entire dictionary of terms to express the finite variations of military or political force which can be carried out. There are also estimates of the likelihood of alternative responses which each might bring. The whole subject is presented as a vast semantic war game in which all the variations of the players now have names of their own. It is now possible to annihilate the whole human race and to have a name for every step of the way by the verbal rules of the game. There is a common blindness in this military mentality which sees all problems as quantitative, and which fails to see that qualitative alterations occur to any culture when the quantity of devastation it is willing to entertain increases.

In a recent book by retired General Nathan F. Twining he expresses his consternation that both politicians and civilians should imagine that they have any competence to speak to military men. General Twining was particularly offended by the discussion of "limited war."[22] He believed the discussion aimed to hamstring military leaders from whatever "all-out" strategy they might deem necessary. Since he envisioned the aim of warriors to be the defeat of the enemy, he could not imagine why there should be limitations of the price that a people would be willing to pay for such victory. He blamed the discussion on scientists "with bad conscience," State Department under-secretaries, "moralists," political scientists, defeatists, and unilateral disarmers. It is difficult to imagine what is the more amazing: that a General should believe that military men should be handed over the affairs of State because of their competence in all political and moral areas, or that warriors should be entrusted with the ends as well as the means of war. The entire practice of diplomacy was branded as a sign of weakness, and national strength was equated with willingness to destroy.

The extent to which military control has taken over political control of American foreign policy has been carefully and extensively documented in *The Military Establishment* by John M. Swomley, Jr. This military domination has been overwhelming in Laos, Vietnam, and Berlin, and has been the chief reason why the United States has thus far not participated successfully in negotiations for disarmament and treaties banning nuclear weapons tests.[23] It was the Pentagon that led the United States to withdraw from the peace proposals of 1955 at the very time when Russia had agreed to comply. In place of disarmament the military pressured the political leaders into a program of aerial photography of the Soviet Union. Although Harold Stassen was appointed by President Eisenhower to be a Special Assistant to work on disarmament policy, Stassen was opposed in his efforts by Secretary of State Dulles, Admiral Arthur Radford, Chairman of the Joint Chiefs of Staff, and Lewis Strauss, Chairman of the Atomic Energy Commission. Stassen finally resigned under pressure in 1958. The whole issue of disarmament was now to be handled by the Pentagon, and was thus assured of failure from the start.

Within a nation the actions of armed gangsters produce an antipathetic response from almost the entire culture, and this, in itself, constitutes a partial sanction against violence. Internationally, however, a similar action of armed gangsterism produces almost international approval. While no nation wants to be shot at, virtually all of them agree that every nation has the right to shoot its neighbors. The only debatable question is whether the shooting in question was pragmatically wise. And thus the organized military bloc survives in almost every country, first because it wields political power and cannot be expected to vote for its own demise, and second because it stands as a fetish of economic free-enterprise. To attack the war business is to betray communist or socialist leanings! With these two elements working in behalf of the business of war-waging and war-making, the magnitude of the opposition to either cooperation or adjudication is more understandable.

The myth of war to end war, and of weapons to keep the peace, constitutes one of the chief obstacles to the future survival of mankind, and yet every nation engaged in armed conflict finds this fact the most difficult to comprehend. After every war, nations are full of hindsight experts who see that what they just went through was avoidable, and that they must never make this mistake again. However, war, propaganda for war, and military preparedness for war all eat away at the residue of common humanity, and there seem to be no arguments persuasive enough to combat the simple message of massive armaments and weighty military establishments. There is, obviously, no solution until we do internationally what we have done within our nations, namely, to eliminate the military altogether, and to resort to legislative, economic, and social means commensurate with our cultural claims.

XIII   *Economic Causes of War*

THE CLAIM THAT WARS are economically caused goes back at least as far as Plato, and it thus takes its place as among the oldest and most distinguished explanations for war. Plato saw that the occupation of seeking unlimited wealth was not only the major cause of war but of most of the rest of human ills as well.[1] Because he placed such an importance on economic factors, he believed that soldiers must be prevented from taking part in the race for personal accumulation. Since personal possessions are a primary cause of rivalry, soldiers would soon forget their function if they sought financial gain. He recommended that the soldiers be taught that gold and silver were gifts of the gods so that they would not be encouraged to engage in economic competition.[2] He did not explain how this myth would be taught to soldiers while the businessmen were occupied in amassing wealth. Indeed, with the economic struggle playing such a strategic part it may seem odd that Plato made room for the soldier class at all, let alone that he gave this class such a position of significance. Perhaps the fact that Athens had four times as many slaves as free men influenced this myopia, but quite apart from this possibility, the fact remained that men could be trained to eschew financial gain, and that this training would make war less likely.

Aristotle reached the same essential conclusion about the role of economic rivalry in bringing about war. He expressed this in the

remark that "poverty is the parent of revolution and crime."[3]
If economic inequality is the cause of revolution within states,
then it is this same inequality among states that is the cause of
war. While he felt strongly that international discontent had
economic origins, he did not believe that poverty was the only
irritant to social harmony. "The fact is," he averred, "that the
greatest crimes are caused by excess and not by necessity."[4] But
this does not alter the economic roots of the problem, since the
desire for riches on the part of the wealthy is the reverse side of
the lack of riches. Both may stimulate an exaggerated preoccupation with money and material goods. Men with luxuries want
more luxuries, just as men in desperate want desire the necessities.
His solution to this problem may seem unduly bourgeois, since
he saw the cure to lie in the cultivation of habits of temperance
that would curb immoderate desires, as well as in the devotion
to philosophy whose satisfactions transcend the need for warfare.
The trouble, as Aristotle saw it, did not lie in the system, but
in the immoderate use of the system. The fact remained, however,
that the major cause of war was economic, hence the major cure
for war was economic also.

Aristotle would surely doubt the wisdom of mankind if he were
alive over two millennia later to discover that we still engage in
those economic battles that give rise to war with our economic
neighbors. Aristotle saw that the race for wisdom entailed no
such collision course for men, but apparently men are unwilling
to take those needful steps that would direct their efforts toward
the race for learning instead of toward the suicidal economic
struggle. We still pursue the enterprising occupations and we
still let our economic life be governed by men of immoderation.
Even the name of the system by which we pursue our infinitely
expanding ends, free-enterprise, indicates that we are not willing
to choose those things that make for peace. Death with economic
license is preferred to life with economic control. It is not, however, that men would sooner be dead than bound by law, but
that they know that law puts a social curb on their unbridled
greed. If capitalism is not alone in making war more likely, the

fact remains that a system that teaches individual enterprise as an economic privilege, and that promotes both production and sales of items independently of their constructive usefulness, does have a special obligation to explain the warrant for such industries as munitions of war. The question is not so much whether other economic systems can wage war successfully, but whether any particular systems make war more likely.

The human race seems to have learned its economic lessons poorly. While periodically religious leaders advocated the simple life, saw coveting as degrading, and filling of worldly barns as beneath human dignity, these were looked at by the masses as counsels of perfection. Rarely did anyone imagine that ordinary human relations were implied by these sermonic recommendations. Thus it was that the church which praised an other-worldly parsimony also praised a this-worldly gluttony, and the church itself led the march for economic domination. It was not until the eighteenth century that secular minds came to the rescue, and praised the simple life as other than a monastic ideal. Rousseau, for example, affirmed that property ownership was the root cause of war, and he claimed that the cure for war lay in the abolition of private property. "There can be no injury," he asserted, "where there is no property."[5] He saw the solution to the war-making power of wealth to lie in the prohibition of the accumulation of such wealth by an economic system that takes away both the opportunity and the incentive for miserliness.[6] It would be self-defeating to permit persons to accumulate wealth without limit in the name of freedom, while at the same time curtailing this accumulation in the name of social harmony. It would be simpler and wiser to abolish the acquisitive system. William Godwin, a contemporary of Rousseau, also identified the source of the problem of war to be economic ambition.[7] Wars would never have occurred if men had not been in the position to accumulate property at the expense of their fellows. It is only in an economy in which the exploitation of the many by the few is possible that war is beneficial. The benefit, of course, is only to the exploiting few. In a society where every man lived with plenty, and where there was no advantage to be gained by possessing more than one could use, then selfishness would disappear. All anxieties about food and lodging would vanish, and no man would be an enemy of another.[8] The passions that men now feel for property are generated by the system that makes the ownership of surplus property a sign of status. Any nation which permits economic rivalry can easily be plunged into war. As a consequence of his conviction that this was the case, Godwin considered all attempts to establish universal peace, while still permitting unequal property, to be destined to failure. Once we abolish the game of material accumulation, wars would cease, since they would serve no useful end.

Thomas Malthus (1766–1834) drew the same conclusion that if we would establish a fair way of assuring enough for all, "it might fairly be expected that war, that great pest of the human race, would, under such circumstances, soon cease to extend its ravages so widely and so frequently."[9] The cause of war, Malthus believed, was the imbalance between population growth and food production. War restored the balance by reducing the population. Such an observation on his part was not intended, however, to be taken as a prescription. Moral restraint, or birth control, was the humane cure for imminent starvation. In his *Principles of Political Economy*[10] he noted that the transition from war to peace commonly resulted in economic chaos. Nations that suffered most in war, in the sense that the wars were fought on their land, suffered the least in the peace that followed. Nations that suffered the least in war, on the contrary, experienced the worst economic dislocation during peace. The clue to the explanation of this fact lay in the matter of consumer demand. If the country is not bombed to pieces in the war, then it ends the war with its productivity far ahead of ordinary peace-time demand, hence a recession sets in. Malthus did not envision that political organization would abolish war. If economic misery is the cause of war, then wars should disappear with the elimination of want.

A number of nineteenth-century economists saw the subject of economics as playing an essentially pacific role. Economics was the discipline, above all others, that could teach men the futility of war, since it alone could show authoritatively the disaster which war brings. John Ramsay MacCulloch (1789–1864), professor of political economy at the University of London, and a popularizer of David Ricardo (1772–1823), saw the mission of economics to show men that wars for economic gain rest upon a mistake. Richard Cobden (1804–1865), a British manufacturer and economist, saw war as a money-losing business, and he believed that economists had an obligation to point out this fact. Jean-Baptiste Say (1767–1832), briefly a professor of political economy at the College de France, branded war as an execrable crime and an economic disaster. Frederic Bastiat (1801–1850) developed the thesis that war was an aspect of economic spoliation, which production would, in the long run, destroy. Military disarmament, he maintained, was the first step toward economic health. Gustave de Molinari (1819–1912) concluded that war had no economic reason for being. While ancient wars may have been occasionally profitable, modern wars are simply not worth the effort. With all of this economic analysis of the cause and cure of war, the position of communists and socialists comes naturally. Men like Saint-Simon (1760–1825), Robert Owen (1771–1858), Charles Fourier (1772–1837), Victor Considerant (1809–1893), Constantin Pecqueur (1801–1887), François Vidal (1814–1872), and Louis Blanc (1811–1882) all portrayed war as a manifestation of the capitalist system, and all of them believed that a reorganization of the economic system would abolish war.

Kirby Page, a socialist, remarked that "war grows naturally and luxuriantly in the soil of a competitive society."[11] The chief expressions of this deadly competition are nationalism, with its quest for empire, and capitalism with its quest for private ownership of natural resources. We have lived so long with economic competition that we have become blinded to its destructive influence. This negative result is expressed both in the depreciation of human life and in the maximizing of international rivalry that leads to war. Self-interest on the personal level may merely produce a Silas Marner who can be curbed or rehabilitated by society. Self-interest as a national or international policy, being sheer anarchy, leads to blind and autonomic war reactions. Many of the American socialists shared this same conviction that the causes of war were basically economic, and that capitalism by virtue of its glorification of competition was peculiarly productive of war. Harry Ward expected that the new experiment begun in Russia after World War I would result in a society that did not contribute to war hysteria.[12] Jerome Davis was skeptical of peace conferences because the nations attending the conferences were organized economically so that war was profitable.[13] War was an inevitable part of the culture of capitalism, and it would be abolished only after capitalism had been abolished. Walter Rauschenbusch, another socialist-protestant-minister, pictured the chief hope for the abolition of war as lying in the Christianizing of the economic system from capitalism to socialism.[14] Many of the occasions for war within the United States have been curbed by federal economic control and by national planning for full employment. Internationally, however, business is still being carried out in an eighteenth-century fashion of unrestricted competition. Business assumes that it ought not to be fettered by rules, and this commitment to anarchy is part of the reason that economic competition so easily leads to military conflict. Rauschenbusch believed that far more wars are fought over economic issues than are ever fought for the espoused military clichés. The enterprise that leads to the massive concentration of property in the hands of private persons or corporations constitutes the greatest single threat to international peace, since it stands as the major symbol of lawlessness. The conviction that this was the case led G. F. Nicolai to assert that war would be impossible without property.[15] Indeed, war is the primary means by which inequities of property are maintained. These socialist critics saw no hope that capitalism could be tidied up so that war would disappear. War was basic to the system, and only the abolition of the system could eliminate the need for war.[16]

At the Second Conference on Cause and Cure of War, 1926, the question was raised, "Do international rivalries contribute to the maintenance of the war system?" This was asked also in the reverse: "Does the maintenance of the war system contribute to international economic rivalries?"[17] In answering the above questions Edward Mead Earle observed that the two questions were inseparable. The fundamental causes of war are the consequence of international struggles for raw materials, new markets, and lucrative investments. While the government acts as the arbiter of economic disputes within a nation, once we move into international economic disputes, then governments become the litigants and there is no arbiter. International economics is still autarkical. In 1934 Joseph Stalin agreed with this diagnosis:

> *"The intensified struggle for foreign markets, the abolition of the last vestiges of free trade, prohibitive tariffs, trade war, currency war, dumping and many other analogous measures which demonstrate extreme nationalism in economic policy, have caused the relations between the countries to become extremely acute, have created the soil for military conflicts, and have brought war to the front."*[18]

Thorstein Veblen thought that the nurture of the war-spirit was one of the consequences of the leisure class. This class is the least personally involved in any war, although the members stand to gain the most by its being waged.[19] While John Kenneth Galbraith did not blame capitalism for war, he did indict it for its excessive egoism and its misplacement of value on the production of private consumer goods to the neglect of socially beneficial projects.[20] A man may be praised for making a hula hoop, and condemned as a socialist for proposing public health programs.

It has been easy, however, to dismiss these contemporary analyses because they are made by socialists, just as it has been simple to reject the observations of Plato and Aristotle because they are so ancient. If capitalism is the prevailing American plan, it should not be expected that many defenders of the status quo would rise to admit that the capitalist system is really responsible for modern wars. In addition, the fact is that capitalistic theoreticians have not claimed that socialism or communism tends toward war either. While capitalist writers eschew the thesis that war has economic causes, the socialists have located the problem in the free-enterprise profit system. We do not have to be committed to any special economic panacea, however, to be able to recognize that there are economic causes for war. Economic anarchy does, after all, exist as the international norm, and this is the case whether the national economies are capitalist or communist. We can also see that federal control within nations does avoid some conflict by providing non-militant means of adjudication. In addition, and quite apart from economic theories, the history of imperialism and colonialism makes it evident that both are irritants to war. It is no accident that the United States is a leader in war involvement, and at the same time has taken more square miles of its own continental land by military conquest than any other nation in the world.[21] Thus the nation that leads the world in foreign investments also leads the world in foreign military bases.

Apart from socialist and communist economists, however, there does not seem to be much enthusiasm for the thesis that economic factors cause wars. In a survey of the history of wars and their causes L. F. Richardson felt able to identify only 29% of the wars studied as wars with primary economic causes.[22] Between 1850 and 1941 the national score for war was as follows: Great Britain 20, France 18, Italy 12, Russia 11, China 10, Spain 10, Turkey 10, Japan 9, Germany 8, the United States 7, Austria 6, Poland 5, Netherlands 2, and Denmark 2. Within the space of these 90 years, the countries mentioned experienced a variety of political structures and exhibited both capitalist and pre-capitalist economic systems. With the exception of Russia none was socialist. While it would be absurd to reject the thesis that economics plays a role in war-making, it does not on the face of it seem that any of the existing economic systems has any unique tendencies to contribute to war. It would be foolish, however, to dismiss economic competition, the quest for world markets, and the desire for natural resources as factors. These are the same nations, with one exception, that pledged themselves at the founding of the U.N. in 1945 to replace military diplomacy with peaceful adjudication. Since that time the major delinquents have been the United States and France, who, at the same time, have been the most outspoken advocates of peace talk. Apparently peace-loving nations fight more wars than war-loving nations, and supposedly they do this in the name of peace. This kind of double-talk produces not only self-deception, but a cynicism about the motives of any peace pretender. To wage war to win peace is a kind of arrant nonsense that parades under the disguise of patriotism. If America is considered to be a case of a peace-loving nation, then peace-loving nations are better prepared for war and they wage war more frequently than other kinds of nation. Not only this, but peace-loving nations win more wars and fight them less on their own territory. Peace-loving nations have more troops stationed on other people's land, and are more involved in the politics of other countries than the so-called warlike nations. Great Britain, for example, which is ordinarily listed with the peaceful nations, led the list with 78 out of 278 wars in a study by Quincy Wright.[23] It would be natural for a socialist to observe that, after all, Great Britain was the major colonial power.

It is doubtless true that wars are caused by a complex of factors, of which economic elements are a part. Any war in which territory, natural resources, or industrial complexes are the prizes is obviously one in which economics plays some role. We may ask, therefore, whether it is possible to construct any economic system at all in which war is less likely than in the present milieu. Is it possible to resolve our economic needs on the international level without recourse to war? Can the have and the have-not nations reconcile their conflicts without war? Some minimum lessons appear to be deducible from the ways in which nations now resolve their internal economic conflicts. Within the nation, federal planning has eliminated both the need and the right for taking up arms against our neighbors. Communities are no longer the pawns of battles between financial barons. Private corporations should not go foraging, even in their own states, as if the world were their private garden. Regulations of trade, prices, wages, and transportation make this economic pirating more difficult if not impossible.

The practice of war has created its own special businesses, and this fact creates special problems. War is an industry like the production of medicine, refrigerators, and automobiles. Unlike other businesses, however, the military is the only purchaser, so that there is no competition for price, quality, or customers. Military business competes, if at all, only with other military business, but federal expediters find it easier to deal with cartels and monopolies, so that there is actually no competition at all. Kenneth Boulding coined the term "milorg" for this peculiar military financial organization which is its own consumer.[24] Within this category the Department of Defense of the United States is the largest milorg in the world. Military power is not only an instrument of economic policy, but this military business has become an end in itself, and economic policy is a means to its perpetuation.[25] In the first four years of World War II, for example, about $175 billion in war contracts were given, and almost one-third of this money went to ten companies. It would be naïve to assume that such companies and their employees had no special concern over the possibility that peace might be established prematurely, and thus that the war contracts would cease. It would, however, be even more amazing if our economists saw no way to convert from war production to peace production. If there were no way, then the United States would exhibit the exact manifestations that Karl Marx predicted for capitalist countries, namely that they thrive only when there is war or the threat of war, and that they cannot survive on peaceful production. One of the anomalies in the public reactions to federal planning is expressed in the fact that the most conservative citizen sees no creeping socialism in war contracts, while at the first sign of government spending for medicine, food, or conservation of natural resources the cry of "subversion" and "socialism" is immediately heard. The government stimulation of the economy in education spending has millions of opponents, while far greater sums spent in stimulating war industries arouse no conservative fears. It is one of the paradoxes of our society that it is still easier to justify paying our citizens to kill for the state than it is to justify paying them to think for the state.

Although the first World War ended with the military complex being radically curtailed, plans had been laid during World War II to prevent this from happening again. Donald Nelson, head of the War Production Board, reported that from 1942 onward the Army did its best to make the Board an errand boy for the military.[26] In 1944 Charles E. Wilson, president of General Electric, suggested that every big company appoint a special executive, with the rank of colonel in the reserve, to serve as a liaison with the armed forces.[27] Secretary of the Navy Forrestal furthered this big-business link with the military by founding the National Security Industrial Association to ensure that business and the military be in close contact. By 1952, Air Force Secretary Thomas Finletter claimed that the plant facilities of the Air Force were greater than those of General Motors, Standard Oil of New Jersey, United States Steel, and American Telephone and Telegraph combined. A Special House Committee assigned to investigate the employment of retired military men revealed in 1960 that 261 generals and admirals, and 485 officers above the rank of colonel or Navy captain were employed by the companies that manufacture 80% of our armaments.[28] All of this intimate relation between the economic and the military was promoted by the fiction that war-spending was good for the economy. The fact remains, however, that money spent for war-making means less spent for constructive human needs.

Even where it is admitted that business makes war seem to be the better way for a nation, there is a remarkable chauvinism in judging the enemy by the same criteria that we use to judge ourselves. In summing up the position that there are economic causes for war, Lionel C. Robbins observed with jingoism: "The economic motives of the powers who became involved in the catastrophe of the Great War of 1914–18 were the motives of distrustful and irascible but, for the most part, fairly civilized men. The economic motives of the totalitarian powers are the motives of barbarian hordes."[29] War is big business, in part, because there are big profits. Indeed, the presence of the profits seems to be the sanctifying property which makes attacks on war production appear subversive. The same amount of demonstration against education subsidies or housing grants is, on the other hand, considered to be an expression of patriotic frugality. Educational lobbies are looked on with suspicion, while military lobbies are above suspicion. As we noted in the previous chapter, the private sale of munitions, without control by any national or international agency, has often led to the creation and continuance of wars which might not otherwise have begun. Munitions firms continue to lobby for increasing federal spending in armaments, and surely this constitutes an economic cause of war. Perhaps the issue is moral, rather than economic, whether any business should be permitted to capitalize on human death. Such a question is paralleled by practices, occasionally discovered, of putting habit-forming drugs in a product to encourage and assure its continued sale. Does a drug firm have a free-enterprise right to sell a nostrum with no known curative powers? Eventually we will have to come to terms with the whole issue of financial gain, for whatever end, and by whatever means. If we suspect that poisons should not be permitted to be peddled, even in the name of free-enterprise, we might also come to suspect any business which sets the psychological stage for war by making it both convenient and profitable. Is there, thus, a formal plot of businessmen to sell nations into war? Is war the result of scheming financiers who deliberately arrange the breakdown in international understanding? While there are certainly diabolic industries, there does not seem to be evidence that the diabolism is organized this well. An economic system that is predicated on anarchy, such as capitalism is, probably creates most of the chaos by accident or by designed carelessness, rather than by any systematic plot. The more important matter, in any case, is not whether capitalism is really more conducive to war than other methods, but, rather, whether there is any economic way which can minimize the chances of war. As long as war pays, it will remain as an appealing option.

THE CURES FOR WAR

XIV *Disarmament and the Arms Race*

AFTER SEVEN VOLUMES ON disarmament and six volumes of documents on international affairs, John Wheeler-Bennett published *The Pipe Dream of Peace*. This was in 1935 and his dismal sentiments sum up the brief and frequently optimistic history of disarmament proposals. It would, however, be a mistake to lose heart too soon, since the efforts at arms reduction are relatively contemporary. Disarmament is of recent vintage as a solution to the problem of war. The early seventeenth-century proposals for securing peace did not base themselves on any expectation that there would be disarmament. Indeed, concomitant with the rise of nationalism, there was the conviction that power in the hands of the state was both natural and necessary. States were instruments of power and armaments were natural extensions of this function. With this comfort from natural-law theorists, it was no accident that war was generally conceded to be a fundamental instrument of political policy. When this Machiavellian thesis was implemented by nationalistic aspirations, a new sense of urgency in coming to grips with the war problem emerged. Further, when the manufacture of arms became a major element in international trade, it became clear, in a way that had not previously been the case, that arms by themselves pose a general threat to peace.

The wars of the new rising nations sharpened the concern

with resolving war, since the national right of making war was assumed to be independent of any principles of morality. Legality and morality were either identified so that what was politically needful became automatically what was morally permissible; or legality and morality were sharply divided so that what was politically useful could be done without interference from moral inhibitions. Indeed, morality was equivalent to romanticism and its counsels were dismissed as politically unrealistic. Many valiant efforts were made, however, to put war in some framework of lawfulness. The efforts of Grotius and Pufendorf (1632–1694) were to establish juridical bases for international settlements. The writings of Leibniz (1646–1716), specifically his "Diplomatic Codification of the Law of Nations," and of Christian Wolff (1679–1754) in his "Institutions of the Law of Nature and of Nations," were also intended to develop some diplomatic procedures whereby there would be some legal basis for peace. These attempts were couched in faith in natural law.

As this confidence in laws written into the nature of things waned, the eighteenth century gave birth to a humanitarian approach which aimed, first of all, to reestablish by some positive means the connection between legality and morality. The Abbé de St. Pierre (1737–1814) in his "Sketch of a Project of Permanent Peace," Jean-Jacques Rousseau in "An Opinion on Lasting Peace," and Immanuel Kant in *Perpetual Peace* all urged the reassessment of the whole war issue in the context of some moral principles. One of the consequences of Kant's investigation was the recommendation for the abolition of standing armies at some time in the near future.[1] His bases for this proposal were that the hiring of men for the killing of persons treated them as mere means or things, and that such treatment was contrary to the categorical imperative. In addition he saw standing armies as constant signs of aggressive intent and hence as incitement to wars. After a nation has spent sums of great magnitude on war preparation, there comes a time when war is cheaper than peace and a lot more exciting. Kant did not, however, oppose voluntary citizens' armies to protect a country from invasion from without. This, of course, is precisely what every nation considers itself to be doing. All armies are for defense, and none are for offense. In the light of the history of warfare there is an obvious self-deception in this premise, since at least half of the nations in war must be offensively engaged. Nonetheless, the proposal to limit standing armies was a start in the direction of disarmament.

The universal peace plan of Jeremy Bentham (1748–1832), published posthumously in 1843, laid down the same proposal to hold down the size of the army and navy to that required to curb piracy.[2] He saw, further, that repressive trade agreements and the expansion of colonialism were obstacles to any plan for permanent peace. He envisioned an international court for adjudication that could function without any recourse to the use of arms. He proposed that Great Britain take a first step in this direction by removing all military force from her colonies. As a further step in the minimization of war, Bentham agreed with Kant that secrecy should be abolished as a governmental strategy. Neither legislatures nor diplomats should be permitted to carry out their business in secret from the citizens, or, for that matter, from the other nations. The conviction that secrecy was a primary irritant toward war had prompted Kant to deduce its impropriety from both categorical and hypothetical imperatives. In the contemporary world with its multitude of national espionage systems each spying, tricking, and irritating, and each operating in the general name of national defense, this proposal of Kant and Bentham may seem like a proposal from Venus. In any case, both men aimed to reunite ethics and legality in such a way as to reduce the occasions for war.

There has always been a difference between attempts, on the one hand, to limit the kind, amount, and targets of weapons, and, on the other, to advocate abolition of arms altogether. The former was a way to set rules or limits to war while still retaining it as a viable political tool. The latter intended to abolish war altogether. The limitation on the size of standing armies urged by Kant and Bentham, however, was expected to be followed ultimately by the total abolition of the army. Reduction of arms is a difficult step for any nation to take when it feels itself to be surrounded by armed neighbors. It is far more likely that every move in the direction of weapons innovation or increase will prompt a world-wide escalation of armament building. Montesquieu noted this fact and observed that as nations increase their arms and men, so also do their neighbors. This promotes an endless escalation which is mistakenly assumed to promote peace. He considered this feverish preparedness to be a contagious disease,[3] and he considered the sophistry of armaments as peace-keeping forces as a sign of spiritual and semantic decadence.

In 1893 Friedrich Engels wrote a book called *Can Europe Disarm?* It was written on the eve of a discussion of the military budget of the Reichstag. This assessment took place in the face of twenty-five years of excessive European armament, and, in spite of this, Engels concluded that disarmament was possible and that Germany had both the power and the mission to carry the leadership in such a program. As a first step he proposed that all standing armies be changed to militias. He then advocated a gradual reduction in the term of military service. Germany should propose this to Austria, Italy, and France; and if at least France would agree to progressive disarmament, then Germany should go ahead with her own disarmament. However, if France would not agree to disarm then Germany should not do so either. In a letter to Ludwig Kugelmann, April 12, 1871, Marx had insisted that the next French revolution should not attempt merely to transfer the military bureaucracy from one power to another, but should rather smash the whole military machine. Maxim Litvinov, writing on the issue of the U.S.S.R. and disarmament,[4] observed that the popular clamor for the abolition of war could not be met by a mere reduction of war budgets, but required instead the rejection of war as a national policy instrument. Under the current world economic situation he saw total disarmament as the only means of averting future wars. If nations continue to arm, then no treaties, pacts, protocol, or international organizations will be able to create any real security. There are too many weapons in the world already for a mere reduction in arms production to do any good. Nothing short of beating capitalist swords into socialist plowshares would be sufficient to end militarism. Ultimately militarism could not be destroyed until capitalism had been abolished.

The history of attempts at disarmament is short and dismal. The first successful attempt came in 1817 when the famous Rush-Bagot Agreement was reached between Canada and the United States. It proposed the discontinuance of major naval armaments on the Great Lakes. Unfortunately, this was also the last successful proposal. Nonetheless, between 1845 and 1853 the *British Almanac Companion* or *Year Book* reported that 2,117 petitions in favor of disarmament and against increasing the militia were presented to the House of Commons. These petitions had a combined total of over 600,000 names. In 1848, for example, the 249 petitions were for arbitration and disarmament. In 1850 and 1851 the 213 petitions were for general disarmament and retrenchment. In 1852 there were 1,400 petitions opposed to the Militia Bill. Yet no action was taken to implement the popular sentiment. If anything, history seemed to teach that wars would always be waged to the extent of man's capacity, and that long before man decided to disarm he would exterminate himself simply because the power to do so was present. Indeed, the confidence that armaments promoted security seemed to prosper independently of experience, and this gave rise to the apparently sound conclusion that modern man is more likely to have atomic annihilation than he is to disarm. As the horrors of nuclear war are painted with ever increasing clarity, the same weary arguments for armaments are now given even though survival and living underground in holes turn out to be compatible.

Norman Thomas, the Presbyterian minister and Y.M.C.A. worker turned Socialist, listed disarmament as the second major point in his national program for peace.[5] He believed, however, that disarmament required taking the profit out of war and out of the preparation for war. Long before the Socialist revolution had been effected, he expected that some steps toward peace could be taken. One of these was for the Congress and the President of the United States to declare as national policy that they would not permit military materials to be shipped to belligerents. This would mean that free-enterprise would have to get out of the international arms business, and that the government would officially enforce this. This first step has proved to be a major one, since the nationalization of the arms industries has been consistently opposed by the nations that do not produce their own weapons, since they feared they would not be able to buy arms from nationalized arms firms as easily as from entrepreneurs. Even the Hague Convention of 1907 paid due regard to those nations which were not able to manufacture their own arms, and, after all, this Convention was putatively organized for the promotion of peace. The Report of the Royal Commission (1935–1936) on private manufacture and sale of arms, after admitting that such free-enterprise was the chief thorn in the side of peace, came to the pussyfooting conclusion that its abolition was not practical.[6]

Not only has the plan to nationalize the arms industries failed to curb international trading in the instruments of death, but these same firms have raised the hoary watchword of the right of individual citizens to be armed against their neighbors. Militant Minutemen train with their weapons like vigilante posses from the days of the wildest West. Expostulations of the arms firms that theirs is a business of the greatest pacification, and that no one hates war more than they, are seen as absurd, deceptive, and false in the face of the findings of congressional committees like the Nye Committee that munitions salesmen not only fostered wars as a means of increasing business, but then sold their wares to the participants on both sides. Opponents of this wholesale macabre farce of capitalizing on murder are commonly branded as communist, passivists, and isolationists. It is a peculiar facet of these paradoxical times that the true internationalists are those who help their neighbors to commit mutual suicide, while those who advocate international conversations are called isolationists. This has led to the conundrum that arms embargoes are political, while arms sales are merely business. This has produced some Kafka-like situations. Prior to World War I, for example, Krupp invented a special fuse for hand grenades. The English arms firm, Vickers, expropriated the invention during the War and many Germans were killed with bombs using this fuse. After the War Krupp sued Vickers for one shilling per fuse used. Preposterously, the case was settled out of court with Vickers paying Krupp.[7] After all, business ethics must be maintained in any event.

Many piecemeal attempts have been made to patch up the threat posed by the mere existence of stockpiles of arms and the continued arms race. Noel-Baker urged that military research be abolished and that the scientists be phased into peaceful research.[8] It has been amply demonstrated that there are no economic obstacles to such a plan, but there are political jeremiads that this would be undemocratic. The same opponents who crush medical research when it appears to be socialistic defend military research even when it is clearly atavistic. The series of conferences which advocated the outlawry of various weapons, while still permitting them to be manufactured and sold, were gestures of the same self-defeating kind. In the face of centuries of dismal insecurity from our weapons offensives and defensives, starry-eyed romanticists still sing the siren song of armed defense, while cool-headed realists who urge disarmament are viewed as quixotic. Even Pope Pius XI announced that arms competition was a major cause of national rivalries as well as a drain on the public treasuries.[9] Earlier he had averred that the states must not train their youth to be warriors.[10] But such counsels were offered at the height of secular peace conferences, and not on the eve of war, and they were, hence, gentle whispers rather than thunder from Mount Sinai. All of these gestures were insufficient. As John Dewey remarked, what is called for is not a series of steps toward disarmament, but a radical about-face.[11] It was not a mere moral proposition to abolish wars, but a fundamental motion to abolish the war system as an authorized and legally sanctioned procedure. He reminded men that at the Hague Convention of 1907, called a peace conference, twelve of the fourteen points dealt with the waging of war, and only two with arbitration for peace. The late President John F. Kennedy noted that arms races are national suicide and must be stopped,[12] but even this remark was too pallid to create notice. The arms industry itself is only part of a large milieu of patriotism, nationalism, imperialism, capitalistic jingoism, and mis-valuation. All of these lend an aura of respectability and plausibility to this economy for destruction. As late as 1958 the Senate Subcommittee on Disarmament stated that there were only six or seven persons working full-time on problems of disarmament for the State Department. Obviously the appropriations go where the expectations are, and peace is not in anybody's plan.

As a partial result of the embarrassment which our puny efforts toward peace have caused there has emerged a vocal group who advocate arms control. It is not the elimination, however, but the controlled use of weapons which they have in mind, and the future for such casuistry is dim indeed. Arms control was urged when the cross-bow was first invented, and every new weapon has produced its advocates for moderation. There is, nonetheless, an official Arms Control and Disarmament Agency of the United States government. It assumes that there will be arms, and that the only admissible question will be as to who has the arms, and how much they have. The proposals which come out of this commission have included such Frankenstein monsters as test bans of unclean nuclear bombs and the maintenance of fusion and fission bombs in the hands of our friends.[13] This kind of arms control merely represents a way of racing for weapons superiority, and concedes that the arms race is an accepted fact of the political situation. The object is the sophistic one of finding a strategy of outmaneuvering our neighbors in arming for the nuclear Armageddon.[14] We seem to have come the full circle back to the state of affairs rife in the Middle Ages, when it was presumed that war was a legitimate instrument of national policy, and that the best a thinking person could expect was a new Truce of God. It has been noted, however, that there is something of a conflict between European and American thinking on this matter.[15] Americans talk about arms control, while Europeans speak of disarmament. The British, for example, are less concerned with the strategies of avoiding surprise attack or of mustering a retaliatory reply than they are with the whole business of the arms race.

Within the framework of nuclear arms some gestures have been made since their use at Nagasaki and Hiroshima to curtail or eliminate them. In 1946 the United Nations Atomic Energy Commission was established by the U.N. General Assembly, and it consisted of the permanent members of the security council plus Canada. Since the United States was then the only nation with atomic arms it seemed appropriate that she make the first proposal. In June, 1946, the Baruch Plan was the result. This Plan required that all nations agree to international control and ownership of nuclear development, and that there be a veto-free control body, The International Atomic Development Authority, to administer the program. Russia vetoed this plan. The Soviet counter-proposal in June, 1946, demanded unilateral nuclear disarmament by the United States, with aspects of control of future developments to be discussed later. In view of the fact that the U.S. had the only nuclear weapons, it was probably no surprise that its leaders vetoed the plan. In fact, one of the dilemmas of this entire effort is to figure out what nation would ever agree to limitation as long as it was in the position of arms superiority. By 1948 the U.N.A.E.C. reported back to the General Assembly its inability to come to any resolution. Meanwhile a United Nations Commission for Conventional Armaments was set up in February, 1947. The Soviet called for a straight one-third cut in conventional arms, but the United States was reluctant to consider control of conventional weapons prior to an agreement on nuclear weapons. In 1952 the General Assembly voted to combine the A.E.C. and the Conventional Armaments Commission into one body. The result was the U.N. Disarmament Commission, which likewise had no success. In 1954 a five-man subcommittee of the Disarmament Commission was established. The U.S., U.S.S.R., Britain, France, and Canada presented a three-stage plan: (1) a simple freeze of conventional forces; (2) a 50% cut in conventional forces, plus a cut-off of fissionable material;

and (3) the destruction of nuclear stockpiles and the reduction of the remaining 50% of the conventional weapons. Russia again voted for a "ban the bomb" immediately, and a one-third reduction in conventional forces. In March, 1955, the Western powers made a new proposal: (1) destroy all nuclear weapons halfway through stage three, i.e., after 75% of conventional · weapons had been destroyed; and (2) offered new arms levels for the major countries. Much to the surprise and embarrassment of the U.S. State Department, Russia accepted these new proposals. Noel-Baker called this event "The Moment of Hope." The United States, however, promptly announced that she had changed her mind.

There has been no dearth of imagination in the business of inventing plans for arms disengagement, although most of them still expect that control rather than abolition is the chief aim. A recent book on the subject listed sixty plans and projects presented in the West between 1957 and 1959, and about twenty similar proposals coming from Russia. The two sides in this race for suggestions differ essentially over inspection procedures, particularly when they are proposed unilaterally, rather than through the United Nations. Indeed, one of the sadder sides to the whole arms control issue has been the degree to which the major nations, like the United States, have systematically bypassed the U.N. In a final report of the 19th American Assembly on arms control [16] ten proposals were made. They began with the vague admonition that arms control should be our concern, and ended with the vacuous hope that the United States would inform the citizens about the issues. Depressing as this situation is, it may still be better for the one nation in the world that has outarmed all others, outflanked all others, and outmaneuvered all others to say some small word on behalf of disarmament even though its military actions belie this word. J. F. Kennedy added his good word on behalf of disarmament and urged that some program for implementing it be developed.

In a world of nations, like our own, grown dependent on the big stick and unaccustomed to rational discussion of international problems—witness SEATO, NATO, and OAS, not to mention unilateral conferences in Honolulu, Taipei, and Saigon, all of which bypass and undermine the hope of the United Nations— it comes as no surprise that we are paranoid about the honesty of our opponents in the matter of arms inspection. Military men are especially sensitive about inspection teams, since they look like enemy troops. There is the fear that some nation may have a secret pile of bombs that has not been declared, and that it may attack by surprise and confront us with its armed superiority. Or some nation may secretly add to its store of weapons, and thus cheat on its disarmament agreement. To be sure these are possibilities, but the hope for disarmament · ought not to rest on the worst event that might happen, but on the likelihood of the best that could happen. We do not base our hope for lawful citizens on the possibility of murder, but on the far greater probability that most of them will be decent.

There is also the ever-present fear that no chest-pounding nation will relinquish its "inherent right to self-defense." This tired ploy keeps munitions firms in business, and it is a variation of this gambit that businessmen appeal to when they foster arms sales, invest in the development of the raw materials of other countries for their own benefit, and generally advocate anarchy in economics. The economic thesis that the world is the sales territory for United States businessmen bears a relation to the political thesis that our nation has rights as a political salesman all over the world also. The nations are pictured as arenas where business and political entrepreneurs compete for customers. The United States policy of having armed bases on the major continents and diplomatic intervention in the political future of other countries surely gains whatever rationale it can muster from the myth that the world outside our own nation is one vast colonial frontier waiting for American enlightenment. Under any rational criteria our actions would be called "armed aggression," but in this Looking Glass environment we call it "self-defense." Most of the day-to-day problems of disarmament will be procedural. They will relate to the rights of inspectors to inspect, and of private enterprises to be free from inspection. This kind of issue, however, has been faced before and we have been able to resolve it to the general public benefit. The first attempts at federal inspection of the safety conditions in industries were met with cries of "invasion of privacy," since it was presumed a sacred right of business to exploit whomsoever is willing to be exploited or unable to protect themselves. There are some fears for the adequacy of sanctions to be imposed against violators.

But here again, the military mind leads us astray, and causes us to forget the degree to which political, economic, and social sanctions are actually operative in keeping the law. We tend to forget that most persons in any society are respectful of the laws, while for those who are not so respectful a variety of sanctions do operate. As most sociological studies indicate, it is not the fear of capital punishment that deters crime, and hence it should be seen as equally reasonable that it is not the threat of massive armed force which keeps nations pacific toward each other. If anything, warlike people show an amazing indifference to the risks of war. We have been in enough wars to be able to appreciate this simple fact. There is, of course, the possibility fictionalized by Dr. Strangelove, that some sadistic paranoid will be put in the position of chief button-pusher, and thus no system of control will be better than the persons who have to run it. This is no surprise, but in other areas, where the risks are great, we abolish the enterprise altogether. We make no efforts to keep the heroin trade law-abiding; we abolish the trade. It makes no sense to speak of heroin control, lynching control, or kidnaping control. These, like arms, need to be abolished, not controlled in moderation.

Still, as long as the weapons do exist, and as long as there is no confidence that they can be dispensed with, it is reasonable to attempt some kind of control. Four mechanisms were devised to attempt a control of nuclear expansion in the space of the same number of years. *Euratom* was sponsored by France, West Germany, Italy, and the Benelux countries. It encompassed research, training, information, and a safeguards system. This latter applied automatically to all nuclear fuels and installations not already in nuclear weapons or clearly destined for them. *The European Nuclear Energy Agency* was sponsored by 18 West European nations, overlapping with Euratom on six nations. It runs a fuel processing plant in Mol, Belgium, used by the member nations for the processing of nuclear fuels. Since such fuels must be periodically processed, the plant acted as a simple means of inspection. *The International Atomic Energy Agency,* with headquarters in Vienna, was a direct result of then President Eisenhower's "Atoms for Peace" proposal of 1953. It differed from the foregoing in that it included non-European nations. Finally, there were certain minimum safeguards for arms control implicit in the bilateral agreements between suppliers and purchasers of nuclear fuels. These were, obviously, of interim use only, and each agreement signed since 1956 included provisions for the eventual transfer of the safeguards to *The International Atomic Energy Agency.*

In a most interesting pact signed at Paris, October 23, 1954, and "put into effect" May 6, 1955, Belgium, France, West Germany, Italy, Luxemburg, Netherlands, Great Britain, and Northern Ireland agreed not to manufacture certain types of weapons within their respective countries. These included: atomic weapons, chemical and biological weapons, long-range and guided missiles, warships, mines (except for anti-tank and anti-personnel types), guns larger than 90 mm, tanks and armored vehicles heavier than 10 tons, and aircraft bombs larger than 1000 kg. Apparently every nation knew that if they needed such weapons in a pinch they could always buy them from the United States, which permitted the manufacture of almost anything. The ephemeral nature of such pledges, however, was indicated by the attempt on the part of the British within a few years to develop the Blue Streak Missile for massive retaliation. This attempt was abandoned in the early sixties and the effort taken over by the French. There is, however, something odd about expecting to curb war by removing the weapons of war. The primary problem here is to get persons who have little confidence in any international diplomacy to give up the only weapons in which they do have confidence. This would seem to reverse the order of psychological probability.

In spite of this, the fact remains that within a nation we do expect to minimize the seriousness of unorganized crime by making weapons hard to get, but even here, every citizen has recourse to courts of law, and thus the incentive to take up arms is surely less even where the arms are available. The problem in the international arena is that, in the absence of international legal institutions, the very presence of armaments may serve as an incentive to their use.

The periodic efforts at disarmament are still the wisest course. At worst the advocates of beating swords into plowshares may be guilty of ignorance of the antecedent factors that must precede disarmament. Perhaps many exponents of peace proposals to disarm have overlooked the role of munitions businesses and, indeed, of eighteenth-century economic theses generally in keeping war going. Perhaps it is putting the military cart before the economic horse to seek to abolish militarism before we abolish colonialism, imperialism, and nationalism. The difficulties encountered in abolishing lynch law and vigilante justice in the West may teach us some lessons of hope in this regard. Long before all rascals had been rehabilitated we had agreed to relinquish the "right" to carry a Colt on each hip. If there were risks in this unarmed state, it was infinitesimal compared with the range wars we were thus avoiding.

The United States, as the major economic and military power in the world, has a special duty to make the first gestures. The world does have many countries which do not play the game of quick-shooting cowboys, so that it is apparently possible to achieve some sense of security without a gun. Part of the problem is aggravated by amateur Lone Rangers here at home. The vocal lobbies which attack every effort to curb the sale of weapons to private citizens include the Minutemen, who want their guns to shoot potential communist neighbors whom they sense to be lurking in every dark place. Congress has its vigilante spirits who have never been at ease in discussion, and who doubt that opponents understand anything save physical force. We listened to these martinets warn of the dire consequences that would follow from trying to talk conciliation with the Russians when they thought we should be obliterating them with bombs, but the Russians have proved themselves to be excellent discussants, shrewd diplomats, and able to admit an error, as in the case of Cuba. Would that our own diplomats could show as much good sense about Taiwan, Korea, Germany, Central America, and Vietnam. We have the missile sites all over the world, and yet we insist that the other side is the aggressor. The world, including the United States, is perhaps fortunate at least in that there is only one bomb-happy behemoth at a time out to play the role of Grand Inquisitor to the heathen. These same little Napoleons warn us of permitting China to enter the U.N. as if it were more dangerous to talk to the Chinese than to engage in thermonuclear war with them. They tell us that we ought to continue to support Chiang Kai-shek, who represents no nation, in preference to discussion with Mao, who represents the largest nation in the world.

To the martial spirit every enemy is a Hitler and every ally is a freedom-lover. This either-or mentality dooms us to live in dread of nations with whom we could well live in peace. Perhaps what is needed to speed the possibility of disarmament is a more reliable way of selecting political leaders. It would not be absurd, although it would be unlikely, to expect that one day we would give our leaders periodic psychological tests to see if they are still fit to conciliate. In the same vein one author suggested that we give lie-detector tests to all persons in key positions to see if they have been selling secrets to the potential enemy.[17] Disarmament is counseled by reason as part of the step we must take to learn to live with each other. We cannot afford, for any reason, to keep the shibboleth of the national right to wage war.

XV *World Political Federation*

OUR GREATEST HOPE FOR emerging from the anarchy in which world affairs are carried out doubtless rests on some form of political cooperation or organization. The alternatives to war lie in the areas of international law, international diplomacy, and international organization. If theory and practice still seem far apart, and if the hope for a world community still seems a chimera of naïve peace-lovers, the reasons for our failure to do as well internationally as we have already done nationally are at least no impenetrable mystery. Many of the proposals for world harmony presume that we must begin with a full-blown world government, world judiciary, world army, or world emperor if anarchy is to be displaced. In a world of sovereign nations such world machinery, it is generally conceded, could never be instituted. Thus an impossible solution to an intolerable situation can lead only to despair, and otherwise reasonable persons still expect to solve the international problems with the rough and ready justice of a nineteenth-century vigilante posse in the far West. Affairs of state are still handled with the spirit and machinery of the earlier range wars between cattlemen and sheepmen. The evidence is accumulating, however, that we ought not to underestimate the power of world opinion as it develops through the sheer exigencies of our having to live with other nations in the U.N. We do not need world *government* immediately. What we do need is world *willingness* to feel obliged, to reverence commitments, to make compromise. It is to the historical antecedents which support this expectation that we shall now turn.

Between 1306 b.c. and 1914 a.d. more than 151 different peace plans were discussed as theoretical possibilities, although none of them was ever put into practice. During the period from 1375 b.c. to 1918 a.d. there were 45 practical attempts to establish a basis for peace among the nations, and all of them consisted of plans to create some kind of international organization.[1] Indeed, apart from such proposals to federate the nations of the world, and by this federation to abolish the anarchic aspects of nationalism, there have been no serious plans to establish peace as the normal state of world affairs. Military alliances have always presupposed that wars were both necessary and desirable, and have set an atmosphere where no nation really has to adjudicate its problems amicably if it should prove inconvenient to do so. The most that alliances were intended to accomplish was to dull the edge of likelihood of attack, at a partial price, of course, that if war did come it would be maximal rather than minimal. On the other extreme, some peace plans proposed to train nations to be unwarlike in a world where war was the easiest and most likely option in any contest of national wills. Apart from some form of international organization and law under which the nations of the world would live, however, attempts to curb war are merely nibbling at the periphery of secondary causes. It is like trying to solve inequities in economics by the promotion of alms-giving, rather than by a reassessment of the basic system.

Clearly, the history of human warfare reveals that nationalism, for all its assets, is still the soil in which wars germinate best, and that in such an environment it is futile to expect diplomacy or discussion to kill the anarchic germ which produces war. Individual nations have demonstrated that they could avoid this chaos of lawlessness within their boundaries by political arrangements roughly corresponding to those in the United States, Canada, England, or the U.S.S.R. The fifty "sovereign" United

States avoid civil war by the expedient of relinquishing some autonomy to a federal government, and, with one notable exception, this arrangement has maintained the domestic tranquillity intended by the founding fathers. It took time for a feeling of security to be established in the minds of the leaders of the states that their individuals' needs would not be ignored by such a union. States now know that they do not need to call out the militia to resolve inter-state disagreements. The advantages of federal adjudication far outweigh the risk that the decision may be unfavorable. Still the current civil-rights disputes and the problems of implementing federal laws with regard to equal treatment for all citizens indicate that, even within a relatively literate nation, masses of persons assert the right to be irresponsible as being more basic than the obligation to be right. Generally, however, even where states may fail to achieve all that they would wish to attain, there is agreement that the domestic harmony more than compensates for the internecine warfare which would be the alternative. If some states lose before a court of law, the result cannot compare to the magnitude or quality of loss which everyone suffers in war.

It is, therefore, surprising that the nations of the world have been so hesitant and unwilling to resolve their international anarchy by a similar kind of political federation. It is even more amazing in view of the age of this knowledge. The ancient Greeks made such a cogent case for federalism, both through affirmative plans and through the negative descriptions of the desolation brought about by their Peloponnesian wars, that it is astounding that the world should have struggled along with the cultivation of warfare and the planned extermination of peoples when there were obviously better alternatives.

Part of the reason for this reluctance may stem from the same factors that gave rise to early American reservations toward federalism. Indeed, we still have a strong nucleus of citizens who fear every expansion of federal services on the grounds that it signalizes a corresponding decrease in what are euphemistically called "state's rights." This fear of losing autonomy is variously expressed as a concern for individual liberty, local integrity, economic enterprise, or personal incentive. These were, of course, all arguments used by free-wheeling cowboys of the far West. Negatively, the fear of having to live under law is claimed to stem from some innate fear of central authority to be Freudianly accounted for, or to suspicions that administration means bureaucracy and will soon result in the enforcement of monolithic values. We should not be too critical of the slow progress of the United Nations, for in spite of all the obvious advantages enjoyed in the United States as a consequence of federalism, there are still chauvinistic factions who would just as soon revert to the anarchy of unfettered "state's rights." In view, therefore, of this state of suspicion even in a country where federalism has demonstrated its value, it should not be surprising that proposals for world federalism or world law awaken fears of a political leviathan. Thus, although almost every believer in the possibility of world peace knows that it is impossible without world law and world government, most concrete proposals for the conditions that will banish anarchy are viewed with fear and trembling. Men speak of law as entailing dictatorship, and they picture anarchy as the precondition of peace.

This unwillingness to give up the Hobbesian and Rousseau-like "state of nature" still obstructs even minimal attempts at arbitration. The former League of Nations was not able to attract even the leaders of the United States because of their fear of losing sovereignty. The current United Nations did attract them, however, primarily because the large nations were assured that their sovereignty would not be lessened by membership. It suffers, therefore, through this initial unwillingness of nations to submit to international conciliation, let alone to international control. The countries always know that if their membership in the United Nations becomes too demanding, too inconvenient, or too inimical to their self-interest, they can secede from membership and go their own neolithic way. In fact, they may commonly do this without jeopardizing their United Nations status. At the founding meeting in 1945 the organizers of the U.N. precluded that it be a final arbiter of international dispute by insisting that no nation be required to relinquish national sovereignty in order to become a member. This same confusion that identifies sovereignty with lawlessness is one that has become famous in the mouths of white race supremacists. But in spite of attempts to make the United Nations an organization of convenience, it has served amazingly well, as we shall see, as a platform for arbitration and as a center for conciliatory study.

The idea that there should be some federation of relatively sovereign states is quite ancient. The Greeks envisioned it beginning with the amphictyonies of religiously compatible city states, and the Romans attempted to implement federation on a larger scale. It was, however, the Renaissance that opened the era of genuine federative peace proposals. Pierre Dubois was the medieval herald of all the modern projects for world organization. He wrote a series of pamphlets between 1300 and 1314 advocating a federation of Christian states. France would play the leading role. He proposed an international court of arbitration and urged boycotts against powers that made war, and thus anticipated the sanctions of the League of Nations covenant. The punishment for defeated offenders was that they be sent off to colonize the Holy Land. The pretentious religious chauvinism of the plan obviously prevented it from ever becoming more than a political weapon for religious proselyting. In the same century Dante called for a world state under an all-powerful emperor. He assumed that Rome would take the lead, although he did envision a separation of the powers of church and state. Also in the fourteenth century, Marsilius of Padua proposed in his *Defensor Pacis* a joint church and state leadership in the development of a world order. These proposals, however, still breathed the aura of military alliances and were not relevant even to the kind of world in which they were announced.

The turning point was symbolized in the 1461 plan of Antoine Marini, chancellor of George Podebrod, king of Bohemia. The design provided for a federation of Christian princes from France, Germany, Italy, and Spain to preserve the peace and to protect

Christianity from the Turks. While it was presumed that the Pope would provide moral support, neither the Pope nor the Emperor was to be permitted any role of power. The significant part of the plan stipulated that the member states relinquish to the federation their right to wage war. It was this last item that proved the major obstacle to the adoption of the program, and, indeed, of every similar plan since. The putative claim of sovereign nations to a "right to wage war" has been a virile one, and even after centuries of destruction from the exercise of this "right" it still appeals to patriots. Nation-centered politics, like nation-centered economics, has the predominant support of citizens everywhere, and neither political nor economic panaceas for war have been able to achieve acceptability if they advocated any undermining of international anarchy.

In 1513 there was a peace plan announced by William of Ciervia and John Sylvagius. It called for a congress of kings at Cambray, and included Germany, France, England, and the Low Countries. According to Erasmus, the plan was scuttled by war profiteers. Indeed, it was at the suggestion of John Sylvagius that Erasmus wrote *The Complaint of Peace* in 1517. Erasmus directed his plea to kings, whom he believed to be the instigators of wars. He recommended that the right to declare war be taken away from the kings and given to the whole people. He assumed, hopefully though vainly, that he would have the support of the clergy, who would exercise their power by refusing the religious rites to those who died in battle.

Lodovicus Molina, a Jesuit priest, wrote a book in 1614 in which he recommended that the Pope serve as the international arbiter. Such a plan, however, suffered from religious chauvinism as seriously as the plans of world communism or world Americanism suffer from political chauvinism. It would be presumptive to imagine that Moslems, Jews, Hindus, Buddhists, let alone Protestants, would feel secure if the affairs of state were in the hands of a power to whom they were already unwilling to trust their religious destinies.

The New Cyneas of Emeric Cruce in 1623 conceded the unlikelihood of world peace through religious enforcement. His plan was also directed to the kings. He envisioned that world trade would diminish the occasions for war on the grounds that the hope of profit would accustom nations to fraternize. The plan called for an assembly of ambassadors from each country. Before this tribunal nations would come to plead their cases. Recalcitrant princes would be kept in line by the majority. While he did not believe that religion was a major cause of war, he did think that both Luther and Calvin heaped fuel on the flames of war by their religious chauvinism. Since he believed that national harmony was a precondition to international harmony, he denounced dueling and advocated good laws and moderation in punishment.

The Grand Design, once credited to Henry IV of France, but most likely the product of his minister of finance, Sully, appeared over a period of years 1638–1662. It entailed a European plan of independent states, a balance between Roman Catholic, Protestant, and Reformed (Calvinist) Christian groups. The design was not so grand, however, as to permit new or non-Christian religions in the plan. Fifteen powers of Europe were to be recognized, and there was to be a general council of ministers from each of the countries which would meet constantly as a senate. Among its proposals was the quite non-pacific aim to eject the Turks from Europe, and a military alliance to capture sections of North Africa. The whole plan was doomed to remain utopian since it proposed a complete remapping of European boundaries, and would, if implemented, have precipitated a European war. In spite of its obvious visionary nature the *Design* still influenced the proposals of Saint-Pierre, William Penn, and Rousseau. Even Leibniz, under the pseudonym Caesarinus Furstenerius, wrote a peace plan.

In 1712 Saint-Pierre wrote *A Project for Settling an Everlasting Peace in Europe,* and he credited *The Grand Design* as being the inspiration for his plan to federate the nations of Europe in a continual diet. Following this same scheme, William Penn (1644–1718) also advocated a European Parliament or diet. Penn noted that nations which were internally federated tended to avoid civil wars, and he saw no reason why this should not operate equally well for affairs between nations. He expected that if the nations of Europe were to band together, they would be more than powerful enough to compel obedience from any dissident European exception.[2] In 1710, John Bellers, another Quaker, reproduced Penn's plan combined with *The Grand Design* in an essay, *Some Reasons for an European State*. By the nineteenth century the writers seemed agreed that some form of federalism was the only way to make war unneccessary. J. G. Fichte proposed a confederation which would begin with the European states for the maintenance of law and for the punishment of unjust states. As this confederation became extended to the whole earth he envisioned an "eternal peace."[3] William Ladd, a nineteenth-century American writer, portrayed a Congress of Nations which would make war functionless, and hence extinct. There was a time, he noted, when persecution was believed to be essential to the promotion of religion. Just as that position is now discredited, the time will come when the same is seen for the presumption that war is needed for the promotion of political proselyting.[4] Ralph Waldo Emerson spoke with enthusiasm about Ladd's plan, particularly if it were developed in the "favorable" environment of American culture.[5]

The relinquishment of national sovereignty, which any plan for federation involves, is, however, a step that few national leaders seem to have been willing to take. The very idea of an international authority generates the darkest fears in the minds of those over whom the authority is to be exercised. National leaders commonly visualize being directed to commit national suicide, to give away their national heritage, or to sell their political birthright for a pottage of doubtful nutrition. Visions of potential tyrannical world leaders cast suspicion on the very idea of confederation. We know what kind of fears the relatively simple question of water resources generates among the leaders of the Western states, where those states possessing water suspect a plot to drain their reserves to irrigate some desert that never should have been inhabited in the first place. We can recall the historic debates in the new country of America when federation was first being entertained, and the genuine concerns that the wishes of individuals would be lost under a government so large and so remote. This fear has been proved to have been more supposition than fact, save on the part of those whose concept of liberty presupposes the absence of law or government. If, like Herbert Hoover, we identify liberalism with economic freedom, and economic freedom with the absence of government control, then every expansion of political relevance will be viewed as opposed to "free enterprise." It was this concern, for example, that prompted Hoover to assert that liberty had its greatest support from local rather than federal government. Friedrich A. Hayek echoed this same concern that a planned economy with federal control meant the death of economic democracy. There is, then, a fertile breeding ground for discontent with government in any form located in the economic milieu. Some of the objections to the Federal Trade Commission, Civil Service, Pure Food and Drug laws, and to anti-trust legislation arise from business groups who correctly assess these steps of government as bringing about a corresponding decrease in private enterprise.

The complaint, however, is not solely economic. The threats of southern Bilbos to secede from the Union if the federal government interferes with the "right" of white southerners to oppress the Negroes are not simply economic, although there are surely economic considerations. The perennial sniping at the United Nations by super-patriotic American clubs doubtless arises from more than economic or racial fears, nor is it simply explained as a paranoid suspicion of foreigners. It is more an unwillingness to respond to authority at all. The sweeping broadsides fired by the Birchite mind against Cabinet members, Supreme Court Judges, and Congressmen all indicate that there are still deep-seated suspicions that government of any kind means loss of liberty. Anarchy is appealing when one is in the position of being chastised by authority. The chief enemies of the U.N. or of U.N.I.C.E.F. are those who do not believe in government at all.

The opposition is not from those who fear mismanagement of government, but from those who fear the very principle of government. After all, if one suspects that corruption may occur, the cure is not the abolition of government but more adequate controls. This should follow also for resolving corruption in local, municipal, or state affairs. The answer to Hitler's rise to power is not the anarchic dissolution of national government, but the democratic involvement of persons in the establishment and administration of government. The suspicion that law means loss of sovereignty has been hard to allay. Large nations, like the U.S.A. and the U.S.S.R., still prefer to be their own judges and juries, and thus both international organization and international law operate under handicaps.

Before turning specifically to the two valiant attempts of the twentieth century to supply the missing organizational ingredient for the adjudication of international conflict, let us note that military alliances still flourish and commonly under the guise of being gestures to promote world peace. This merely confirms the confusion implicit in such expressions as "wars to make peace," and "the army is the best peace-keeping force." Clarence Streit advocated an Anglo-American alliance in *Union Now*. Walter Lippmann recommended a three-power alliance to include Great Britain, Russia, and the United States. He chose these three nations because they were the military arsenals of the world. Henry Luce proposed an "American Century" where the United States would control the political, economic, and social fate of the world. Colonel Robert R. McCormick recommended the incorporation into the American federal union of the self-governing nations which now fly the British and Irish flags. These federations are, however, simply disguised forms of national chauvinism, and if nationalism is an irritant making for war, these arrangements will merely foster bigger cataclysms. What is needed is some structure to dull the edge of national sovereignty and to make it unnecessary for militant anarchy to prevail. Anything less than international organization and the national willingness to live under law will be a futile palliative.

Here, however, the conventional diplomatic mind comes to a cognitive halt. Such persons cannot conceive of trading national free-enterprise for anything so chimerical as national security. Like Churchill, they do not propose to sit idly by while American dominance is undermined by any potential international obligations. Like Ramiro DeMaeztu, they see international government as the death of humanity, progress, and freedom.[6] War may be more violent, but they believe it to be less evil than bowing to adjudication. Treitschke (1834–1896) spoke for these persons when he avowed that the grandeur of history lay in the perpetual warfare of nations, and that it would be both foolish and immoral to attempt to curb the "right of national self-defense." He quoted Gustavus Adolphus with favor: "I recognize no power over me but God and the conqueror's sword." Treitschke concluded, thus, that "the establishment of a permanent international Arbitration Court is incompatible with the nature of the State."[7] Von Moltke (1800–1891) concurred in this judgment that war was simply one of the prices paid for national vitality, and that to abolish the occasion for war would result in the sapping of the national spirit.[8] And thus the nations continue to propose the piecemeal panacea of unilateral agreements, and by this unwillingness to bring themselves under law they perpetuate and promote the gigantic arms race. Ralph Barton Perry saw world organization as the one and only moral solution,[9] and John Dewey said that the cause of war is not warlikeness but the absence of organization.[10]

Two major efforts in the twentieth century, The League of Nations and The United Nations, have been undertaken to establish the start of world organization.° When we consider that

---

° A regional alliance such as that of the OAS (the Organization of American States), while it has had limited success, is hardly to be included in the attempts at international justice. The OAS has been essentially an effort of the United States, and would surely prove helpless if the U.S. were the aggressor, in addition to the fact that the arrangement is more like benevolent colonialism than international law. Both SEATO and NATO are further instances of the same kind of regional alliance.

each of these was joined by nations unwilling to do what had to be done to make the organizations viable, it is remarkable that they accomplished as much as they actually did. The League of Nations was founded after World War I as a loose confederation of essentially sovereign nations. In spite of the unwillingness of the American congress to permit the country to become a member of the League, it served briefly as a distinguished adjudicator of international issues. Between 1920 and 1939, 66 political controversies came before the League of Nations. Fifty-five of these were handled successfully either by the League or by agencies to which the League assigned them. Ten of the 66 controversies involved armed hostilities.

When the League was established in 1920, Article 10, to preserve members against external aggression, and Article 16, to authorize members to apply sanctions against aggressors, were thought to provide the basis of League action to maintain peace. Actually, however, Article 11 proved to be the easiest basis for action, since it did not require war to have been declared and the Council or the Assembly could make an investigation without having to count the votes of the dissenting parties. In the cases involving hostilities the Council developed the following steps in its mediation: (1) The President of the Council issued a warning and a cease-fire to the disputants. Failure to abide by the cease-fire left the offending nation open to the classification of aggressor. (2) The immediate convening of the Council with representatives of the disputing nations. (3) The appointment of a commission to supervise the cessation of hostilities. (4) The establishment of a commission to make recommendations for a resolution to the dispute.

Whenever the large nations were in accord, the League succeeded, and, with the exception of the Vilna case, the Council efforts to maintain peace were successful from 1920 to 1930. After 1930, Japan, Italy, Germany, and Russia proved stronger than the efforts of the League. Japan was the first of the powerful nations to reject completely the report of a Commission of Inquiry, and when the report on the case in Manchuria was adopted by the Assembly, the Japanese delegate walked out of the meeting and Japan withdrew from the League. It was this event which marked the downfall of the League as the international adjudicator.

Henri Bergson commented concerning the League that its results were already far beyond what had been hoped.[11] However, a condition basic to its success was missing from the beginning. The governments and the people of the states were still unwilling to accept unpleasant limitations imposed on their right of national action. The League was still, in the desperate case, a mere pool of arms for independent powers who could and would do whatever was most convenient for their national ends. Such a League was not a federal government but a loose alliance of independent states adrift in a sea of potential anarchy. If the states of the United States had been as uncommitted to our federation as this, then that first trial between the states would have caused the secession, then and later, of any state which found it inconvenient to abide by law. One of the practical problems of the League was the nature of the sanction which the League should hold over recalcitrant nations. Some had asserted, unsuccessfully, that the League army should possess the world's most powerful or dangerous weapons. At the time the League was formed this weapon was believed to be airpower. Today it would be thermonuclear weapons. Even though Pope Pius XI[12] had held that the *Summa* of Saint Thomas contained the doctrinal support for a real League of Nations, this theological bulwark did not save the experiment. The League perished in the inundation of World War II.

If the grand experiment of the League appeared incapable of making World War II unnecessary because it could not accomplish what nations were unwilling to do for themselves, this seems to be a most unfair denigration of an organization which never claimed to be able to establish a warless world, particularly as long as strong nations refused to have their cases adjudicated. On a lesser scale the League had been preceded by some very successful international accomplishments. The Geneva Convention of 1864, which grew out of the Crimean War, resulted in the establishment of the international Red Cross in 1906. The Paris conference of 1863, called to consider a postal union, was consummated in 1874 by the establishment of the Universal Postal Union. At the invitation of President Arthur a Washington conference succeeded in establishing the Prime Meridian in 1884. There was a successful international sanitary conference in Washington, D.C., in 1881 and another in Paris in 1903. A convention for the protection of industrial property held in 1883 in Paris, and amended in 1891 and 1900, made progress in establishing some international protocol for the protection of foreign property owners. A convention in Paris in 1884 led to agreement on the protection of submarine cables. A general act for the repression of the slave trade in Africa and for the prohibition of the importation and sale of liquor and firearms into Africa was signed in 1890 and ratified in 1892. An international meeting in Paris in 1875 established an international bureau of weights and measures. A convention in 1906 established international rules on the use and management of wireless telegraphy and confirmed the Morse code as the standard. These events were landmarks both as achievements in international organization and in international law. Even though it was commonly supposed that the existence of an international court to adjudicate international law raised the question of national sovereignty, in these areas, at least, men saw that international rules relieved nations of the ambiguity of having their rights determined by the unilateral assertions of their adversaries, and gave them instead the security of arbitration by law. Nations are virtually the only entities left which insist that they have a right to act as their own judges, and only in this case is sovereignty equated with lawlessness.

The other great experiment of the twentieth century is still in operation, and in spite of its putative friends and avowed enemies, the United Nations stands as one of the few citadels of refuge from anarchy. To be sure the U.N. began with the same essential limitations as did the League, but it does have the membership of a majority of the nations of the world. It also contains the major nations, with few exceptions, and provides a diplomatic environment for what would otherwise be mere unilateral power struggles. It is a loose confederation of sovereign states which could at any moment, in principle, vote not to be bound by any adjudication which went against their wishes. National sovereignty is still enshrined in the U.N., and the wonder is that it has accomplished as much as it has considering the limitations under which it operates.

The U.N. charter provides in Article 33 that nations which are likely to break international peace should first seek to solve their dispute by peaceful means. The initial action by the U.N. may come from any one of three sources. (I) Under Article 34 the Security Council has the authority to investigate any dispute or any situation that might lead to a dispute. Under Article 36 the Security Council may make recommendations for settlement. Such recommendation would not, however, be binding on the parties to the dispute, and even the decision to investigate could be vetoed by any member of the Security Council. (II) Under Articles 11 and 12 of the Charter the General Assembly can discuss any question relating to peace and security and make recommendations to the Security Council. Two-thirds of the Assembly can initiate the use of peace-observation measures, but if the parties in the dispute do not consent, even the observation cannot be carried out. (III) The third way in which peace discussions may originate, under Article 99, is from the Secretary-General. However, the peace-observations even here would have only the limited objective of determining whether a situation was indeed a threat to peace. Here also the parties in the controversy would have to agree to make some adjustment. In spite of what are rigid limits to the power of the U.N. in its role of intermediary, its efforts have met with some success. But if the United Nations cannot legally compel states to comply with its decisions, there do appear to have been moral sanctions at work which aided in the resolution of some controversies.

While states may evade the U.N. by unilateral maneuvers, and large states may veto action in the Security Council, unilateral citation is possible. What this means is that if two states conflict, one of them may cite the other for the offense without the second state having to admit that there is a problem. Admission of a problem has always been a legal stalemate in international affairs. No nation is ever at war unless its duly authorized body for making such a decision admits that there is, indeed, a war. One of the debated interpretations of Chapter VII of the U.N. Charter concerns this problem in a special way. The issue arose specifically during the Palestine question, i.e., does the Council have to admit the existence of a threat to peace, or may it ignore this threat on the grounds that the Council is not equipped to handle the matter? Does the Council have discretionary powers to determine when a threat exists? Both France and the United States have insisted that the Council has no choice in the matter; while Britain, Belgium, and Canada have said that the Council should be allowed to act pragmatically.[13] Even if the Council must act, it faces the other debated aspect of the issue as to whether a threat to the peace really exists. In one of the sessions, for example, when the problem was to clarify the meaning of the expression "potential danger," the Mexican delegate observed that such an expression is self-contradictory. Actual dangers are determinable, while potentially dangerous situations, apart from expressing everything, designate nothing.

At its 123rd plenary meeting on November 21, 1947, the General Assembly of the U.N. established the International Law Commission. The aim of the Commission was to "initiate studies and make recommendations for the purpose of encouraging the progressive development of international law and its codification."[14] On December 12, 1960, the General Assembly adopted a resolution to solicit views from the member states as to topics for continuing research by the Commission. At the head of the list with 47, 46, 24, and 14 states voting respectively were topics such as: Law of Treaties, State Responsibility, Succession of State and Governments, and Special Missions. At the other extreme, only five small states were interested in Outer Space or Air Space; only two small states were interested in Sovereignty over Natural Resources; only one state proposed that the Commission study the rights of states to determine their own political form; only Austria proposed a study of Laws of War; only Afghanistan mentioned the Prohibition of War; and only Czechoslovakia suggested Prohibition of Aggressive War, Mass Weapons of Destruction, and Responsibility for Breaches of Peace. The large states were interested in the general theories, while the small states wanted to discuss more specific applications of these principles.[15]

Law seems to have fared better than organization. The Permanent Court of International Justice of the League of Nations survived the death of the League. Its prestige was taken over by the International Court of Justice of the U.N. in February, 1946. There was strong support in 1920 when the Permanent Court was instituted and again in 1945 when the International Court was established to give each Court obligatory jurisdiction. The majority of the smaller nations wished this, but in 1945 the opposition of the United States and the Soviet Union defeated the principle. The Soviets appeared to have been prompted by the Marxian fear that in a world of capitalist nations law will be the expression of this dominant power group, and thus the Soviet position would not receive a fair hearing. The United States insisted on the right to except its own domestic issues as well as disputes arising from a multilateral treaty.[16] International law can aid in the development of world peace only when states are willing to be subservient to this law, but, in the interim, some cases have been adjudicated where war was too costly to resolve the issue. At least the Court is in existence against the time when that conciliatory day comes and in the meantime it is working on the development of less ambiguous international law.

It would, however, be fatuous to criticize the U.N. for its built-in limitations, and those who doomed it from the start have failed to take account of the degree to which the necessities of U.N. discussion have led to an international conscience on national obligation to the world community. The sight of great nations discussing in the Council chambers must surely give more cause for hope than all the military might of the Western world arrayed against the East. A great advantage of inter-cultural fraternity is that it helps to remove one of the obstacles to cultural understanding, namely strangeness. In fact, through the alchemy of necessary discussion, in a setting where authorities may be heard, men do develop a conscience that transcends the boundaries of their respective nations. As one psychologist observed during World War II, "our faith in the potentialities of human learning leads us to believe that most, if not all, people could acquire an international conscience quite readily provided the necessary learning conditions were arranged." [17]

Jacques Maritain, for example, concurred in the general thesis. He saw the problem as the establishment of world government, and he envisioned the first step to bring this about to be a federation where sovereignty was progressively diminished or relinquished. Sovereignty, he insisted, belonged only to the body politic as a perfect society. Since we do not live anywhere near this end, ordinary political states can surrender their autonomy, and should do so, whenever they recognize that confederation offers more than independence. [18] There is, no doubt, more reification of the state than its function warrants, and the tendency to give states lives of their own, independent of the citizens, does contribute to the charisma of national claims to the right of survival.

It was the unwillingness of large nations to subject their claims to U.N. adjudication that led to the formation of NATO, SEATO, OAS, and like alliances. These are steps to bypass international law and to frustrate the hopes of U.N. members in their expectation for law in place of anarchy. Peace negotiations which are not carried out through the United Nations are also inimical to the hope for a world community of conscience and obligation. If we believe in the principle and practice of law, then the U.N. must be used by large as well as small nations for the discussion and resolution of their problems. We would not expect to solve labor-management disputes where each group acted as its own judge and jury. Within the nation we have courts where problems like these can be discussed and where a ruling can eventuate from law. The old days when labor and management fought like sheepherders and cattlemen outside the law are fortunately gone. When we consider the damage to the bystanders, it must baffle a rational mind that nations let each other wage war when the minimal means for more pacific adjudication are at hand. The hope does not lie in the direction of personal or national pledges to renounce war as long as there is no tribunal. Nor will conferences aiming at the "softening of the horrors" of war help. As has already been noted, the more rigorous rules for war of the modern era are accompanied by less observance of even the minimal medieval rules of war.[19]

The solution seems so obvious, and the risks of neglecting the solution so cosmic, that the bellicose individualism of the large nations of the world must seem like either heresy or subversion. We must band together as our own founding fathers did almost two centuries ago to insure internationally what they secured within the nation. Otherwise we contribute to the demise of mankind. Americans of an individualistic bent may insist upon their egocentric rights to promote anarchy in the world, but we cannot find·security or survival in this fashion. Nor does it suffice to couch the law of the jungle in the tired euphemisms of military alliances. The hope for world community will not come about through the unilateral leadership of any single nation no matter how wise, benevolent, or virtuous. In this, the powerful nations like the United States, the U.S.S.R., Great Britain, France, or Canada must take the initiative, for the little nations cannot be expected to bring the behemoths to the table. Surely the alternative to anarchic chaos has always been organization, and the wider the scope of that organization, the better the chances that it will serve as an effective alternative to Armageddon.

NOTES

Chapter I.

[1] Quincy Wright, *A Study of War.* Two Volumes. Chicago: University of Chicago Press, 1942.

[2] Quincy Wright, *op. cit.,* Volume II, Chapter XVII.

[3] Quincy Wright, "Criteria for Judging the Relevance of Researches on the Problems of Peace," in *Research for Peace.* Amsterdam: North-Holland Publishing Company, 1954.

[4] Saint Thomas Aquinas, *Summa Theologica,* Part II, Second Part, Question 41, Article 1, Vol. IX. London: Burns, Oates, and Washburne, 1916.

[5] Giovanni da Legnano, *The Law of War,* Chapter 76. Oxford: Oxford University Press, 1917.

[6] Pierino Belli, *A Treatise on Military Matters,* Part I, Chapter III. Oxford: The Clarendon Press, 1936.

[7] Francisco Suarez, *The Three Theological Virtues: On Charity,* Disputation 13. Oxford: The Clarendon Press, 1944.

[8] Alberico Gentili, *On the Law of War,* I, 2. Oxford: The Clarendon Press, 1933.

[9] Hugo Grotius, *On the Law of War and Peace,* I, 1:2. Washington, D.C.: The Carnegie Institution, 1913–1925. See also Cicero, *On Duties.*

[10] Cornelius van Bynkerschoek, *On the Law of War and Peace,* I, 1. Oxford: Oxford University Press, 1923.

[11] Jean J. Rousseau, *The Social Contract,* Chapter IV. New York: Hafner, 1957.

[12] Emmerich de Vattel, *Law of Nations,* Chapter II. Washington, D.C.: Carnegie Institution, 1916.

[13] Luigi Sturzo, *The International Community and the Right of War,* Chapter V, paragraph 20. London: George Allen and Unwin, 1929.

[14] Hans Kelsen, *Law and Peace in International Relations,* pp. 34–35. Cambridge: Harvard University Press, 1942.

[15] Fritz Grob, *The Relativity of War and Peace,* p. 176. New Haven: Yale University Press, 1949.

Chapter II.

[1] Aristotle, *Politics,* Book I, Chapter VIII, 1256. New York: Random House, Inc., 1943.

[2] Cicero, *Offices,* pp. 25–27. London: Lackington, 1820.

[3] Saint Augustine, *City of God,* Book III, Section IV, p. 86. New York: Random House, Inc., 1950.

[4] *Ibid.,* Book III, Section XXX, p. 106.

[5] Franciscus de Victoria, *On the Law of War,* p. 170. Washington, D.C.: The Carnegie Institution, 1917.

⁶Pierino Belli, *A Treatise on Military Matters,* Part II, Chapter I. Oxford: The Clarendon Press, 1936.

⁷John Calvin, *Institutes of the Christian Religion,* Book IV, Chapter XX, paragraph 10. Philadelphia: Presbyterian Board of Christian Education, 1936.

⁸Balthazar Ayala, *On the Law of War,* p. 8. Washington, D.C.: The Carnegie Institution, 1912.

⁹*Loc. cit.*

¹⁰Francisco Suarez, *The Three Theological Virtues: On Charity,* p. 802. Oxford: The Clarendon Press, 1944.

¹¹Alberico Gentili, *On the Law of War,* Book I, Chapter VI, paragraph 48. Oxford: The Clarendon Press, 1933.

¹²Hugo Grotius, *On the Law of War and Peace,* Book I, Chapter I, paragraph 6. Washington, D.C.: The Carnegie Institution, 1913–25.

¹³*Ibid.,* Book I, Chapter III, paragraph 1.

¹⁴Quincy Wright, *A Study of War,* Volume I, p. 330. Chicago: University of Chicago Press, 1942.

¹⁵Charles Montesquieu, *The Spirit of the Laws,* Book X, Chapter II. New York: P. F. Collier and Sons, 1900.

¹⁶*Adam Smith's Moral and Political Philosophy,* "Lectures on Justice, Police Revenue, and Arms," pp. 330–331. New York: Hafner, 1948.

¹⁷William Paley, *Moral and Political Philosophy,* Volume IV, p. 526. London: C. and J. Rivington, 1825.

¹⁸William Godwin, *Enquiry Concerning Political Justice,* Book V, Chapter XVI. New York: A. A. Knopf, 1926.

¹⁹J. G. Fichte, *The Science of Rights,* p. 482. Philadelphia: J. B. Lippincott, 1869.

²⁰John Stuart Mill, *Dissertations and Discussions,* Volume III, "A Few Words on Non-Intervention," pp. 166–167. London: John W. Parker, 1859–75.

²¹R. G. Collingwood, *The New Leviathan,* p. 244. Oxford: The Clarendon Press, 1942.

²²Majid Khadduri, *War and Peace in the Law of Islam,* p. 57. Baltimore: Johns Hopkins Press, 1955.

²³Emil Brunner, *The Divine Imperative,* p. 469. Philadelphia: Westminster Press, 1947.

²⁴John Courtney Murray, "Theology in Modern War," in William J. Nagle, *Morality in Modern Warfare,* p. 75. Baltimore: Johns Hopkins Press, 1960.

²⁵*Op. cit.,* Chapter VI.

²⁶Franziskus Strattman, "War and Christian Conscience," *Cross Currents,* Winter, 1953.

²⁷John K. Ryan, *Modern War and Basic Ethics,* p. 104. Washington, D.C., The Catholic University of America, 1933.

²⁸Hans Kelsen, *Law and Peace in International Relations,* pp. 36–39. Cambridge: Harvard University Press, 1942.

²⁹Robert W. Tucker, *The Just War,* p. 11. Baltimore: Johns Hopkins Press, 1960.

³⁰*Christian Century,* July 20, 1966.

Chapter III.

¹*Matthew* 24:6.

²Tacitus, *History,* Chapter II, paragraph 37. New York: Random House, 1942.

³Herbert Spencer, *Social Statics,* p. 149. New York: D. Appleton, 1897.

[4] Saint Augustine, *City of God*, Book XIX, paragraph 7. New York: Random House, 1950.

[5] *Deuteronomy* 20:2–4.

[6] *Ecclesiastes* 3:8.

[7] *Matthew* 24:6.

[8] Nicolo Machiavelli, *The Prince*, Chapter XIV, p. 53. New York: Random House, 1940.

[9] *Ibid.*, Chapter XVIII, p. 62.

[10] Nicolo Machiavelli, *The Discourses*, Book I, Chapter XXI, p. 175. New York: Random House, 1940.

[11] *Ibid.*, Book III, Chapter VII, p. 436.

[12] *Ibid.*, Book III, Chapter XXIV.

[13] Thomas Hobbes, *Philosophical Rudiments Concerning Government and Society*, Part I, Chapter I, paragraph 12. London: J. Bohn, 1839–45.

[14] *Ibid.*, paragraph 15.

[15] Hugo Grotius, *On the Law of War and Peace*, Book I, Chapter II, paragraph 4. Washington, D.C.: The Carnegie Institution, 1913–25.

[16] Benedict Spinoza, *Tractatus Politicus*, Chapter III, paragraph 13. Oxford: The Clarendon Press, 1958.

[17] John Locke, *Treatise of Civil Government*, "Of the Dissolution of Civil Government," paragraph 235. New York: Random House, 1939.

[18] Jean J. Rousseau, *The Social Contract*, Chapter IV. New York: Hafner, 1957.

[19] Immanuel Kant, *Perpetual Peace*, Section II. New York: Columbia University Press, 1932.

[20] Ralph Waldo Emerson, "War," *Essays*, pp. 166–175. Boston: Houghton Mifflin, 1903–11.

[21] *Ibid.*, pp. 168–169.

[22] Herbert Spencer, *Social Statics*, p. 149. New York: D. Appleton, 1897.

[23] Thomas de Quincey, *Narrative and Miscellaneous Papers*, "On War," p. 201. New York: A. and C. Black, 1896–97.

[24] *Ibid.*, p. 226.

[25] *Ibid.*, p. 231.

[26] G. W. F. Hegel, *Philosophy of Right*, p. 333. Oxford: The Clarendon Press, 1942.

[27] G. W. F. Hegel, *Philosophy of History*, p. 544. New York: George Bell, 1894.

[28] G. W. F. Hegel, *Philosophy of Right*, p. 334. Oxford: The Clarendon Press, 1942.

[29] Johann K. Bluntschli, *The Theory of the State*, p. 293. Oxford: The Clarendon Press, 1895.

[30] Henri Bergson, *The Two Sources of Morality and Religion*, pp. 272–276. New York: Henry Holt, 1935.

[31] George Santayana, *The Life of Reason in Society*, Volume II, pp. 85–87. New York: Charles Scribner's, 1922–32.

[32] Bernard Bosanquet, *Social and International Ideals*, Chapter XIII, pp. 300–301. London: Macmillan, 1917.

[33] William Graham Sumner, "War," in Volume I, *Essays of William Graham Sumner*, pp. 140–141. London: Oxford University Press, 1934.

[34] Peter Kropotkin, *Mutual Aid*, p. 76. New York: McClure, 1907.

[35] Nels Ferré, *Christianity and Society*, pp. 183–195. New York: Harper, 1950.

[36] *Ibid.*, p. 184.

[37] Hoffman Nickerson, *Can We Limit War?* p. 19. New York: Stokes, 1933–34.

[38] G. W. F. Hegel, *Philosophy of History*, p. 22. New York: George Bell, 1894.

[39] Reinhold Niebuhr, *Beyond Tragedy*, pp. 180–181. New York: Charles Scribner's, 1937.

[40] G. W. F. Hegel, *Philosophy of Right*, pp. 66–67. Oxford: The Clarendon Press, 1942.

[41] Benedict Spinoza, *The Ethics*, Part IV, Proposition 37. New York: Tudor, 1936.

[42] Heinrich von Treitschke, *Politics*, Volume II, p. 598. New York: Macmillan, 1916.

[43] Henry Sidgwick, "The Morality of Strife," in *International Journal of Ethics*. 1891.

[44] Francis Bacon, *Advancement of Learning*, Book VIII, Chapter III. London: J. M. Dent, 1934.

[45] G. W. F. Hegel, *Philosophy of Right*, p. 295. Oxford: The Clarendon Press, 1942.

[46] Heinrich von Treitschke, *Politics*, Volume I, p. 66. New York: Macmillan, 1916.

[47] G. W. F. Hegel, *Philosophy of Right*, p. 334. Oxford: The Clarendon Press, 1942.

[48] David Hume, *Of National Characters*. New York: Longmans, Green, 1907.

[49] Adam Smith, *Wealth of Nations*, Book V, Chapter I, Part 1. New York; Random House, 1937.

[50] Ramiro DeMaeztu, *Authority, Liberty, and Function in the Light of War*, pp. 204–205. New York: Macmillan, 1916.

[51] Thomas E. Holland, *Letters on War and Neutrality (1881–1909)*, p. 25. New York: Longmans Green, 1909.

[52] Norman Cousins, *Modern Man Is Obsolete*. New York: Viking, 1945.

[53] James Burnham, *The Struggle for the World*, p. 224. New York: John Day, 1947.

[54] Nicholas Berdyaev, *The Destiny of Man*, p. 200. New York: Harper & Row, 1960.

Chapter IV.

[1] Thucydides, *The Peloponnesian War*, paragraph 140. London: Penguin, 1954.

[2] Aristotle, *Politics*, Book II, Chapter IX, 127b. New York: Random House, 1943.

[3] *Ibid.*, Book V, Chapter V, 1305.

[4] *Ibid.*, Book VII, Chapter II, 1324b.

[5] *Ibid.*, Book VII, Chapter IX, 1329a.

[6] John E. Neale, *Queen Elizabeth*, p. 296. New York: Harcourt, Brace, 1934.

[7] Adam Smith, *Wealth of Nations*, Book V, Chapter I, part 1, New York: Random House, Inc., 1937.

[8] William Godwin, *Enquiry Concerning Political Justice*, Book V, Chapter XVI. New York: A. A. Knopf, 1926.

[9] Friedrich Nietzsche, *Thus Spake Zarathustra*, Volume XI, Part I, Chapter X. London: George Allen and Unwin, 1910–30.

[10] Friedrich Nietzsche, *The Will to Power*, Volume II, paragraphs 728–729. London: George Allen and Unwin, 1910–30.

[11] *Ibid.*, paragraph 748.

[12] John Stuart Mill, *Considerations on Representative Government*, p. 311. London: Longmans, Green, and Co., Inc., 1911.

[13] Herbert Spencer, *The Principles of Ethics*, Volume II, p. 33. New York: D. Appleton, 1897.

[14] Leo Tolstoy, "Patriotism or Peace." New York: R. Field, 1948.

[15] *Ibid.*

[16] Emma Goldman, *Anarchism and Other Essays,* "Patriotism: A Menace to Liberty," p. 134. New York: Mother Earth Publishing Association, 1910.

[17] Thorstein Veblen, *An Inquiry into the Nature of Peace,* p. 22. New York: Macmillan, 1917.

[18] Karl Liebknecht, *Militarism,* p. 62. New York: B. W. Huebsch, 1917.

[19] *Loc. cit.*

[20] *Ibid.,* p. 74.

[21] Josiah Royce, *The Philosophy of Loyalty,* pp. 39–40. New York: Macmillan, 1919.

[22] John Dewey, *The Public and Its Problems,* pp. 78–79. New York: Henry Holt, 1927.

[23] Cited in Julia E. Johnsen, *Compulsory Military Training,* pp. 111–113. New York: H. W. Wilson, 1941.

[24] John M. Swomley, Jr., *The Military Establishment.* Boston: Beacon Press, 1964.

[25] Julia E. Johnsen, *Peacetime Conscription,* pp. 248–255. New York: H. W. Wilson, 1945.

[26] Charles Oman, *A History of the Art of War,* p. 595. New York: A. P. Putnam's, 1898.

[27] John Laird, *A Study in Moral Theory,* p. 241. London: George Allen and Unwin, 1926.

[28] Gene M. Lyons and John W. Masland, *Education and Military Leadership,* p. 167. Princeton: Princeton University Press, 1949.

[29] G. F. Nicolai, *The Biology of War,* p. 250. New York: Century, 1918.

[30] Cited in Florence Boeckel, *The Turn toward Peace,* p. 132. New York: Friendship Press, 1930.

[31] G. B. Shaw, *Platform and Pulpit,* p. 266. New York: Hill and Wang, 1961.

[32] Seymour Melman, *The Peace Race,* p. 38. New York: Ballantine, 1961.

[33] Karl von Clausewitz, *Principles of War,* p. 13. Harrisburg: The Military Publishing Company, 1942.

[34] Michael Howard (ed.), *Soldiers and Government,* p. 18. Bloomington: Indiana University Press, 1959.

[35] Franz Schurmann, Peter Dale Scott, and Reginald Zelnik, *The Politics of Escalation in Vietnam.* Greenwich: Fawcett, 1966.

[36] Newton D. Baker, *Why We Went to War,* p. 160. New York: Harper, 1936.

[37] Lyndon B. Johnson, *Why Vietnam,* August 20, 1965 (government White Paper). Franz Schurmann, *op. cit.* (citizens' White Paper).

[38] Rene A. Wormser, *The Myth of the Good and the Bad Nations,* p. 3. Chicago: Regnery, 1954.

[39] H. D. Lasswell, *Propaganda Technique in the World War,* p. 32. New York: A. A. Knopf, 1927.

Chapter V.

[1] Saint Cyprian, *Epistle to Donatus,* paragraph 6. *The Ante-Nicene Fathers,* Volume V. New York: The Christian Literature Company, 1890.

[2] *Complete Writings of Thucydides,* pp. 188–189. London: Penguin, 1954.

[3] *Thoreau's Writings,* Volume VII. *The Journal,* Volume I, p. 101. Boston: Houghton Mifflin, 1884–93.

[4] *Ibid.*, p. 335.

[5] *Ibid.*, p. 246.

[6] B. Malinowski, *Freedom and Civilization*, pp. 282–283. New York: Roy, 1944.

[7] Paul Peeters, *Massive Retaliation: The Policy and Its Critics*, p. 78. Chicago: Henry Regnery, 1959.

[8] David Starr Jordan, *War's Aftermath*, p. 78. Boston: Houghton Mifflin, 1914.

[9] François Voltaire, *Philosophical Dictionary*, p. 194. New York: Philosophical Library, 1961.

[10] Raymond Aron, *On War*, p. 102. New York: Doubleday, 1954.

[11] B. Beau, "A Defense of Cannibalism," in *International Conciliation*, Number 78, 1914.

[12] T. H. Green, *Principles of Political Obligation*, "The Right of the State over the Individual," paragraph 163. New York: Longmans, Green, 1937.

[13] Leon Trotsky, *Their Morals and Ours*, p. 14. New York: Pioneer, 1942.

[14] William Jay, *War and Peace*, pp. 47–50. New York: Oxford University Press, 1919.

[15] Norman Thomas, *War: No Glory, No Profit, No Need*, p. 150. New York: Frederick A. Stokes, 1935.

[16] R. G. Collingwood, *The New Leviathan*, Chapter XXX, 30:34. Oxford: The Clarendon Press, 1942.

[17] Bert Cochran, *The War System*, pp. 157–159. New York: Macmillan, 1965. See also Tristram Coffin, *The Passion of the Hawks*, p. 14. New York: Macmillan, 1964.

[18] "The Case for Shelters," Herman Kahn, in Seymour Melman (ed.) *No Place to Hide*, pp. 56–57. New York: Grove, 1962.

[19] Paul W. Blackstock, *The Strategy of Subversion*, pp. 299, 319–320. Chicago: Quadrangle, 1964.

[20] *Ibid.*, pp. 319–320.

[21] V. Lenin, *Toward the Seizure of Power*, Book I, p. 215. Moscow: Foreign Languages Publishing House, 1947.

[22] Karl Marx, *Selected Works*, Volume II, p. 441. Moscow: Foreign Languages Publishing House, 1955.

[23] V. Lenin, *Collected Works*, Volume XIX. "A Caricature of Marxism and 'Imperialist Economism,'" p. 216. Moscow: Foreign Languages Publishing House, 1950.

[24] V. Lenin, *The Soviet Union and the Cause of Peace*, p. 12. New York: International, 1936.

[25] V. Molotov, "Soviet Initiative for the Preservation of Peace," in V. Lenin, *op. cit.*, p. 45.

[26] Thucydides, *Complete Writings of Thucydides*, p. 189. London: Penguin, 1954.

[27] Henry Thoreau, *Journal*, Volume VIII, p. 189. Boston: Houghton Mifflin, 1884–1893.

[28] Friedrich Nietzsche, *Thoughts Out of Season*, "David Strauss," p. 3. London: George Allen and Unwin, 1910–1930.

[29] Herbert Spencer, *Principles of Ethics*, Volume II, p. 23. New York: D. Appleton, 1897.

[30] L. T. Hobhouse, *Social Development*, p. 110. New York: Henry Holt, 1924.

[31] Friedrich Nietzsche, *Human, All-Too-Human*, Part I, paragraph 444. London: George Allen and Unwin, 1910–1930.

[32] Herbert Spencer, *Principles of Ethics*, Volume II, pp. 20–23.

[33] *Essays of William Graham Sumner*, Volume I. "War," pp. 168–173. London: Oxford University Press, 1934.

[34] *Works of Voltaire,* Volume XIV, "Philosophical Dictionary," p. 198. New York: E. R. DuMont, 1901–1903.

[35] Seymour Melman, *No Place to Hide,* p. 84. New York: Grove, 1962.

Chapter VI.

[1] John C. Bennett, *Christians and the State,* p. 165. New York: Charles Scribner's Sons, 1958.

[2] Umphrey Lee, *The Historic Church and Pacifism,* p. 39. New York: Abingdon-Cokesbury, 1943.

[3] C. J. Cadoux, *The Early Christian Attitude toward War.* London: Headley, 1919, and *The Early Church and the World.* Edinburgh: T. and T. Clark, 1925.

[4] Leyton Richards, *Realistic Pacifism,* p. 72. New York: Willett, Clark, 1935.

[5] Carl David Soule, "The New Testament and War and Peace," p. 237, in Edwin Prince Booth, *New Testament Studies.* New York: Abingdon-Cokesbury, 1942.

[6] E. N. Wright, *Conscientious Objectors in the Civil War,* p. 18. Philadelphia: University of Pennsylvania Press, 1937.

[7] George Fox, *Journal,* pp. 356–357, 400. London: W. Richardson and S. Clark, 1765.

[8] *Ibid.,* p. 402.

[9] *Ibid.,* p. 399.

[10] John C. Bennett, *op. cit.,* pp. 167–168. New York: Charles Scribner's Sons, 1958.

[11] Leo N. Tolstoy, "Nobel's Bequest," in *Essays, Letters, and Miscellanies,* Volume II, p. 1. New York: Charles Scribner's Sons, 1925.

[12] Norman Thomas, *War: No Glory, No Profit, No Need,* p. 156, New York: Stokes, 1935.

[13] Merle E. Curti, *The American Peace Crusade, 1815–1860,* p. 145. Durham: Duke University Press, 1929.

[14] A. J. Muste, "Pacifism and Class War," in Devere Allen (ed.), *Pacifism in the Modern World,* pp. 93–95. New York: Doubleday, 1929.

[15] Norman Thomas, *War: No Glory, No Profit, No Need.* New York: Stokes, 1935.

[16] M. K. Gandhi, *Non-Violence in Peace and War,* p. 1. Ahmedebad: Navajivan, 1948–49.

[17] A. D. Lindsay, *Pacifism As a Principle and Pacifism As a Dogma,* pp. 13–17. London: Student Christian Movement Press, 1939.

[18] O. Nathan and H. Norden (eds.), *Einstein on Peace,* p. 117. New York: Simon and Schuster, 1960.

[19] *Ibid.,* p. 229.

[20] Gustave Hervé, *My Country, Right or Wrong,* p. 158. London: A. C. Field, 1910.

[21] *Ibid.,* p. 159.

[22] John C. Bennett, *op. cit.,* p. 172.

[23] O. Nathan and H. Norden, *op. cit.,* p. 462.

[24] E. N. Wright, *op. cit.,* p. 129.

[25] *Ibid.,* p. 129.

[26] *Ibid.,* p. 224.

[27] *Ibid.,* p. 240.

[28] Charles Tare Russell, "The Unfinished Mystery," quoted by R. H. Abrams, *Preachers Present Arms,* p. 183. New York: Round Table, 1933.

29 *Ibid.,* p. 197.

30 Mulford Sibley and Philip Jacob, *Conscription of Conscience,* p. 464. Ithaca: Cornell University Press, 1952.

31 John C. Bennett, *op. cit.,* p. 179. New York: Charles Scribner's Sons, 1958.

32 Reinhold Niebuhr, *Christianity and Power Politics,* p. 4. New York: Charles Scribner's Sons, 1940.

33 Nels Ferré, *Christianity and Society,* p. 190. New York: Harper, 1950.

34 *Ibid.,* p. 203.

Chapter VII.

1 Cornelius van Bynkerschoek, *On the Law of War and Peace,* pp. 16–17. Oxford: Oxford University Press, 1923.

2 Jean J. Rousseau, *The Social Contract,* Chapter IV. New York: Hafner, 1957.

3 Guglielmo Ferrero, *Peace and War,* p. 56. London: Macmillan, 1933.

4 Saint Thomas Aquinas, *Summa Theologica,* Question 40, Article 4, Part II, Second Part. London: R. and T. Washburne, 1912–1941.

5 Pierino Belli, *A Treatise on Military Matters,* p. 81. Oxford: The Clarendon Press, 1936.

6 J. G. Fichte, *The Science of Rights,* p. 482. Philadelphia: J. B. Lippincott, 1869.

7 Benjamin Franklin, *Franklin's Writings,* Volume II, "Observations on War." New York: Macmillan, 1905–1907.

8 William Ladd, *Congress of Nations,* p. 15. New York: Oxford University Press, 1916.

9 R. E. Osgood, *Limited War: The Challenge to American Strategy,* p. 13. Chicago: University of Chicago Press, 1957. A similar military distaste for the idea of any limitation on war was expressed by General Nathan F. Twining in his *Neither Liberty nor Safety,* pp. 102–120. New York: Holt, Rinehart and Winston, 1966.

10 Walter F. Hahn and John C. Neff (eds.), *American Strategy for the Nuclear Age,* p. 251. New York: Doubleday, 1960.

11 *Ibid.,* p. 266.

12 Dietrich Bonhoeffer, *Ethics,* pp. 116–117. New York: Macmillan, 1955.

13 Saint Augustine, *The City of God,* Book I, Section 7. New York: Random House, 1950.

14 R. H. Abrams, *Preachers Present Arms,* p. 65. New York: Round Table, 1933.

15 *Ibid.,* p. 67.

16 Saint Thomas Aquinas, *ibid.,* Articles 2 and 3.

17 *Ibid.,* Article 3.

18 William Godwin, *Enquiry Concerning Political Justice,* Book V, Chapter 8. New York: A. A. Knopf, 1926.

19 William Paley, *Moral Philosophy,* Vol. IV, p. 531. London: C. & J. Rivington, 1825.

20 Immanuel Kant, *Perpetual Peace,* Sec. I, paragraph 6. New York: Liberal Arts, 1948.

21 J. G. Fichte, *The Science of Rights,* p. 484. Philadelphia: J. B. Lippincott, 1869.

22 Guglielmo Ferrero, *op. cit.,* p. 61.

23 "C'est une Vive Satisfaction," September 14, 1939.

24 Adolf Hitler, *My New Order,* p. 951. New York: Reynal and Hitchcock, 1941.

[25] Carnegie Endowment for International Peace, Pamphlets 1–22.

[26] I. S. Bloch, *The Future of War*, p. 150. New York: Doubleday, 1902.

[27] Hiram Maxim, *Defenseless America*, p. 83. New York: Hearst, 1915.

[28] O. Nathan and H. Norden, *Einstein on Peace*, p. 521. New York: Simon and Schuster, 1960.

[29] Raymond Aron, *On War*, p. 159. New York: Doubleday, 1959.

[30] J. D. Bernal, *World Without War*, p. 15. London, 1958.

[31] Emil Brunner, *The Divine Imperative*, p. 471. Philadelphia: Westminster, 1947.

[32] Paul Ramsay, *War and the Christian Conscience*, p. 167. Durham: Duke University Press, 1961.

[33] *Ibid.*, p. 170.

[34] P. M. S. Blackett, *Fear, War, and the Bomb*, p. 208. New York: Whittlesey, 1948.

[35] Walter F. Hahn and John C. Neff (eds.), *American Strategy for the Nuclear Age*, Herman Kahn, "The Nature and Feasibility of War and Deterrence," p. 221. New York: Doubleday, 1960.

[36] William J. Nagle (ed.), *Morality and Modern Warfare*, Thomas E. Murray, "Morality and Security," p. 65. Baltimore: Helicon, 1960.

[37] *Ibid.*, John R. Connery, "Morality of Nuclear Armament," p. 92.

[38] Sheldon Glueck, *War Criminals: Their Prosecution and Punishment*, p. 155. New York: A. A. Knopf, 1944.

[39] William J. Nagle, *op. cit.*, p. 103, "The Hydrogen Bombing of Cities."

Chapter VIII.

[1] William E. Lecky, *History of European Morals*, Volume II, p. 255. New York: Appleton, 1900.

[2] Jean J. Rousseau, *The Social Contract*, Chapter 8. New York: Hafner, 1957.

[3] Marsilius of Padua, *The Defensor Pacis*, Discourse II, Chapter 26, paragraph 15. New York: Columbia University Press, 1951–1956.

[4] John Calvin, *Institutes of the Christian Religion*, IV:20:11–12. Philadelphia: Presbyterian Board of Christian Education, 1936.

[5] John Calvin, *Tracts and Treatises on the Doctrine and Worship of the Church*, Volume II, "Forms of Prayer for the Church," p. 106. London: Oliver and Boyd, 1958.

[6] Ernst Troeltsch, *The Social Teaching of the Christian Churches*, Volume II, p. 920. New York: Harper, 1960.

[7] Vilfredo Pareto, *The Mind and Society*, Volume III, paragraph 1950. New York: Harcourt, Brace, 1935.

[8] Shailer Matthews, *Patriotism and Religion*, p. 80. New York: Macmillan, 1918.

[9] L. T. Hobhouse, *Morals in Evolution*, p. 262. New York: Henry Holt, 1906.

[10] Willard L. Sperry (ed.), *The Religion of Soldier and Sailor*, Paul L. Moody, "The Precedent of the First World War," p. 19. Cambridge: Harvard University Press, 1945.

[11] *Ibid.*, John E. Johnson, "The Faith and Practice of the Raw Recruit," p. 67.

[12] The author had the personal experience, along with others in 1944, of being rejected for the chaplaincy on the grounds that he would not sign a non-pacifist pledge.

[13] Pope Pius XII, Address: "Nel Mese di Luglio," July 10, 1940.

[14] G. J. Heering, *The Fall of Christianity*, p. 230. New York: Fellowship, 1943.

[15] Harry C. Koenig, *Principles for Peace*, p. xv. Washington, D.C.: National Catholic Welfare Conference, 1943.

[16] *Ibid.*, Pope Leo XIII, Encyclical: *Inscrutabili Dei*, April 21, 1878.

[17] William H. Prescott, *The Conquest of Mexico*, Volume I. New York: Harpers, 1848.

Chapter IX.

[1] C. J. Cadoux, *The Early Christian Attitude to War*, p. 229. London: Headley, 1919.

[2] Saint Justin Martyr, *The First Apology*, Chapter XIV, *The Ante-Nicene Fathers*, Volume I. New York: The Christian Literature Company, 1890.

[3] *Ibid.*, Chapter XXXIX.

[4] Saint Justin Martyr, *Dialogue with Trypho*, Chapter CX, *op. cit.*

[5] Tatian, *Address to the Greeks*, Chapter XI, Volume II, *op. cit.*

[6] Clement of Alexandria, *Exhortation to the Heathen*, Chapter III, Volume II, *op. cit.*

[7] Tertullian, *Apology*, Chapter XLII, Volume III, *op. cit.*

[8] Tertullian, *On Idolatry*, Chapter XIX, *op. cit.*

[9] Tertullian, *The Chaplet*, Chapter I, *op. cit.*

[10] *Ibid.*, Chapter XI.

[11] Origen, *Against Celsus*, Book V, Chapter XXXIII, Volume IV, *op. cit.*

[12] *Ibid.*, Book, VIII, Chapter LXXIII.

[13] *Ibid.*, Book VII, Chapter XXVI.

[14] *Ibid.*, Book VIII, Chapter LXXV.

[15] *Ibid.*, Book VIII, Chapter LXX.

[16] Saint Cyprian, *The Good of Patience*, Chapter XIV, Volume V, *op. cit.*

[17] Saint Cyprian, *To Donatus*, Chapters VI and VII, *op. cit.*

[18] Saint Cyprian, *To Demetrian*, Chapter XVII, *op. cit.*

[19] *The Octavius of Minucius Felix*, Chapter XXX, Volume IV, *op. cit.*

[20] Arnobius, *The Case Against the Pagans*, Book I, paragraph VI, Volume VI, *op. cit.*

[21] Lactantius, *The Divine Institutes*, Book VI, Chapter XX, Volume VII, *op. cit.*

[22] Saint Athanasius, *The Incarnation of the Word of God*, Paragraph LII, Volume IV, *op. cit.*

[23] C. J. Cadoux, *op. cit.*, p. 166.

[24] Council of Chalcedon, Canon 7, in H. J. Schroeder, *Disciplinary Decrees of the General Councils*. Saint Louis: Herder, 1937.

[25] See Chapter VII, pp 115, for a discussion of the Truce of God.

[26] Council of Vienne, Canon 9, H. J. Schroeder, *op. cit.*

[27] Desiderius Erasmus, *The Complaint of Peace*, pp. 17–23. New York: Scholar's Facsimile and Reprints, 1946.

[28] *Ibid.*, pp. 33–34.

[29] *Ibid.*, p. 39.

[30] Leo Tolstoy, "Letter to a Non-Commissioned Officer," *Works*, Volume II, p. 35. New York: Charles Scribner's, 1913.

[31] Eugene Debs, *Writings and Speeches*, p. 449. New York: Hermitage, 1948.

[32] *Statements of Religious Bodies on the Conscientious Objector*. Compiled and printed by the National Service Board for Religious Objectors, 1963.

[33] C. J. Cadoux, *op. cit.*, p. 245.

Chapter X.

[1] Roland H. Bainton, *Christian Attitudes toward War and Peace,* Chapter IV. New York: Abingdon, 1960.

[2] Tertullian, *De Fuga,* Chapter XIII, Volume III, *Ante-Nicene Fathers.* New York: The Christian Literature Company, 1890.

[3] Clement of Alexandria, *Christ the Educator,* Paragraph 65, Volume XXIII. New York: Fathers of the Church, 1954.

[4] *Ibid.,* paragraph 100.

[5] *Nicene and Post-Nicene Fathers,* Volume XIV, pp. 27–28. New York: The Christian Literature Company, 1890.

[6] C. J. Cadoux, *The Early Christian Attitude to War,* p. 586, footnote 1. London: Headley, 1919.

[7] Eusebius, *Oration on Constantine,* Chapter XVI, paragraphs 3–8. Westminster, Md.: Ancient Christian Writers, 1949.

[8] Saint Ambrose, *Letters to Laymen,* "Letter to Studius," Letter 90, Volume XXVI. New York: Fathers of the Church, 1954.

[9] Saint Augustine, *Letter 189,* Volume XXX, *op. cit.*

[10] Saint Augustine, *Letter 138,* Volume XX, *op. cit.*

[11] John of Salisbury, *Policraticus,* Book VI, Chapter VII. New York: A. A. Knopf, 1927.

[12] *Ibid.,* Book VI, Chapter VIII.

[13] Martin Luther, *Works,* Volume III, "Secular Authority: To What Extent It Should Be Obeyed," pp. 228–236. Philadelphia: A. J. Holman, 1915–1932.

[14] *Ibid.,* "That Soldiers, Too, Can Be Saved," p. 166. Washington, D.C.: The Carnegie Institution, 1917.

[15] *Ibid.,* p. 36.

[16] Franciscus de Victoria, *On the Law of War,* p. 166. Washington, D.C.: The Carnegie Institution, 1917.

[17] William E. Lecky, *History of European Morals,* Volume II, pp. 253–254. New York: D. Appleton, 1900.

[18] John Calvin, *Institutes of the Christian Religion,* Book IV, Chapter XX, paragraph 12. Philadelphia: Presbyterian Board of Christian Education, 1936.

[19] Francisco Suarez, *The Three Theological Virtues: On Charity,* Disputation XIII, Section 1. Oxford: The Clarendon Press, 1944.

[20] Giovanni da Legnano, *The Law of War,* Chapter LXXXVI. Oxford: Oxford University Press, 1917.

[21] William Paley, *Works,* Volume IV, *Moral and Political Philosophy,* p. 520. London: C. and J. Rivington, 1825.

[22] "The Sword and Christianity," in *The Boston Review Devoted to Theology and Literature,* III, pp. 257–261, cited in Abrams, *op. cit.*

[23] W. H. P. Faunce, *Religion and War,* p. 78. New York: Abingdon, 1918.

[24] Ray H. Abrams, *Preachers Present Arms,* p. 4. New York: Round Table, 1933.

[25] *Ibid.,* p. 57.

[26] *Ibid.,* p. 69.

[27] Walter Van Kirk, *Religion and the World of Tomorrow.* New York: Willett, Clark and Company, 1941.

[28] Reinhold Niebuhr, "Why I Leave the F.O.R.," *The Christian Century,* January, 3, 1934.

[29] Ray H. Abrams, "The Churches and the Clergy in World War II," *The Annals of the American Academy of Political and Social Science,* March, 1948, p. 111.

[30] *Ibid.*, p. 117.

[31] John C. Bennett, "Swords and Plowshares: A Critical Look at Pacifism," p. 15. *United Church Herald*, October, 1966.

Chapter XI.

[1] Thomas Hobbes, *The Citizen*, Part I, Chapter I, Section 4. New York: Appleton-Century-Crofts, 1949.

[2] *James* 4:1.

[3] Giovanni da Legnano, *The Law of War*, p. 222. Oxford: Oxford University Press, 1917.

[4] Samuel A. Stouffer and others, *The American Soldier: Combat and Its Aftermath*, Volume II, p. 108. Princeton: Princeton University Press, 1949.

[5] *Ibid.*, Volume I, pp. 462–465.

[6] National Research Council, *Psychology for the Fighting Man*, p. 348. Washington, D.C.: *Infantry Journal*, 1943.

[7] John T. MacCurdy, *War Neuroses*, p. 129. Cambridge: The University Press, 1918.

[8] William McDougall, *An Introduction to Social Psychology*, Chapter XI. Boston: John W. Luce, 1915.

[9] Sigmund Freud, *Collected Papers*, Volume IV, "Thoughts for the Times on War and Death," p. 294. London: Hogarth, 1949.

[10] *Ibid.*, p. 300.

[11] Laurence Dennis, *The Dynamics of War and Revolution*, p. 26. New York: The Weekly Foreign Letter, 1940.

[12] Bertrand Russell, *Why Men Fight*, p. 8. New York: Century, 1916.

[13] Hadley Cantril (ed.), *Tensions That Cause Wars*, Gordon Allport, "The Role of Expectancy," p. 43. Urbana: University of Illinois Press, 1950.

[14] George Santayana, *The Life of Reason in Society*, Volume II, pp. 85–87. New York: Charles Scribner's Sons, 1922–1932.

[15] G. W. Crile, *A Mechanistic View of War and Peace*, p. 64. New York: Macmillan, 1917.

[16] Carl G. Jung, *The Collected Works*, Volume VII, p. 270. New York: Pantheon, 1953–1956.

[17] Gardner Murphy (ed.), *Human Nature and Enduring Peace*, p. 13. Boston: Houghton Mifflin, 1945.

[18] T. H. Pear (ed.), *Psychological Factors of Peace and War*, H. J. Eysenck, "War and Aggressiveness," p. 52. New York: Philosophical Library, 1950.

[19] *Ibid.*, J. C. Flugel, "Neglected Aspects of World Integration," p. 131.

[20] *Ibid.*, G. W. Allport, "Guidelines for Research in International Cooperation," p. 147.

[21] George K. Pratt, *Soldier to Civilian*, p. 32. New York: McGraw-Hill, 1944.

[22] O. Nathan and H. Norden, *Einstein on Peace*, p. 199. New York: Simon and Schuster, 1960.

[23] E. F. M. Durbin and John Bowlby, *Personal Aggressiveness and War*, pp. 93–94. New York: Columbia University Press, 1939.

[24] T. W. Adorno, *The Authoritarian Personality*. New York: Harper, 1950. Gordon Allport, *The Nature of Prejudice*. New York: Cambridge University Press, 1954.

[25] Edward Glover, *War, Sadism and Pacifism*, pp. 12–13. London: George Allen and Unwin, 1946.

[26] Pryns Hopkins, *The Psychology of Social Movements*, p. 128. London: George Allen and Unwin, 1938.

[27] *Ibid.*, pp. 90–91.

[28] *Ibid.*, p. 117.

[29] Carl I. Hovland and others, *Experiments on Mass Communication*, Volume III, pp. 224–225. Princeton: Princeton University Press, 1949.

[30] Charles E. Osgood, *Perspectives in Foreign Policy*. Privately Printed, 1965.

[31] Samuel A. Stouffer and others, *op. cit.*, pp. 158, 583–595.

[32] *Ibid.*, p. 553.

[33] Edward C. Tolman, *Drives toward War*, p. 102. New York: D. Appleton-Century, 1942.

Chapter XII.

[1] Adam Smith, *Wealth of Nations*, Book V, Chapter I, part 1. New York: Random House, Inc., 1937.

[2] Thorstein Veblen, *An Inquiry into the Nature of Peace*, pp. 19–20. New York: Macmillan, 1917.

[3] George Santayana, *The Life of Reason in Society*, p. 81. New York: Charles Scribner's Sons, 1922–1932.

[4] *Ibid.*, p. 83.

[5] Homer Lea, *The Valor of Ignorance*, p. 88. New York: Harpers, 1909.

[6] Friedrich von Bernhardi, *Britain As Germany's Vassal*, pp. 206–207. New York: George H. Doran, n.d.

[7] *Fourth Conference on Cause and Cure of War*, Captain Thomas Schneider, "Necessity of Preparedness for Defense," p. 75. New York: 1929.

[8] *Soviet Total War*, Volume I, General Curtis LeMay, "Strategic Air Command and World Peace," p. 386. Washington, D.C.: House Committee on Un-American Activities, 1956.

[9] Philip Noel-Baker, *The Arms Race*, p. 558. London: Stevens, 1958.

[10] Paul Peeters, *Massive Retaliation: The Policy and Its Critics*, p. 16. Chicago: Henry Regnery, 1959.

[11] John S. Tompkins, *The Weapons of World War III*, p. xiv. New York: Doubleday, 1966.

[12] T. H. Pear (ed.), *Psychological Factors of Peace and War*, L. F. Richardson, "Threats and Security," pp. 224–225. New York: Philosophical Library, 1950.

[13] Philip Noel-Baker, *The Private Manufacture of Armaments*, pp. 287–289. New York: Oxford University Press, 1937.

[14] *Ibid.*, p. 19.

[15] *Ibid.*, p. 20.

[16] *Ibid.*, p. 318.

[17] Julia E. Johnsen, *International Traffic in Arms and Munitions*. New York: Wilson, 1934. Stephen and Joan Rauschenbush, *War Madness*. Washington, D.C.: National Home Library Foundation, 1937.

[18] L. DuPont, *The DuPont Company and Munitions*, p. 5. Wilmington, Delaware: 1934.

[19] *Ibid.*, p. 7.

[20] *Ibid.*, p. 27.

[21] Herman Kahn, *Thinking About the Unthinkable*, p. 81. New York: Horizon, 1962.

[22] Nathan F. Twining, *Neither Liberty nor Safety*, pp. 106–114. New York: Holt, Rinehart and Winston, 1966.

[23] John M. Swomley, Jr., *The Military Establishment*, pp. 139–176. Boston: Beacon Press, 1964.

Chapter XIII.

[1] Plato, *The Republic*, Book II, sections 373–375. *The Dialogues of Plato*, Volume I. New York: Random House, 1937.

[2] *Ibid.*, Book III, sections 416–417.

[3] Aristotle, *Politics*, Book II, Chapter VII, section 1265. New York: Random House, 1943.

[4] *Ibid.*, section 1266.

[5] Jean J. Rousseau, *Discourse on the Origin of Inequality*, Part II, p. 213. New York: E. P. Dutton 1941.

[6] Jean J. Rousseau, *Discourse on Political Economy*, p. 267. New York: E. P. Dutton, 1941.

[7] William Godwin, *Enquiry Concerning Political Justice*, Book V, Chapter XVI. New York: A. A. Knopf, 1926.

[8] *Ibid.*, Book VIII, Chapter III.

[9] Thomas Malthus, *On the Principle of Population*, Volume II, p. 164. New York: E. P. Dutton, n.d.

[10] Thomas Malthus, *Principles of Political Economy*. New York: A. M. Kelley, 1951.

[11] Kirby Page, *Must We Go to War?* pp. 30–31. New York: Farrar and Rinehart, 1937.

[12] Harry Ward, *In Place of Profit*, Chapter I. New York: Charles Scribner's Sons, 1933.

[13] Jerome Davis, *Capitalism and Its Culture*, pp. 215–218. New York: Farrar and Rinehart, 1935.

[14] Walter Rauschenbusch, *Christianity and the Social Crisis*, p. 350. New York: Macmillan, 1907.

[15] G. F. Nicolai, *The Biology of War*, p. 17. New York: Century, 1918.

[16] Scott Nearing, *War*, Chapter VIII. New York: Vanguard, 1931.

[17] *Report of the Second Conference on Cause and Cure of War*, p. 52. Washington, D.C., 1926.

[18] Joseph Stalin, *The Political and Social Doctrine of Communism*, p. 389, in *International Conciliation*. New York: Carnegie Endowment, 1934.

[19] Thorstein Veblen, *The Theory of the Leisure Class*, p. 247. New York: Macmillan, 1912.

[20] John Kenneth Galbraith, *The Affluent Society*, p. 272. Boston: Houghton Mifflin, 1958.

[21] C. Wright Mills, *The Causes of World War III*, p. 63. New York: Ballantine, 1958.

[22] T. H. Pear (ed.), *Psychological Factors of Peace and War*, L. F. Richardson, "Statistics of Deadly Quarrels," pp. 248–249. New York: Philosophical Library, 1950.

[23] Quincy Wright, *A Study of War*, pp. 220–223. Chicago: University of Chicago Press, 1942.

[24] Emile Benoit and Kenneth Boulding, *Disarmament and the Economy*, p. 7. New York: Harper, 1963.

[25] C. Wright Mills, *op. cit.*, p. 67.

[26] John M. Swomley, *The Military Establishment*, p. 99. Boston: Beacon Press, 1964.

[27] *Ibid.*, p. 100.

[28] *Ibid.*, p. 106.

[29] Lionel C. Robbins, *The Economic Causes of War*, p. 85. London: Jonathan Cape, 1939.

Chapter XIV.

[1] Immanuel Kant, *Perpetual Peace*, Section I, Part 3. New York: Columbia University Press, 1932.

[2] Jeremy Bentham, *Economic Writings*, Volume II, Essay IV. London: George Allen and Unwin, 1952–1954.

[3] Charles Montesquieu, *Spirit of the Laws*, Book XIII, Chapter XVII. New York: P. F. Collier, 1900.

[4] Maxim Litvinov, "U.S.S.R. and Disarmament," in *The Soviet Union and the Cause of Peace*, p. 102. New York: International, 1936.

[5] Norman Thomas, *War: No Glory, No Profit, No Need*, p. 194. New York: Frederick A. Stokes, 1935.

[6] *Royal Commission on the Private Manufacture and Trading in Arms*, Part VIII, Chapter XII. London: H. M. Stationery Office, 1935–1936.

[7] H. C. Engelbrecht and F. C. Hanighen, *Merchants of Death*, p. 6. New York: Dodd, Mead, 1934.

[8] Philip Noel-Baker, *The Arms Race*, p. 561. London: Stevens, 1958.

[9] Encyclical: *Nova Impendet*, October 2, 1931.

[10] *Ecco Una*, May 4, 1929.

[11] John Dewey, *Intelligence in the Modern World*, p. 523. New York: Random House, 1939.

[12] John F. Kennedy, *The Strategy of Peace*, p. 26. New York: Harper, 1960.

[13] Louis Henkin (ed.), *Arms Control*. Englewood Cliffs, N.J.: Prentice-Hall, 1961.

[14] Donald G. Brennan (ed.), *Arms Control, Disarmament, and National Security*. New York: Braziller, 1961.

[15] *Ibid.*, p. 443.

[16] Louis Henkin (ed.), *op. cit.*, pp. 202–203.

[17] Donald G. Brennan, *op. cit.*, Lewis C. Bohn, "Non-Physical Inspection Techniques."

Chapter XV.

[1] Edith Wynner and Georgia Lloyd, *Searchlight on Peace Plans*. New York: E. P. Dutton, 1944.

[2] William Penn, "An Essay Towards the Present and Future Peace of Europe by the Establishment of an European Diet, Parliament or Estates" (1693). New York: Carnegie Endowment for International Peace, 1943.

[3] J. G. Fichte, *The Science of Rights*, pp. 488–489. Philadelphia: J. B. Lippincott, 1869.

[4] William Ladd, *An Essay on a Congress of Nations*, p. 86. New York: Oxford University Press, 1916.

[5] R. W. Emerson, "War." New York: Houghton Mifflin, 1903–1911.

[6] Ramiro DeMaeztu, *Authority, Liberty and Function in the Light of War*, pp. 525–527. New York: Macmillan, 1916.

[7] Heinrich G. von Treitschke, *Politics*, Volume I, p. 29. New York: Macmillan, 1916.

[8] Helmuth von Moltke, *The Franco-German War of 1870–71*, Part I. London: Harper, 1907.

[9] Ralph Barton Perry, *Our Side Is Right*, p. 137. Cambridge: Harvard University Press, 1942.

[10] John Dewey, *Intelligence in the Modern World*, p. 511. New York: Random House, 1939.

[11] Henri Bergson, *The Two Sources of Morality and Religion*, p. 276. New York: Henry Holt, 1935.

[12] Pope Pius XII, Encyclical: *Studiorum Ducem*, June 29, 1923.

[13] Eduardo Jiménez De Aréchaga, *Voting and the Handling of Disputes in the Security Council*, pp. 159–160. New York: Carnegie Endowment for International Peace, 1950.

[14] Herbert W. Briggs, *The International Law Commission*, p. 20. Ithaca: Cornell University Press, 1965.

[15] *Ibid.*, pp. 332–337.

[16] Oliver J. Lissitzyn, *The International Court of Justice: Its Role in the Maintenance of International Peace and Security*, pp. 63–65. New York: Carnegie Endowment, 1951.

[17] Mark A. May, *A Social Psychology of War and Peace*, p. 229. London: Oxford University Press, 1943.

[18] Jacques Maritain, *Man and the State*, pp. 194–195. Chicago: University of Chicago Press, 1951.

[19] Quincy Wright, *A Study of War*, Volume I. Chicago: University of Chicago Press, 1942.

BIBLIOGRAPHY

Chapter I. The Definition of War

AQUINAS, SAINT THOMAS, *Summa Theologica*. Question 41, Article 1.

BELLI, PIERINO, *A Treatise on Military Matters*. Oxford: The Clarendon Press, 1936.

BYNKERSCHOEK, CORNELIUS, *On the Law of War and Peace*. Oxford: Oxford University Press, Inc., 1923.

GENTILI, ALBERICO, *The Law of War*. Oxford: The Clarendon Press, 1933.

GROB, FRITZ, *The Relativity of War and Peace*. New Haven: Yale University Press, 1949.

GROTIUS, HUGO, *On the Law of War and Peace*. Washington, D.C.: The Carnegie Institution, 1913–1925.

KELSEN, HANS, *Law and Peace in International Relations*. Cambridge: Harvard University Press, 1942.

LEGNANO, GIOVANNI DI, *The Law of War*. Oxford: Oxford University Press, Inc., 1917.

ROUSSEAU, JEAN JACQUES, *The Social Contract*. New York: Hafner Publishing Company, Inc., 1957.

STURZO, LUIGI, *The International Community and the Right of War*. London: George Allen and Unwin Limited, 1929.

WRIGHT, QUINCY, "Criteria for Judging the Relevance of Researches on the Problems of Peace," in *Research for Peace*. Amsterdam: North-Holland Publishing Company, 1954.

WRIGHT, QUINCY, *A Study of War*. Two Volumes. Chicago: University of Chicago Press, 1942.

Chapter II. The Just War

ARISTOTLE, *Politics*. New York: Random House, Inc., 1943.

AUGUSTINE, SAINT, *The City of God*. New York: Random House, Inc., 1950.

AYALA, BALTHAZAR, *On the Law of War*. Washington, D.C.: The Carnegie Institution, 1912.

BELLI, PIERINO, *A Treatise on Military Matters*. Oxford: The Clarendon Press, 1936.

BRUNNER, HEINRICH EMIL, *The Divine Imperative*. Philadelphia: The Westminster Press, 1947.

CALVIN, JOHN, *Institutes of the Christian Religion*. Philadelphia: Presbyterian Board of Christian Education, 1936.

CICERO, *De Officiis: Or His Treatise Concerning the Moral Duties of Mankind*. London: Lackington, 1820.

COLLINGWOOD, R. G., *The New Leviathan*. Oxford: The Clarendon Press, 1942.

FICHTE, J. G., *The Science of Rights*. Philadelphia: J. B. Lippincott Company, 1869.

GENTILI, ALBERICO, *The Law of War*. Oxford: The Clarendon Press, 1933.

GODWIN, WILLIAM, *Enquiry Concerning Political Justice*. New York: A. A. Knopf, 1926.

GROTIUS, HUGO, *On the Law of War and Peace*. Washington, D.C.: The Carnegie Institution, 1913–1925.

KELSEN, HANS, *Law and Peace in International Relations*. Cambridge: Harvard University Press, 1942.

KHADDURI, MAJID, *War and Peace in the Law of Islam*. Baltimore: The Johns Hopkins Press, 1955.

MILL, JOHN STUART, "A Few Words on Non-Intervention." *Dissertations and Discussions*. Volume III. London: John W. Parker, 1859–1875.

MONTESQUIEU, CHARLES, *The Spirit of the Laws*. New York: P. F. Collier and Son, 1900.

NAGLE, WILLIAM J. (ed.), *Morality and Modern Warfare*. Baltimore: The Johns Hopkins Press, 1960.

PALEY, WILLIAM, *Moral Philosophy*. Volume IV. London: C. and J. Rivington, 1825.

RYAN, JOHN K., *Modern War and Basic Ethics*. Washington, D.C.: The Catholic University of America Press, Inc., 1933.

SUAREZ, FRANCISCO, *The Three Theological Virtues*. Oxford: The Clarendon Press, 1944.

TUCKER, ROBERT W., *The Just War*. Baltimore: The Johns Hopkins Press, 1960.

VICTORIA, FRANCISCUS, *On the Law of War*. Washington, D.C.: The Carnegie Institution, 1917.

WRIGHT, QUINCY, *A Study of War*. Two Volumes. Chicago: University of Chicago Press, 1942.

Chapter III. The Inevitability of War

AUGUSTINE, SAINT, *The City of God*. New York: Random House, Inc., 1950.

BACON, FRANCIS, *The Advancement of Learning*. London: J. M. Dent and Sons, 1934.

BERGSON, HENRI, *The Two Sources of Morality and Religion*. New York: Henry Holt and Company, 1955.

BLUNTSCHLI, JOHANN K., *The Theory of the State*. Oxford: The Clarendon Press, 1895.

BOSANQUET, BERNARD, *Social and International Ideals*. London: Macmillan and Co. Limited, 1917.

BURNHAM, JAMES, *The Struggle for the World*. New York: The John Day Company, 1947.

DEQUINCY, THOMAS, *On War*. New York: A. and C. Black, 1896–1897.

FERRÉ, NELS, *Christianity and Society*. New York: Harper and Row Publishers, Inc., 1950.

HEGEL, G. W. F., *The Philosophy of History*. New York: George Bell and Sons, 1894.

HEGEL, G. W. F., *The Philosophy of Right*. Oxford: The Clarendon Press, 1942.

HOBBES, THOMAS, *Liberty*. Volume II. London: J. Bohn, 1839–45.

HOLLAND, THOMAS ERSKINE, *Letters to "The Times" upon War and Neutrality (1881–1909)*. New York: Longmans, Green, and Co., Inc., 1909.

HUME, DAVID, *Of National Characters*. New York: Longmans, Green, and Co., Inc., 1907.

KANT, IMMANUEL, *Perpetual Peace*. New York: Columbia University Press, 1932.

KROPOTKIN, PETER, *Mutual Aid*. New York: McClure, 1907.

LOCKE, JOHN, *Second Treatise on Civil Government*. New York: Random House, Inc., 1939.

MACHIAVELLI, NICOLO, *The Discourses*. New York: Random House, Inc., 1940.

MACHIAVELLI, NICOLO, *The Prince*. New York: Random House, Inc., 1940.

NICKERSON, HOFFMAN, *Can We Limit War?* New York: Stokes, 1933–34.

NIEBUHR, REINHOLD, *Beyond Tragedy*. New York: Charles Scribner's Sons, 1937.

MAEZTU, RAMIRO DE, *Authority, Liberty and Function in the Light of War*. New York: The Macmillan Company, 1916.

SANTAYANA, GEORGE, *The Life of Reason in Society*. Volume II. New York: Charles Scribner's Sons, 1922–32.

SPENCER, HERBERT, *Social Statics* together with *Man Versus the State*. New York: D. Appleton-Century, 1897.

SPINOZA, BENEDICT, *The Ethics*. New York: The Tudor Publishing Company, 1936.

SPINOZA, BENEDICT, *The Political Works, Tractatus Politicus*. Oxford: The Clarendon Press, 1958.

SUMNER, WILLIAM GRAHAM, *Essays*. London: Oxford University Press, Inc., 1934.

TREITSCHKE, HEINRICH G. VON, *Politics*. Two Volumes. New York: The Macmillan Company, 1916.

Chapter IV. Patriotism and the Military Spirit

BAKER, NEWTON DIEHL, *Why We Went to War*. New York: Harper and Brothers, 1936.

CLAUSEWITZ, KARL VON, *Principles of War*. Harrisburg: The Military Service Publishing Company, 1942.

GODWIN, WILLIAM, *Enquiry Concerning Political Justice*. New York: A. A. Knopf, 1926.

GOLDMAN, EMMA, *Anarchism and Other Essays*. New York: Mother Earth Publishing Association, 1910.

HOWARD, MICHAEL (ed.), *Soldiers and Governments*. Bloomington: Indiana University Press, 1959.

JOHNSEN, JULIA EMILY (ed.)., *Compulsory Military Training*. New York: H. W. Wilson Company, 1941.

JOHNSEN, JULIA EMILY, *Peacetime Conscription*. New York: H. W. Wilson Company, 1945.

LASSWELL, H. D., *Propaganda Technique in the World War*. New York: A. A. Knopf, 1927.

LIEBKNECHT, KARL, *Militarism*. New York: B. W. Huebsch, 1917.

LYONS, GENE M., and JOHN W. MASLAND, *Education and Military Leadership*. Princeton: Princeton University Press, 1959.

NICOLAI, G. F., *The Biology of War*. New York: The Century Company, 1918.

OMAN, CHARLES, *A History of the Art of War*. New York: G. P. Putnam's Sons, 1898.

ROYCE, JOSIAH, *The Philosophy of Loyalty*. New York: The Macmillan Company, 1919.

SCHURMANN, FRANZ, PETER DALE SCOTT, REGINALD ZELNICK, *The Politics of Escalation in Vietnam*. Greenwich, Conn.: Fawcett Publications, Inc., 1966.

VEBLEN, THORSTEIN, *An Inquiry into the Nature of Peace*. New York: The Macmillan Co. 1917.

Chapter V. The Attack on the War System

ARON, RAYMOND, *The Century of Total War*. New York: Doubleday and Company, Inc., 1954.

ARON, RAYMOND, *On War.* New York: Doubleday and Company, Inc., 1959.

BEAU, B., "A Defense of Cannibalism." *International Conciliation,* Number 78, 1914.

BLACKSTONE, PAUL W., *The Strategy of Subversion.* Chicago: Quadrangle Books, 1964.

COCHRAN, BERT, *The War System.* New York: The Macmillan Company, 1965.

COFFIN, TRISTRAM, *The Passion of the Hawks: Militarism in Modern America.* New York: The Macmillan Company, 1964.

COLLINGWOOD, R. G., *The New Leviathan.* Oxford: The Clarendon Press, 1942.

GREEN, T. H., *Lectures on the Principles of Political Obligation.* New York: Longmans, Green, and Company, Inc., 1937.

JAY, WILLIAM, *War and Peace.* New York: Oxford University Press., Inc., 1919.

MALINOWSKI, B., *Freedom and Civilization.* New York: Roy Publishers, 1944.

PEETERS, PAUL, *Massive Retaliation: The Policy and Its Critics.* Chicago: Henry Regnery Co., 1959.

THOMAS, NORMAN, *War: No Glory, No Profit, No Need.* New York: Frederick A. Stokes, 1935.

THOREAU, HENRY, "Civil Disobedience." *Works.* Boston: Houghton Mifflin Co., 1884–1893.

TROTSKY, LEON, *Their Morals and Ours.* New York: Pioneer Publications, 1942.

Chapter VI. Conscientious Objection and Pacifism

ABRAMS, RAY H., *Preachers Present Arms.* New York: Round Table Press, 1933.

ALLEN, DEVERE, *Pacifism in the Modern World.* New York: Doubleday, Doran, 1929.

BENNETT, JOHN C., *Christians and the State.* New York: Charles Scribner's Sons, 1958.

CURTI, MERLE E., *The American Peace Crusade, 1815–1860.* Durham: Duke University Press, 1929.

GANDHI, MOHANDAS K., *Non-Violence in Peace and War.* Ahmedabad: Navajivan Publishing House, 1948–49.

HERVÉ, GUSTAVE, *My Country Right or Wrong.* London: A. C. Field, 1910.

LINDSAY, A. D., *Pacifism As a Principal and Pacifism As a Dogma.* London: Student Christian Movement Press, 1939.

NATHAN, OTTO, and HEINZ NORDEN, *Einstein on Peace.* New York: Simon and Schuster, Inc., 1960.

NIEBUHR, REINHOLD, *Christianity and Power Politics.* New York: Charles Scribner's Sons, 1940.

SIBLEY, MULFORD, and PHILIP JACOB, *Conscription of Conscience.* Ithaca: Cornell University Press, 1952.

TOLSTOY, LEO, *The Law of Love and the Law of Violence.* New York: R. Field, 1948.

WRIGHT, EDWARD N., *Conscientious Objectors in the Civil War.* Philadelphia: University of Pennsylvania Press, 1937.

Chapter VII. Humane and Inhumane War Practices

BERNAL, J. D., *World without War.* London: 1958.

BLACKETT, P. M. S., *Fear, War, and the Bomb.* New York: Whittlesey House, 1948.

BLOCH, I. S., *The Future of War.* New York: Doubleday and Company, Inc., 1902.

FERRERO, GUGLIELMO, *Peace and War.* London: The Macmillan Company, 1933.

GLUECK, SHELDON, *War Criminals: Their Prosecution and Punishment.* New York: A. A. Knopf, 1944.

HAHN, WALTER F., and JOHN C. NEFF (eds.), *American Strategy for the Nuclear Age.* New York: Doubleday and Co., Inc., 1960.

LADD, WILLIAM, *An Essay on a Congress of Nations.* New York: Oxford University Press, Inc., 1916.

MAXIM, HUDSON, *Defenseless America.* New York: Hearst's International Library, 1915.

NAGLE, WILLIAM J. (ed.), *Morality and Modern Warfare.* Baltimore: Helicon Press, 1960.

OSGOOD, R. E., *Limited War.* Chicago: University of Chicago Press, 1957.

RAMSAY, PAUL, *War and the Christian Conscience.* Durham: Duke University Press, 1961.

TWINING, NATHAN F., *Neither Liberty nor Safety.* New York: Holt, Rinehart, and Winston, 1966.

Chapter VIII. Religion and War

CALVIN, JEAN, *Tracts and Treatises in Defense of the Reformed Faith.* London: Oliver and Boyd, 1958.

HEERING, G. J., *The Fall of Christianity.* New York: Fellowship Publications, 1943.

HOBHOUSE, L. T., *Morals in Evolution.* New York: Henry Holt, 1906.

KOENIG, HARRY C. (ed.), *Principles for Peace.* Washington, D.C.: National Catholic Welfare Conference, 1943.

LECKY, W. E. H., *History of European Morals.* New York: D. Appleton, 1900.

MARSILIUS OF PADUA, *The Defensor Pacis.* New York: Columbia University Press, 1951–56.

MATTHEWS, SHAILER, *Patriotism and Religion.* New York: The Macmillan Company, 1918.

SPERRY, WILLARD L. (ed.), *Religion of Soldier and Sailor.* Cambridge: Harvard University Press, 1945.

TROELTSCH, ERNST, *The Social Teaching of the Christian Churches.* New York: Harper and Row Publishers, Inc., 1960.

Chapter IX. War Is Unchristian

BENEDICT, MARION J., *The God of the Old Testament in Relation to War.* New York: Columbia University Press, 1927.

CADOUX, C. JOHN, *The Early Christian Attitudes to War.* London: Headley Brothers, 1919.

CHANNING, WILLIAM E., *Works.* Volumes III and IV. Boston: G. G. Channing, 1849.

ERASMUS, DESIDERIUS, *The Complaint of Peace.* New York: Scholar's Facsimile and Reprints, 1946.

FOX, GEORGE, *Journal.* London: W. Richardson and S. Clark, 1765.

GARVIE, ALFRED E., *The Christian Ideal for Human Society.* New York: Richard Smith, 1930.

MACFARLAND, CHARLES S., *Pioneers for Peace through Religion.* New York: Fleming H. Revell Co., 1946.

MOFFATT, JAMES, *Love in the New Testament.* New York: Richard Smith, 1930.

NEARING, SCOTT, *War.* New York: Vanguard Press, 1931.

YODER, MICHAEL L. (ed.), *Statements of Religious Bodies on the Conscientious Objector.* Washington, D.C.: National Service Boards for Religious Objectors, 1963.

Chapter X. Can Christians Be Soldiers?

BENNETT, JOHN C. (ed.), *Nuclear Weapons and the Conflict of Conscience.* New York: Charles Scribner's Sons, 1962.

FAUNCE, WILLIAM H. P., *Religion and War.* New York: Abingdon Press, Inc., 1918.

GARNETT, A. CAMPBELL, *Religion and the Moral Life.* New York: The Ronald Press Co., 1955.

GRANT, ROBERT M., *The Sword and the Cross.* New York: The Macmillan Co., 1955.

HENSON, HERBERT H., *Christian Morality.* Oxford: The Clarendon Press, 1936.

LUTHER, MARTIN, *Works.* "That Soldiers Too Can Be Saved." Philadelphia: A. J. Holman Company, 1915–1932.

MAYER, ELI, *War and Religion.* Philadelphia: University of Pennsylvania Press, 1918.

NIEBUHR, REINHOLD, *Moral Men and Immoral Society.* New York: Charles Scribner's Sons, 1932.

NIEBUHR, REINHOLD, *The Nature and Destiny of Man.* Volume II. Charles Scribner's Sons, 1941–43.

NIEBUHR, REINHOLD, *Reflections on the End of an Era.* New York: Charles Scribner's Sons, 1934.

NIEBUHR, RICHARD, *Christ and Culture.* New York: Harper and Row Publishers, Inc., 1951.

SCHROEDER, H. J., *Disciplinary Decrees of the General Councils.* Saint Louis: B. Herder, 1937.

SIMON, EDITH, *The Piebald Standard: A Biography of the Knights Templars.* Boston: Little, Brown, and Co., Inc., 1959.

SOLT, LEO F., *Saints in Arms.* Stanford: Stanford University Press, 1959.

WESTERMARCK, EDWARD A., *Christianity and Morals.* New York: The Macmillan Co., 1939.

Chapter XI. Psychological Causes of War

ARISTOPHANES, *The Acharnians.* London: The Macmillan Co., 1909.

BOAS, FRANZ, "An Anthropologist's View of War," in *International Conciliation.* New York: March, 1912.

BOURNE, GEOFFREY, *War, Politics and Emotion.* New York: Liveright Publishing Corp., 1941.

CANTRIL, HADLEY, *Tensions That Cause Wars.* Urbana: University of Illinois Press, 1950.

CHRISTIANSEN, BJORN, *Attitudes towards Foreign Affairs As a Function of Personality.* Oslo: Oslo University Press, 1959.

DUNN, FREDERICK S., *War and the Minds of Men.* New York: Columbia University Press, 1939.

FROMM, ERICH, *The Sane Society.* New York: Rinehart, 1955.

GLOVER, EDWARD, *War, Sadism and Pacifism.* London: George Allen and Unwin, 1946.

GRINKER, ROY R., and JOHN P. SPIEGEL, *War Neuroses.* Philadelphia: The Blakiston Company, 1945.

HOPKINS, PRYNS, *The Psychology of Social Movements.* London: George Allen and Unwin, 1938.

HOVLAND, CARL I., and others, *Experiments on Mass Communication.* Volume III. Princeton: Princeton University Press, 1949.

JAMES, WILLIAM, "The Moral Equivalent of War." New York: American Association for International Conciliation, 1910.

MacCURDY, J. T., *War Neuroses.* Cambridge, England: The University Press, 1918.

MAY, MARK, *A Social Psychology of War and Peace.* London: Oxford Press, 1943.

MURPHY, GARDNER (ed.), *Human Nature and Enduring Peace.* Boston: Houghton Mifflin Co., 1945.

PEAR, T. H. (ed.), *Psychological Factors of Peace and War.* New York: Philosophical Library, 1950.

RUSSELL, BERTRAND, *Why Men Fight.* New York: The Century Company, 1916.

STRACHEY, ALIX, *The Unconscious Motives of War.* London: Allen and Unwin, 1957.

YOUNG, KIMBALL, "The Psychology of War," in Jesse D. Clarkson and Thomas C. Cochran, *War As a Social Institution.* New York: Columbia University Press, 1941.

Chapter XII. Military Causes of War

ATWATER, ELTON, *American Regulation of Arms Exports.* Washington, D.C.: Carnegie Endowment for International Peace, 1941.

BANSE, EWALD, *Germany Prepares for War.* New York: Harcourt, Brace and World, Inc., 1934.

BERNHARDI, FRIEDRICH VON, *Britain as Germany's Vassal.* New York: George H. Doran, no date.

BROCKWAY, ARCHIBALD F., *The Bloody Traffic.* London: Victor Gollancz, Ltd., 1933.

BRODIE, B. (ed.), *The Absolute Weapon.* New York: Harcourt, Brace and World, Inc., 1946.

BROOKE, TUCKER, and HENRY S. CANBY, *War Aims and Peace Ideals.* New Haven: Yale University Press, 1919.

BUSH, VANNEVAR, *Modern Arms and Free Men.* New York: Simon and Schuster, Inc., 1949.

CHORLEY, KATHERINE, *Armies and the Art of Revolution.* London: Faber and Faber, Ltd., 1943.

CLARKSON, JESSE D., and THOMAS C. COCHRAN, *War As a Social Institution.* New York: Columbia University Press, 1941.

COBLENTZ, STANTON A., *Marching Men.* New York: The Unicorn Press, 1927.

DOUHET, GIULIO, *The Command of the Air.* New York: Coward-McCann, 1942.

HERZOG, ARTHUR, *The War-Peace Establishment.* New York: Harper, 1963.

HUNTINGTON, S. P., *The Soldier and the State.* Cambridge: Harvard University Press, 1957.

JOMINI, ANTOINE HENRI, *Art of War.* Harrisburg, Pennsylvania: The Military Service Publications Co., 1947.

JOUVENAL, BERTRAND DE, *On Power.* New York: The Viking Press, Inc., 1949.

KELLER, A. G., *Man's Rough Road.* New Haven: Yale University Press, 1932.

LEA, HOMER, *Valor of Ignorance.* New York: Harper, 1909.

MENNE, BERNARD, *Blood and Steel.* New York: L. Furman, 1938.

MILLIS, WALTER, *Arms and the State.* New York: The Twentieth Century Fund, 1958.

MILLS, C. WRIGHT, *The Causes of World War III.* New York: Ballantine Books, Inc., 1958.

NEWMAN, JAMES R., *The Tools of War.* New York: Doubleday and Co., Inc., 1942.

NOEL-BAKER, PHILIP, *The Private Manufacture of Armaments.* New York: Oxford University Press, Inc., 1937.

PALMER, JOHN M., *America in Arms.* London: Oxford University Press, Inc., 1941.

PRATT, GEORGE K., *Soldier to Civilian.* New York: McGraw-Hill Book Co., Inc., 1944.

SCHELLING, THOMAS C., *Arms and Influence.* New Haven: Yale University Press, 1966.

STOUFFER, SAMUEL A., *The American Soldier: Combat and Its Aftermath.* Volume II. Princeton University Press, 1949.

SWOMLEY, JOHN M., JR., *The Military Establishment.* Boston: Beacon Press, 1964.

Chapter XIII. Economic Causes of War

BRAILSFORD, H. N., *The War of Steel and Gold.* New York: Harcourt, Brace, and World, Inc., 1915.

BROCKWAY, ARCHIBALD F., and FREDERICK MULLALLY, *Death Pays a Dividend.* London: Victor Gollancz, Ltd., 1944.

CLARK, G. N., *War and Society in the 17th Century*. Cambridge University Press, 1958.

CLARKE, R. W. B., *The Economic Effort of War*. London: George Allen and Unwin, Ltd., 1940.

DEGRAS, JANE (ed.), *The Communist International, 1919–1943*. London: Oxford University Press, 1956.

DuPONT, L., *The DuPont Company and Munitions*. Wilmington, Delaware, 1934.

EAGLETON, CLYDE, *Analysis of the Problem of War*. New York: The Ronald Press Co., 1937.

EDDY, SHERWOOD, *The Abolition of War*. New York: George H. Doran, 1924.

LEHMANN-RUSSBULDT, OTTO, *War for Profits*. New York: A. H. King, 1930.

LENIN, V., *State and Revolution*. New York: International Publishers Co., Inc., 1932.

LENIN, V., J. STALIN, V. MOLOTOV, and others, *The Soviet Union and the Cause of Peace*. New York: International Publishers Co., Inc., 1936.

LEWINSOHN, RICHARD, *The Profits of War through the Ages*. London: G. Routledge and Sons, 1936.

PORRITT, ARTHUR (ed.), *The Causes of War*. London: The Macmillan Co., 1932.

ROBBINS, LIONEL C., *The Economic Causes of War*. London: Jonathan Cape, Ltd., 1939.

ROYCE, JOSIAH, *War and Insurance*. New York: The Macmillan Co., 1914.

SILBERNER, EDMUND, *The Problem of War in Nineteenth Century Economic Thought*. Princeton University Press, 1946.

TROTZKY, LEON, *The Bolsheviki and World Peace*. New York: Boni and Liveright, 1918.

WALLER, WILLARD W. (ed.), *War in the Twentieth Century*. New York: Random House, Inc., 1940.

Chapter XIV. Disarmament and the Arms Race

BALDWIN, HANSON W., *The Great Arms Race*. New York: Frederick A. Praeger, Inc., 1958.

BARNET, RICHARD J., *Who Wants Disarmament?* Boston: The Beacon Press, 1960.

BARNET, RICHARD J., and RICHARD A. FALK, *Security in Disarmament*. Princeton University Press, 1965.

BENOIT, EMILE, and KENNETH BOULDING (eds.), *Disarmament and the Economy.* New York: Harper and Row Publishers, Inc., 1963.

BRADLEY, DAVID J., *No Place to Hide.* Boston: Little, Brown, and Co., Inc., 1948.

BRENNAN, DONALD G. (ed.), *Arms Control, Disarmament, and National Security.* New York: George Braziller, 1961.

BULL, HEDLEY, *The Control of the Arms Race.* New York: Frederick A. Praeger, Inc., 1961.

COALE, AINSLEY J., *The Problem of Reducing Vulnerability to Atomic Bombs.* Princeton University Press, 1947.

GILPIN, ROBERT G., *American Scientists and Nuclear Weapons Policy.* Princeton University Press, 1962.

KAHN, HERMAN, *On Escalation.* New York: Frederick A. Praeger, Inc., 1965.

KAHN, HERMAN, *On Thermonuclear War.* Princeton University Press, 1961.

KAHN, HERMAN, *Thinking About the Unthinkable.* New York: Horizon Press, Inc., 1962.

LEFEBURE, VICTOR, *Scientific Disarmament.* New York: The Macmillan Co., 1931.

NOEL-BAKER, PHILIP, *The Arms Race.* London: Stevens, 1958.

RICHARDSON, LEWIS F., *Arms and Insecurity.* Pittsburgh: The Boxwood Press, 1960.

RICHARDSON, LEWIS F., *Statistics of Deadly Quarrels.* Chicago: Quadrangle Books, 1960.

SEVERUD, FRED N., and ANTHONY F. MERRILL, *The Bomb, Survival and You.* New York: Reinhold Publishing Corporation, 1954.

SPEIER, HANS, *German Rearmament and Atomic War.* Evanston: Row, Peterson and Company, 1957.

WHEELER-BENNETT, J. W., *Information on the Reduction of Armaments.* London: G. Allen and Unwin, Ltd., 1925.

Chapter XV. World Political Federation

ANGELL, NORMAN, *The Great Illusion—Now.* Middlesex, England: Penguin Books, Inc., 1938.

ARÉCHAGA, EDUARDO JIMÉNEZ DE, *Voting and the Handling of Disputes in the Security Council.* New York: Carnegie Endowment for International Peace, 1950.

BARCLAY, SIR THOMAS, *New Methods of Adjusting International Disputes and the Future.* London: Constable, 1917.

BRIGGS, HERBERT W., *The International Law Commission.* Ithaca: Cornell University Press, 1965.

Feis, Herbert, *Between War and Peace: The Potsdam Conference.* Princeton University Press, 1960.

Grey, Viscount of Falloden, "The League of Nations," in *International Conciliation,* October, 1918, No. 131.

The Hague Declarations of 1899–1907. Washington, D.C.: The Carnegie Endowment, 1915.

Holborn, Louise W. (ed.), *War and Peace Aims of the United Nations, September 1, 1939–December 31, 1942.* Vol I. Boston: World Peace Foundation, 1943.

Holborn, Louise W. (ed.), *War and Peace Aims of the United Nations, January 1, 1943–September 1, 1945.* Vol. II. Boston: World Peace Foundation, 1948.

Holcombe, Arthur N., *Organizing Peace in the Nuclear Age.* New York: New York University Press, 1959.

Huddleston, Sisley, *Popular Diplomacy and War.* Richard R. Smith, 1954.

Lissitzyn, Oliver J., *The International Court of Justice: Its Role in the Maintenance of International Peace and Security.* New York: Carnegie Endowment, 1951.

McNair, Arnold Duncan, *Legal Effects of War.* Cambridge University Press, 1944.

Mannheim, Hermann, *War and Crime.* London: Watts, 1941.

Osgood, Charles E., *Perspectives in Foreign Policy.* Privately printed, 1965.

Penn, William, *An Essay towards the Present and Future Peace of Europe.* New York: Carnegie Endowment, 1943.

Pompe, C. A., *Aggressive War and International Crime.* The Hague: Martinus Nijhoff, 1953.

Puttkammer, Ernst W., *War and the Law.* Chicago: University of Chicago Press, 1944.

Wright, Quincy, *Research in International Law Since the War.* Carnegie Endowment for International Peace, Pamphlet 51, 1930.

INDEX

(The Roman numerals refer to chapters.)